BLOOD
ON THE
ALTAR

THOMAS HORN

BLOOD
ON THE
ALTAR

The Coming War Between
Christian vs. Christian

Contributing Authors: Gary Stearman, Chuck Missler, Cris Putnam,
Michael Lake, Sharon Gilbert, Derek Gilbert, Larry Spargimino,
Paul McGuire, Douglas W. Krieger, S. Douglas Woodward, & Terry James

DEFENDER

CRANE, MO

Blood on the Altar: The Coming War between Christian vs. Christian

Defender

Crane, MO 65633

©2014 by Thomas Horn

A collaborative work by Thomas Horn, Stephen Quayle, Chuck Missler, Sharon K. Gilbert, Michael K. Lake, Gary Stearman, Larry Spargimino, Paul McGuire, Derek Gilbert, Cris Putnam, Douglas W. Krieger, S. Douglas Woodward, and Terry James.

All rights reserved. Published 2014.

Printed in the United States of America.

ISBN: 978-0-9856045-7-8

A CIP catalog record of this book is available from the Library of Congress.

Cover illustration and design by Daniel Wright: www.createdwright.com.

All Scripture quotations are from the Holy Bible, Authorized King James Version.

CONTENTS

FOREWORD

By Stephen Quayle

But whosoever shall deny me before men, him will I also deny before my Father, who is in heaven. Think not that I am come to send peace on earth; I came not to send peace, but a sword. For I am come to set a man at variance against his father, and the daughter against her mother, and the daughter-in-law against her mother-in-law. And a man's foes shall be they of his own household.

—Matthew 10:33–36

This know, also, that in the last days perilous times shall come. For men shall be lovers of their own selves, covetous, boasters, proud, blasphemers, disobedient to parents, unthankful, unholy, Without natural affection, trucebreakers, false accusers, incontinent, fierce, despisers of those that are good, Traitors, heady, high-minded, lovers of pleasures more than lovers of God, Having a form of godliness, but denying the power of it; from such turn away.

—2 Timothy 3:1–5

These things have I spoken unto you, that ye should not be offended. They shall put you out of the synagogues; yea, the time cometh, that whosoever killeth you will think that he doeth God service. And these things will they do unto you, because they have not known the Father, nor me.

—John 16:1–3

The world is now at the time when the bloodiest period of war and betrayal lies at the doorsteps of the Christian faith. As the new world church and the New World Order "emerge," there is a considerable effort being espoused by religious megastars to embrace one world faith based on agreements that we all serve the same god. This is total rebellion and heresy against the faith of the apostles and the prophets and the revealed will of the Living God.

There are two households in which this battle will be waged, and the stakes are eternal. The first household is that of faith—brother will turn against brother, and where they once broke bread together, one will seek to do the other great harm. Faith has always been persecuted by unbelief, and that is the way it is going to play out in the months and years ahead. When you see prominent Christian authors being featured in the mainstream press and talking about Christianity and Islam serving the same god, you know that the battle is looming.

The nuclear family of the Christian is also under an unusual attack, with one member of the family understanding the lateness of the hour versus other members, spouse, or children being in an antagonistic position against the warning partner, parent, or child who "gets it." The church of Jesus Christ, made up of those in right relationship with Him through believing in His death, resurrection, blood, and Second Coming, have already been designated "terrorists" and "enemies of the state" by the US military and the US Justice Department, and this designation has been brought out into the open more graphically lately. The question I am asked more than ever from those with eyes to see, ears to hear, and mouths that pray is "Will my husband or kids betray me?" The answer is yes, unless they have had a transformational encounter with Jesus that puts them on the same side of redemption as you. If you believe that the mainstream apostate church will stand up against this threat against your brethren, think again, and look back in history to the Lutheran church and its surrender to Hitler in not standing up against godless fascism as it slaughtered Jews, Christians, the elderly, Gypsies and "misfits."

Each man, woman, and child must seek God to lead him or her *not* into this heretical evil, and also to deliver him or her from betrayal. Just as a house divided against itself cannot stand, neither will the mainstream Christian church, which has forsaken and denied the blood of Jesus.

A war is coming. By the end of this book, you will believe that. And you will know what to do about it.

FORGOTTEN ASPECT OF BIBLE PROPHECY

The Lucifer Effect and the Coming War between Christian vs. Christian

---

By Thomas Horn

In January 2014, the Pew Research Center (PRC)—a prestigious think tank based in Washington, DC (which provides information on social issues and demographic trends shaping the world)—published *Religious Hostilities Reach Six-Year High*. In this important report, the worldwide public-opinion surveyors chronicled the steady growth of religious persecution around the world and found that social hostilities involving religion are currently most frequently directed against people of Christian faith. The sharpest increase was in the Middle East, which, the reporters surmise, is the result of the 2010–2011 political uprisings known as the Arab Spring. That region's score on the Social Hostilities Index rose from 5.4 in 2011 to 6.4 in 2012, three times the global median. A January 8, 2014, Breitbart news feature with the headline "A Report from the Non-Denominational Group Open Doors Says the Number of Christians

Martyred around the World for Their Faith Nearly Doubled in 2013"[1] separately confirmed the discoveries of the PRC cited above. Besides the Middle East, the Pew findings also detail an escalation in the United States from the lowest category of government restrictions on Christian expressions as of mid-2009 to an advanced category in only three years,[2] where it appears poised to continue upward at the time of the publishing of this book. If recent activity is any indication, it may not be long before "one nation under God" joins those red-listed countries where Bible-based believers find themselves under the most severe discrimination. Indeed, National Review Online recently posted a critical review by Raymond Ibrahim, a Shillman fellow at the David Horowitz Freedom Center, who cites the 2014 World Watch List (which ranks the fifty nations where Christians are most persecuted) to determine that "the U.S. is the chief facilitator of the persecution of Christians around the world today."[3] While Ibrahim's assertion mostly reflects American involvement in foreign conflicts, examples of repression in the US against people of Christian faith are growing and are easily obtained online. A simple and quick web search produced the following headlines and statistics in just a few minutes:

- A January 25, 2014, news story at Christian News Network is entitled "Legal Group Reports 'Dramatic Increase' in Hostility toward Christian Students in Public Schools." An important distinction in this story is that the upswing in incident reports does not pertain to bullying from other students, but rather to mistreatment *by school officials*. "[The reports all surround] hostility from teachers and school administrators who are curtailing the students' free speech rights simply because they're Christians and they might express a Christian worldview," the article quotes Bob

Tyler, general counsel of Advocates for Faith and Freedom (AFF), as saying. Incidents include:

○ A Boston-area mother of a seventh grader called the AFF to report that one of her child's teachers, an atheist, had belittled the student's faith. "The atheist teacher said, 'We atheists laugh at you Christians. No one will believe in God [in fifty years] because science has proven that there is no God.'"

○ Another incident concerned a California teacher who threw away a gift from a first grader because it was spiritual in nature. "[The teacher] said, 'Jesus is not allowed in school,' and proceeded to throw [the present] in the trash," Tyler outlined, noting that the professing Christian principal sided with the teacher in the matter.

○ Another first grader, who was giving a religious presentation in class, was told to stop when her teacher realized the student was referring to biblical passages. "The teacher said, 'Stop right there. You cannot talk about the Bible in school,'" Tyler said. "And for [the student]…all of a sudden you feel like you're in trouble because of what just happened."[4]

• **A February 2, 2014, CBS story** outlines how a North Carolina high school football coach was ordered to cease baptisms and leading prayers for students *even when not on school grounds* (the baptism in question was performed at the Charles Mack Citizen Center, a church in town that many team members attend and the coach was simply invited to be there). "'It is a violation of the Constitution for the Mooresville High School football coach to organize, lead, or participate in prayers or other religious proselytizing before, during, *or after games and practices*,' Patrick Elliott, attorney for Freedom from Religion Foundation, wrote to the school's district attorney last fall. 'It is well settled that public schools, *and by extension public school officials, may not advance or promote religion.*'"[5]

- **A very well written, January 10, 2014, American Thinker opinion piece** by Fay Voshell titled "Establishing a US State Religion" details a modest group of nuns who have devoted their lives to the care of the elderly for 175 years—"a generally thankless task," Voshell notes, "as they are dealing with human beings who are physically debilitated and most often mentally frail as they come to the end of their earthly existence." The nuns have come under intimidation by the US government for "refusing to obey the Obamacare Affordable Health Care mandate to include abortion-inducing drugs as part of the insurance policies offered to the orders' employees. Such provisions violate the nuns' religious beliefs concerning the sacredness of life from conception to death." Voshell notes that Beverly Monk's report on Citizen Link indicates that the nuns "have been told they must offer the abortifacient or sign a government form that delegates the action to a third party." The Department of Health and Human Services and the Department of Justice (DOJ), Voshell says, "are essentially saying to the nuns, 'You yourselves don't have to do it, but you have to allow someone else to do it on behalf of your order.' That's legal casuistry at its most serpentine. Monk also reports the DOJ demands…'the Little Sisters must sign a "self-certification" form claiming eligibility for an exemption from the mandate, or pay millions in fines.' In other words, sign the paper or else."[6]
- **A December 31, 2013, ABC News story** reports of Houston,

4

Texas, city bus drivers who were reprimanded for praying with a coworker after her twelve-year-old girl was hit by a car and later died of the injuries.[7]

- **A January 3, 2014,** *Daily Caller* **feature** article titled "House Committee: Obama Administration Banned Christmas Carols and Cards for Veterans" by Patrick Howley states how "the Obama administration's Department of Veterans Affairs (VA) prohibited veterans from hearing Christmas carols or receiving gifts wrapped in Christmas-themed wrapping paper.... Additionally, the VA Medical Center in Augusta, Georgia—which treats veterans—banned Christmas carolers from singing Christmas songs with religious references in public areas."[8]

- **A December 9, 2013,** *Charisma News* **report** by Matt Barber details how "Blogging Gays Urge Murder, Castration of Christians."[9]

- **A February 7, 2014, story at WorldNetDaily** features an interview with US Lieutenant General Jerry Boykin under the stinging headline, "General: US Christians Targeted For Murder."[10]

- **Finally, a November 10, 2013, Associated Press report**—while not a direct story of Christian persecution—details how "Atheist 'Mega-Churches' Are Taking Root across US, World."[11]

There are, of course, hundreds more such examples in media at this time, and, again, these stories are just samples found in a few moments with a simple web query. But what these bullet points fail to mention is the developing emergence on the world scene of what will become one of the greatest threats ever raised against the authentic body of Christ—*Religious Christians.*

Social Hostilities Around the World

Level of social hostilities in each country as of December 2012

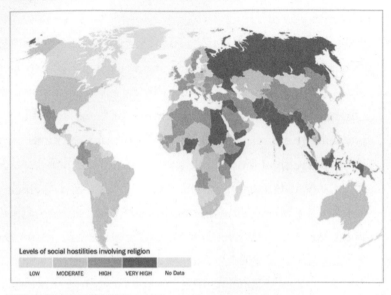

Levels of social hostilities involving religion

LOW   MODERATE   HIGH   VERY HIGH   No Data

"Religious Hostilities Reach Six-Year High," January 2014
PEW RESEARCH CENTER

Pew Research map shows United States as a growing menace to real Christianity.

Cry "Havoc!" and Let Slip the Dogs of War

For some students of prophecy, the facts outlined previously were not only predictable, but were a prophesied prelude to a period in history wherein true believers will be "beheaded for the witness of Jesus, and for the word of God, and....[for] not worship[ing] the beast, neither his image, neither... [receiving] his mark upon their foreheads, or in their hands" (Rev. 20:4).

Yet, when discussing this end-times scenario, and in particular the subject of rigorous persecution, often overlooked is the role that religious "Christians" are being shaped today to play against the true body of Christ.

Even the subtitle of this book and the concept of a coming war between Christians could seem beyond credulity if it were not for what the inspired texts themselves convey. Jesus predicted a time when "whosoever killeth you will think that he doeth God service" (John 16:2), and in Matthew 24, He told His disciples:

> Then shall they deliver you up to be afflicted, and shall kill you; and ye shall be hated of all [groups of people] for my name's sake.
>
> And then shall many be offended, and shall betray one another, and shall hate one another.
>
> And many false prophets shall rise, and shall deceive many.
>
> And because iniquity shall abound, the love of many shall grow cold. (Matt. 24:9–12)

Elsewhere in the Bible is described this coming era of Great Tribulation, as when the Antichrist will have power "to make war with the saints, and to overcome them" (Rev. 13:7; see also Dan. 7:21). Immediately following those verses, there is description of a second beast with "two horns like a lamb" who speaks "like a dragon" (Rev. 13:11). Most evangelical scholars identify this second "beast" as the leader of the end-times religious institution who will be under Satan's control. The phrase "like a lamb" indicates he will pretend to represent the Lamb of God and the Christian church, while the expression "speaks like a dragon" identifies the devilish source of his authority and power. This final, global, super-church leader will be a murderer not unlike the Antichrist, and will cause "that as many as would not worship the image of the beast should be killed" (Rev. 13:15).

Thus, the book of Revelation outlines how the political figure of Antichrist derives ultranational dominance from the world's religious faithful through the influence of an ecclesiastical leader (also called the

False Prophet) who will not hesitate to swim in the blood of the genuine saints of God.

In the days between now and when these men of sin are identified, this reality—that latter-day churchgoers will soon believe they are serving the kingdom of God by participating in or approving the death of conservative Christians—is not a concept lost on all contemporary churchmen. There are those who see things taking shape even now for a war that will eventually pit religious "Christians" against the real members of the body of Christ. For example, the Archbishop of Canterbury, Justin Welby, stated early in 2014 that "modern Christians" will now be "'called' to suffer and even die for the faith" in a new era "of martyrdom."[12] But a clarifying document that was not supposed to be made public and which was authored by a senior advisor to Welby's predecessor details how such a time of great persecution is coming because true believers will, according to the letter, be driven underground by liberal Christians and will become a dissident association comparable to resistance movements during World War II.[13] Dr. J. Vernon McGee, one of America's most beloved Bible teachers of the past century, taught the same and clarified that these true biblical believers would ultimately be driven "underground" by none other than latter-day denominational churches. Another of the twentieth century's most perceptive writers was pastor and author A. W. Tozer (who was not usually given to prognostication), who likewise wrote:

> Let me go out on a limb a little bit and prophesy. I see the time coming when all the holy men whose eyes have been opened by the Holy Spirit will desert worldly Evangelicalism, one by one. The house [institutional Christianity] will be left desolate and there will not be a man of God, a man in whom the Holy Spirit dwells, left among them.[14]

These Holy-Spirit-devoid church attenders will join other "religious types" to constitute Antichrist's apostate religious and political order (connected to "Mystery Babylon" in Revelation 17) and, as unfathomable as it may sound, will seek to formulate perhaps the most egregious rank among the Man of Sin's Gestapo members in their appetite for destroying latter-day, truly born-again believers.

Impossible, some might say? Tell that to the trainloads of Jews who vanished beneath the brutality of Nazi Germany members *who maintained their Protestant faith* or to the hundreds of thousands of men, women, and children who have died since the days of Christ's crucifixion and the martyrdom of His disciples at the hands of institutional church authorities and holy temple leaders. The European wars of religion (sixteenth and seventeenth centuries) are further examples of such mayhem by very religious people, as could also be considered the Muslim conquests (seventh to nineteenth centuries), the Crusades (eleventh to thirteenth centuries), the Spanish Reconquista (eighth to fifteenth centuries), the Ottoman wars in Europe (fifteenth to nineteenth centuries), and the Inquisition of the Roman Catholic Church (twelfth to fourteenth centuries).

But now, what was old is new again, and as a militant spirit of evil pushes through the veil toward a final supernatural conflict (in which blood will flow to the horses' bridles), violent clashes over matters of faith are once more boiling around the globe. Consequently, brutality wrought by the final Antichrist and his end-time Christian assassins will soon make the combined depravities of those wars mentioned above look like child's play. When he raises his fist, "speaking great things...in blasphemy against God, to blaspheme his name, and his tabernacle, and them that dwell in heaven" (Rev. 13:5–6), at his right hand will stand those devoted house-of-worship attendees who are vividly described in the final book of the Bible as "drunk with the blood of the saints, and with the blood of the martyrs of Jesus" (Rev. 17:6) as they dance and sing "in the spirit" of their mega-church "habitation of demons, and the hold of every foul spirit" (Rev. 18:2).

How could such a nightmarish reality develop in modern times and within advanced society? Part of the answer includes a unique, if not disturbing, study in human psychology, repeatedly verified in university and military experiments, which we will now briefly consider.

Stanford and the Lucifer Effect

Perhaps unknown to some readers is a most notorious experiment that took place in America more than forty years ago. Commonly referred to today as "The Stanford Prison Experiment," in 1971, a group of student recruits participated in a study at Stanford University, where they were instructed to act out roles of detainees and guards in a makeshift prison in the basement of the school. What resulted in the test was an unexpected and almost immediate breakdown in normative social behavior that illustrated such astonishing cruelty on the part of the participants that it was quickly shut down, leading the organizer and director, Professor Philip Zimbardo, to embark on a larger quest of discovery regarding how "the majority of us can be seduced into behaving in ways totally atypical of what we believe we are."[15] The program graphically illustrated that, given the right set of circumstances, a majority of people are capable of monstrous inhumanity against others. The Wikipedia entry on the Stanford Prison Experiment explains what happened:

> Participants were recruited and told they would participate in a two-week prison simulation. Out of 70 respondents, Zimbardo

and his team selected the 24 males whom they deemed to be the most psychologically stable and healthy. These participants were predominantly white and middle-class. The group was intentionally selected to exclude those with criminal background, psychological impairments or medical problems. They all agreed to participate in a 7–14-day period and received $15 per day (roughly equivalent to $85 in 2012).

The experiment was conducted in the basement of Jordan Hall (Stanford's psychology building). Twelve of the twenty-four participants were assigned the role of prisoner (nine plus three alternates), while the other twelve were assigned the role of guard (also nine plus three alternates). Zimbardo took on the role of the superintendent, and an undergraduate research assistant the role of the warden. Zimbardo designed the experiment in order to induce disorientation, depersonalization and deindividualization in the participants.

The researchers held an orientation session for guards the day before the experiment, during which they instructed them not to physically harm the prisoners. In the footage of the study, Zimbardo can be seen talking to the guards: "You can create in the prisoners feelings of boredom, a sense of fear to some degree, you can create a notion of arbitrariness that their life is totally controlled by us, by the system, you, me, and they'll have no privacy....We're going to take away their individuality in various ways. In general what all this leads to is a sense of powerlessness. That is, in this situation we'll have all the power and they'll have none."

The researchers provided the guards with wooden batons to establish their status, clothing similar to that of an actual prison guard (khaki shirt and pants from a local military surplus store), and mirrored sunglasses to prevent eye contact. Prisoners wore uncomfortable ill-fitting smocks and stocking caps, as well as a chain around one ankle. Guards were instructed to call prisoners by their assigned numbers, sewn on their uniforms, instead of by name.

The prisoners were arrested at their homes and charged with armed robbery. The local Palo Alto police department assisted Zimbardo with the arrests and conducted full booking procedures on the prisoners, which included fingerprinting and taking mug shots. They were transported to the mock prison from the police station, where they were strip searched and given their new identities.

The small mock prison cells were set up to hold three prisoners each. There was a small space for the prison yard, solitary confinement, and a bigger room across from the prisoners for the guards and warden. The prisoners were to stay in their cells all day and night until the end of the study. The guards worked in teams of three for eight-hour shifts. The guards did not have to stay on site after their shift.

After a relatively uneventful first day, on the second day the prisoners in Cell 1 blockaded their cell door with their beds and took off their stocking caps, refusing to come out or follow the guards' instructions. Guards from other shifts volunteered to work extra hours to assist in subduing the revolt, and subsequently attacked the prisoners with fire extinguishers without being supervised by the research staff. Finding that handling nine cell mates with only three guards per shift was challenging, one of the guards suggested that they use psychological tactics to control them. They set up a "privilege cell" in which prisoners who were not involved in the riot were treated with special rewards, such as higher quality meals. The "privileged" inmates chose not to eat the meal in order to stay uniform with their fellow prisoners. After only 36 hours, one prisoner began to act "crazy," as Zimbardo described: "#8612 then began to act crazy, to scream, to curse, to go into a rage that seemed out of control. It took quite a while before we became convinced that he was really suffering and that we had to release him."

Guards forced the prisoners to repeat their assigned numbers to reinforce the idea that this was their new identity. Guards soon used these prisoner counts to harass the prisoners, using physical punishment such as protracted exercise for errors in the prisoner count. Sanitary conditions declined rapidly, exacerbated by the guards' refusal to allow some prisoners to urinate or defecate anywhere but in a bucket placed in their cell. As punishment, the guards would not let the prisoners empty the sanitation bucket. Mattresses were a valued item in the prison, so the guards would punish prisoners by removing their mattresses, leaving them to sleep on concrete. Some prisoners were forced to be naked as a method of degradation. Several guards became increasingly cruel as the experiment continued; experimenters reported that approximately one-third of the guards exhibited genuine sadistic tendencies [doing things we will not publish here]. Most of the guards were upset when the experiment concluded after only six days....

Zimbardo argued that the prisoners had internalized their roles, since, even though some had stated that they would accept "parole" even if it would mean forfeiting their pay, they did not quit when their parole applications were all denied. Zimbardo argued they had no reason for continued participation in the experiment after having lost all monetary compensation, yet they did, because they had internalized the prisoner identity.

Prisoner No. 416, a newly admitted stand-by prisoner, expressed concern over the treatment of the other prisoners. The guards responded with more abuse. When he refused to eat his sausages, saying he was on a hunger strike, guards confined him to "solitary confinement," a dark closet: "The guards then instructed the other prisoners to repeatedly punch on the door while shouting at 416." The guards stated that he would be released from solitary confinement only if the prisoners gave up their blankets and slept on their bare mattresses, which all but one refused to do.

Zimbardo aborted the experiment early when Christina Maslach, a graduate student in psychology whom he was dating (and later married), objected to the conditions of the prison after she was introduced to the experiment to conduct interviews. Zimbardo noted that, of more than fifty people who had observed the experiment, Maslach was the only one who questioned its morality. After only six days of a planned two weeks' duration, the Stanford prison experiment was discontinued.[16]

Following the Stanford Prison Experiment, Zimbardo wanted to continue his research into the dark side of human psychology to decipher under what conditions "it" can be uncaged. His next big opportunity came a decade ago, in April 2004, while on a business trip to Washington, DC. That's when he saw the American television show *60 Minutes* airing images taken from the Abu Ghraib prison in Iraq of naked detainees forced to simulate fellatio in front of mocking US soldiers. Other prisoners were unclothed and made to lie atop each other; a female soldier was seen leading a naked Iraqi around like a dog, complete with leash and collar, and electric wires were attached to a hooded inmate who was balancing on a small box. Later, it was learned that this type of torture had become sexualized and included examples of a male prisoner being sodomized by a guard using a chemical light and a female prisoner being raped. While Americans were aghast at the images and information, Zimbardo had seen such sadism before, right there at Stanford University years earlier, where his undergraduates had forced fellow students to simulate sodomy, among other things. Although Zimbardo's "guards" knew their classmates had actually done nothing to deserve the maltreatment, he later wrote, "some…were transformed into perpetrators of evil," illustrating that "most of us can undergo significant character transformations when we are caught up in the crucible of social forces."[17]

In January 2008, Random House published Zimbardo's impressive yet chilling study on the subject in a book titled *The Lucifer Effect: Understanding How Good People Turn Evil.* In it, Zimbardo, who was called as an expert psychologist to testify during the trial of one of the Abu Ghraib guards, dismantled what happened at that military facility while also reflecting on his earlier Stanford experiment to conclude that wherever conditions allow for what he calls "deindividualization," the foundations for the towers of evil are laid and a line between good and evil can be crossed in nearly any heart.

Interestingly, Zimbardo actually drew parallels between his findings and the biblical story of the fall of that once-powerful angel named Lucifer:

According to various scenarios of early Christian Church Fathers (from Cyprus, Armenia, Greece, and France), Lucifer was God's favorite angel…. His sin, and the origin of his transformation into the Devil, stems from his envy of man and disobedience to God… Apparently a cosmic battle ensued in which…Lucifer and the fallen angels were cast out of heaven into Hell. Lucifer is transformed into Satan, the Devil, following his fall from grace.… Thus, "The Lucifer Effect" represents this most extreme transformation imaginable from God's favorite Angel into the Devil. My work has focused on lesser transformations of human character not as dramatic as this one, in which ordinary, even good people begin to engage in bad deeds, for a short time or longer, that qualify as "evil."[18]

Zimbardo goes on to describe how, given the right situational conditions, ordinary persons can be transformed from good to evil and will proceed to engage in malevolent activity, even to the point of setting aside "personal attributes of morality, compassion, or sense of justice and fair play."[19]

Of course, what Zimbardo's research reflects was revealed beforehand in the Bible: "The [unredeemed] heart is deceitful above all things, and desperately wicked" (Jer. 17:9). Given these facts about fallen human nature, is it much of a stretch to imagine the role the Lucifer Effect will play in the lead-up to—and during the reign of—Antichrist and his religious followers?

Milgram Experiment on Obedience to Authority Figures

Similar to the findings of the Stanford Prison Experiment but in many ways more disturbing was the 1961 "Milgram Experiment" that has since been repeated on numerous occasions with consistent results. The test measures the willingness of participants to obey authority figures who order them to go against expected restrictions of human conscience in performing acts of cruelty against other study participants.

The original tests began at Yale University in the early 1960s under psychologist Stanley Milgram. At the time, it was just three months into the trial of Nazi war criminal Otto Adolf Eichmann, a German Nazi colonel deemed highly responsible for organizing the Holocaust, and Milgram had designed his test to try to answer the burning question on people's minds then: "Could it be that Eichmann and his million accomplices in the Holocaust were just following orders?"[20] Milgram came to believe that much of that sentiment was true, and that "the essence of obedience consists in the fact that a person comes to view himself as the instrument for carrying out another person's wishes, and he therefore no longer regards himself as responsible for his actions."[21] Milgram first described his research in 1963 in the *Journal of Abnormal and Social Psychology*, then later in greater detail in his 1974 book, *Obedience to Authority: An Experimental View*. Milgram explained how participants were taken into a laboratory and, in the context of a learning experiment, were told to give increasingly severe electrical shocks to another person (who was actually an actor). The purpose of the assessment was to see how far a subject would proceed before refusing to comply with the experimenter's instructions.

The test used three individuals: #1 was THE EXPERIMENTER— the *authority* figure running the trial; #2 was THE LEARNER—an *actor* pretending to be a test subject; and #3 was THE TEACHER—a *volunteer* who believed he or she was actually to administer voltage to THE LEARNER whenever he or she failed to answer a question correctly.

The wiki on the way this test proceeded says the TEACHER and the LEARNER (actor) both drew slips of paper to determine their roles, but unknown to the TEACHER, both slips said "teacher." The actor would always claim to have drawn the slip that read "learner," thus guaranteeing that the unwitting volunteer would always be the "teacher."

At this point, the "teacher" and "learner" were separated into different rooms where they could communicate but not see each other. In one version of the experiment, the confederate was sure to mention to the participant that he had a heart condition.

The "teacher" was given an electric shock from the electro-shock generator as a sample of the shock that the "learner" would supposedly receive during the experiment. The "teacher" was then given a list of word pairs which he was to teach the learner. The teacher began by reading the list of word pairs to the learner. The teacher would then read the first word of each pair and read four possible answers. The learner would press a button to indicate his response. If the answer was incorrect, the teacher would administer a shock to the learner, with the voltage increasing in 15-volt increments for each wrong answer. If correct, the teacher would read the next word pair.

The subjects believed that for each wrong answer, the learner was receiving actual shocks. In reality, there were no shocks. After the confederate was separated from the subject, the confederate set up a tape recorder integrated with the electro-shock generator, which played pre-recorded sounds for each shock level. After a number of voltage level increases, the actor started to bang on the wall that separated him from the subject. After several times banging on the wall and complaining about his heart condition, all responses by the learner would cease.

At this point, many people indicated their desire to stop the experiment and check on the learner. Some test subjects paused at 135 volts and began to question the purpose of the experiment. Most continued after being assured that they would not be held responsible. A few subjects began to laugh nervously or exhibit other signs of extreme stress once they heard the screams of pain coming from the learner.

If at any time the subject indicated his desire to halt the experiment, he was given a succession of verbal prods by the experimenter, in this order:

Please continue.

The experiment requires that you continue.

It is absolutely essential that you continue.

You have no other choice, you must go on.

If the subject still wished to stop after all four successive verbal prods, the experiment was halted. Otherwise, it was halted after the subject had given the maximum 450-volt shock three times in succession.

The experimenter also gave special prods if the teacher made specific comments. If the teacher asked whether the learner might suffer permanent physical harm, the experimenter replied, "Although the shocks may be painful, there is no permanent tissue damage, so please go on." If the teacher said that the learner clearly wants to stop, the experimenter replied, "Whether the learner likes it or not, you must go on until he has learned all the word pairs correctly, so please go on."[22]

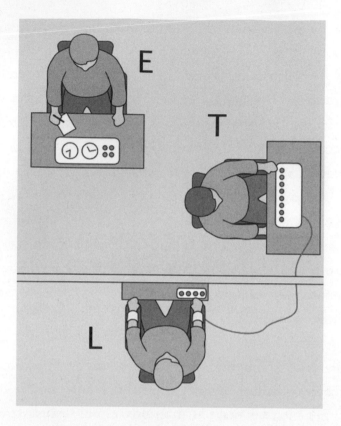

The experimenter (E) orders the teacher (T), the subject of the experiment, to give what the latter believes are painful electric shocks to a learner (L), who is actually an actor and confederate. The subject believes that for each wrong answer, the learner was receiving actual electric shocks, though in reality there were no such punishments. Being separated from the subject, the confederate set up a tape recorder integrated with the electro-shock generator, which played pre-recorded sounds for each shock level.[23]

The amazing findings from this experiment tallied 65 percent of the volunteers (including women) administering the final, massive, 450-volt shock even though they exhibited signs that they were uncomfortable doing so (pausing, questioning, sweating, trembling, biting their lips, digging their fingernails into their skin, and/or laughing nervously), but in the end they did it anyway on the advice of the authority figure (the experimenter). When some ethical criticisms were made in opposition to Milgram following his original study and conclusions (which have since been repeated around the world in different social settings with similar results), he said he believed the arguments developed because his research revealed *something disturbing and unwelcome about human nature*. He then summarized his findings and warned in his 1974 article, "The Perils of Obedience":

> The legal and philosophic aspects of obedience are of enormous importance, but they say very little about how most people behave in concrete situations. I set up a simple experiment at Yale University to test how much pain an ordinary citizen would inflict on another person simply because he was ordered to by an experimental scientist. Stark authority was pitted against the subjects' [participants'] strongest moral imperatives against hurting others, and, with the subjects' [participants'] ears ringing with the screams of the victims, authority won more often than not. The extreme willingness of adults to go to almost any lengths on the command of an authority constitutes the chief finding of the study and the fact most urgently demanding explanation.
>
> Ordinary people, simply doing their jobs, and without any

particular hostility on their part, can become agents in a terrible destructive process. Moreover, even when the destructive effects of their work become patently clear, and they are asked to carry out actions incompatible with fundamental standards of morality, relatively few people have the resources needed to resist authority.[24]

Besides similarities between the Milgram and Stanford experiments, Philip Zimbardo reveals that none of the few participants who refused to administer the final shocks in the Milgram test insisted that the experiment itself be shut down. And when they were finished with their participation, none bothered to check the health of the victim they believed was potentially severely traumatized and/or physically harmed.[25] Years later, when researchers Charles Sheridan and Richard King speculated that some of the Milgram Experiment volunteers in the role of TEACHER may have suspected their victims were faking the trauma, they set up a similar trial using a "cute, fluffy puppy," which obviously would not know how to "fake it." In this case, the electrical shocks were real—albeit, unknown to the participants, harmless. Their findings— published as "Obedience to Authority with an Authentic Victim"—were reported during the proceedings of the eightieth annual convention of the American Psychological Association and surprisingly verified Milgram's conclusion. As in the Yale University experimentation, most subjects in the Sheridan-King research illustrated high levels of distress during the ordeal, yet 50 percent of the male subjects and 100 percent of the females obeyed the authority figure and continued to "electrocute" the puppy until the end.[26]

Not to be redundant, but again, what could this research suggest the majority of people might be willing to do when the utmost fearsome "authority figure" ever to walk planet earth arrives (a time when Jesus said people's hearts will fail them for fear [see Luke 21:26]) and begins ordering his followers to kill all who will not accept his leadership?

Beast Tech Provides Conditions for Global "Lucifer Effect"

In 2013, retired California police detective Terry Cook and I wrote a book titled *Beast Tech*. In it we considered how much of technology today appears to be sufficient for use by the coming Man of Sin—in particular, human tracking and monitoring utilities, including versions of embeddable smart tattoos and biochip devices that may provide for the mark of the Beast. A related area of equal concern we did not have time to address in that book involves the social implications involving *technology* and how it can be used by *unseen forces* to challenge religious faith or to open channels for spiritual warfare. This has been illustrated in thousands of ways down through time—from the creation of Ouija boards for contacting the spirit world to online pornography gateways. But, lately, the course on which technology and transhumanist philosophy seems to be taking mankind threatens to quantitatively elevate the potential for a global Lucifer Effect.

How so?

Given that the key to Dr. Milgram's and especially professor Philip Zimbardo's findings involved the need to deindividualize the victims of abuse, the Internet and associated forms of electronic information-driven technology are important to understand in light of how they are creating a new kind of society by "rewiring our brains'" ability to sympathize with others, says Nora Volkow, world-renowned brain scientist and director of the National Institute of Drug Abuse. For one thing, the lure of "digital stimulation" can actually produce dopamine releases in the brain that affect the heart rate and blood pressure and lead to drug-like highs and lows. Studies show this addictive craving for digital stimulation is leading to the electronic equivalent of Attention Deficit Disorder (ADD) among a growing population in which constant bursts of information and digital stimulation undermine one's ability to focus—especially in children (tomorrow's adults), whose brains are still developing and who naturally struggle to resist impulses or to neglect priorities. A growing body of literature is connecting such digital dependence to personality fragmentation, cyber relationships over personal ones, and the very type of psychosocial issues that were manifest in the Stanford Prison and Milgram experiments. Today, Volkow and similar researchers see these antisocial trends leading to widespread, diminished empathy between people—what Antichrist will need—as a result of humans paying more and more attention to iPads, cell phones, and computer screens than to each other, even when sitting in the same room. New research shows this situation becoming an electronic pandemic as people escalate their detachment from traditional relationships while consuming three times as much digital information today as they did only a decade ago, checking e-mails, texting thirty-seven times per hour, and spending twelve hours per day on average taking in other e-media. Add to this phenomenon how brain-machine interfacing (BMI)—one of the hottest emerging trends in the marketplace—will multiply the divide between human-to-human relationships versus human-machine integration, and substantial concern for readers should be raised for several reasons, including how: 1) BMI will naturally exasperate the decline of the family unit and interpersonal relationships upon which society has historically depended; 2) the increase of euphoric cybernetic addiction will multiply as cerebral stimulation of the brain's pleasure centers is added to existing natural senses—sight, hearing, taste, smell, and touch; and 3) the threat of computer viruses or hijackers disrupting enhanced human neural or cognitive pathways will develop as cyber-enhanced individuals evolve. To illustrate the latter, Dr. Mark Gasson, from the School of Systems Engineering at the University of Reading in the United Kingdom, intentionally contaminated an implanted microchip in his hand that allows him biometric entry through security doors and that also communicates with his cell phone and other external devices. In the experiment, Dr. Gasson (who agrees that the next step in human evolution is the transhuman vision of altered human biology integrated with machines) was able to show how the computer virus he infected himself with spread to external computer systems in communication with his microchip. He told BBC News, "With the benefits of this type of technology come risks. We [will] improve ourselves…but much like the improvements with other technologies, mobile phones for example, they become vulnerable to risks, such as security problems and computer viruses."[27]

Such threats—computer viruses passing from enhanced humans to enhanced humans via future cybernetic systems—are the tip of the iceberg. The real danger, though it may be entirely unavoidable for some, will be the loss of individuality (or, as Zimbardo phrased it, social deindividualizaton), anonymity, privacy, and even free will as a result of cybernetic integration. Dr. Christopher Hook contends, "If implanted devices allow the exchange of information between the biological substrate and the cybernetic device," such a device in the hippocampus (the part of the brain involved in forming, storing, and processing memory) for augmenting memory, for instance, "would be intimately associated with the creation and recall of memories as well as with all the emotions inherent in that process." Hook continues:

> If this device were…to allow the importation of information
> from the Internet, could the device also allow the memories and

thoughts of the individual to be downloaded or read by others? In essence, what is to prevent the brain itself from being hacked [or hijacked by Antichrist]? The last bastion of human privacy, the brain, will have been breached.[28]

Despite these significant ethical and social dangers, industry and government interest in the technological dream of posthumanism, as documented in the highly recommended book *Forbidden Gates*, is more than *laissez-faire*. The steady migration toward the fulfillment of biologically and cybernetically modified humans, combined with corporate and national investments, will predictably fuse this century, ultimately leading to strong cultural forces compelling all individuals to get "plugged in" to the grid. Whoever resists will be left behind as inferior Luddites (those who oppose new technology), or worse, considered enemies of the collectives' progress, as in former counterterrorism czar Richard Clark's *Breakpoint,* which depicts those who refuse technological enhancement as "terrorists."

According to the work *Human Dignity in the Biotech Century*, this pressure to become enhanced will be dramatic upon people in all social strata, including those in the middle class, law, engineering, finance, professional fields, and the military, regardless of personal or religious views:

Consider…whether the military, after investing billions in the development of technologies to create the cyborg soldier…would allow individual soldiers to decline the enhancements because of religious or personal qualms. It is not likely. Individuals may indeed dissent and decline technological augmentation, but such dissenters will find job options increasingly scarce.

Because the network of cyborgs will require increasing levels of cooperation and harmonious coordination to further improve efficiency, the prostheses will continue to introduce means of controlling or modulating emotion to promote these values. Meanwhile, the network [will be] increasingly controlled by central planning structures to facilitate harmony and efficiency. While everyone still considers themselves fully autonomous, in reality behavior is more and more tightly controlled. Each step moves those who are cybernetically augmented toward becoming like the Borg, the race of cybernetic organisms that inhabit the twenty-sixth century of the *Star Trek* mythology. The Borg, once fully human, become "assimilated" by the greater collective mind, losing individuality for the good of the whole.[29]

Lest anyone think the writers of *Human Dignity in the Biotech Century* are overly paranoid, consider that NBIC (Nanotechnology, Biotechnology, Information Technology, and Cognitive Science) Director Mihail Roco, in the US government report, *Converging Technologies for Improving Human Performance*, wrote:

Humanity would become like a single, distributed and interconnected "brain" based in new core pathways in society…. A networked society of billions of human beings could be as complex compared to an individual being as a human being is to a single nerve cell. From local groups of linked enhanced individuals to a global collective intelligence, key new capacities would arise from relationships arising from NBIC technologies…. Far from unnatural, such a collective social system may be compared to a larger form of biological organism…. We envision the bond of humanity driven by an *interconnected virtual brain* of the Earth's communities searching for intellectual comprehension and conquest of nature.[30]

Nowhere will the struggle to resist this human biological alteration and machine integration be more immediate than in those religious homes where transhumanism is seen as an assault on God's creative genius, and where, as a result, conservative Christians will seek to maintain their humanity. Yet the war against such believers is poised to emerge over the next decade as much from inside the "organized church" as it will from external social influences.

Already, the Internet "has unlocked something dark in humanity," says acclaimed author Anthony Horowitz in a recent newspaper interview.[31] Horowitz, a best-selling children's fiction writer in the UK, was speaking at the Oxford Literary Festival when he described how parts of the Internet are "foul, disgusting and cruel" and that "evil is getting the upper hand."[32] His passionate comments came on the heels of relentless and vicious online feedback he received following a television appearance. Mr. Horowitz is certainly not alone in this experience, as any notable writer can attest—especially Christians who pen edgy, newsworthy, or prophetic material.

And yes, that includes me and people like me. In fact, every leader with whom I am associated in news, print, television, and social media has been under growing attack the last few years, and not from those you would expect. Religious Christians, not unbelievers per se, form the largest part of the swelling ranks of warfare aimed at silencing our work. Because such discontents cannot (yet) stop people from hearing our voices, they (and/or the spirit behind them) at a minimum seek to divide and confuse ungrounded babes in Christ who, while seeking a deeper relationship with Jesus, end up online. Those who would destabilize these believers have always existed, of course. I witnessed ingrates in every town where I pastored throughout the 1970s–1990s. But today the Internet has given such malcontents a place to hive and to hide behind screens while using spiritual-sounding titles and websites to voice their ungraciousness. And while their audiences are very small at this time, their contaminated spirits threaten to take root and could explode under the coming legions that will fuel the empire of the Son of Perdition. In fact, I can say unequivocally from decades of experience that the most powerful instruments of satanic conflict by far are those *demons of religion* who can infect and infest institutional Christianity. As we noted in *Forbidden Gates*:

> Just as a lying spirit filled the mouths of the prophets in 2 Chronicles 18, and just as Jesus confronted unclean spirits inside the synagogue (Mark 1:23) and connected some of the priestly leaders of the Temple to the strongest power of Satan on earth (John 8:44; Matt. 13:38 and 23:15), robust *echon daimonion* exists today from the lowest to the highest levels of denominational establishment among institutional members who are possessed (whether they perceive it as such or not) by luciferian ambition. This will come as no surprise to seasoned spiritual warriors, as it is the result of a common military strategy. The church represents the single establishment on earth capable of undoing Satan's plans, and is therefore the natural enemy of the kingdom of darkness and the epicenter against which all spiritual wickedness must ultimately be focused. The church, through its hierarchies and institutional constructs, is therefore the primary target for infiltration by agents of darkness wherever human weakness allows for penetration by *daimonions*. Among others, the apostle Paul recognized this

specific danger, warning the church in Corinth that "false apostles" were masquerading among them as ministers of Christ. "And no marvel," he revealed, "for Satan himself is transformed into an angel of light. Therefore it is no great thing if his ministers also be transformed as the ministers of righteousness" (2 Cor. 11:13–15).[33]

Writing about such activity within evangelical institutions, Rev. David Wilkerson reported a short while before his death that:

A number of [former] witches are…warning that Satanists are infiltrating the church—especially charismatic churches. Some of these [are] telling of a diabolical plot by evil witches to enter congregations posing as super-spiritual Christians.… Many of these evil witches, they say, are already firmly established in numerous churches, controlling both the pastor and congregation and causing great confusion, wickedness, divorce—even death. We have received many letters in our office from people who say they believe their pastor must be under some kind of demonic influence—and I believe many of these letters are very legitimate.[34]

Wilkerson, who at one time was a member of the same organization we [Tom and Nita Horn] served, was correct in asserting that some of those who pose as super-spiritual Christians, online "teachers," department leaders, pastors, and even state office holders and denominational headquarters executives are in fact instruments of evil. Thankfully, there are other church members, pastors, and leaders who, as sincere believers, have become increasingly aware of this sinister invasion into organizations by *daimonions* and in recent years have made special efforts to teach their congregations how to identify the differences between "religious spirits" and true Christianity.

Sometimes "identifying" their misdeeds is not really all that hard to do.

For example, just about every solid Bible expositor I know has been tirelessly harassed online the last few years by fake defenders of the faith. Yet, not once have these self-proclaimed "guardians of the truth" actually followed the Bible's mandates themselves, mandates that very specifically outline how believers are to deal with error in the church. The New Testament books of Matthew, Galatians, Thessalonians, Romans, and others provide guidelines for dealing with differences between true believers. These verses teach us that if we perceive a brother or sister as falling into error, we are to go to him or her PRIVATELY in a spirit of humility and redemption. If those we approach will not receive our advice, we go to the elders of the church PRIVATELY and share our concern. If the elders believe the issue is legitimate, they go to the person PRIVATELY in hopes of restoring him or her. If the person still refuses council, the church is to have nothing more to do with him or her. With that in mind, the next time you are online reading some diatribe about Chuck Missler, Gary Stearman, Steve Quayle, David Flynn, J. R. Church, L. A. Marzulli, Cris Putnam, Jonathan Cahn, yours truly, or any of the other current favorite targets, ask yourself if the hatchet people attacking them ever bothered to obey Scripture and go to the person PRIVATELY with their concerns in a loving spirit of restoration (they haven't), and then "be careful little eyes what you read," because destructive forces seek to contaminate your mind and spirit (see Prov. 4:23–27) in order to prep you for service to the dark side.

Be absolutely clear about this, too: NOTHING in Scripture allows for setting up websites, blogs, or other mediums to PUBLICALLY and routinely lambast believers with accusations—*that is the job of Satan and*

his followers! He is the father of lies and the "accuser of our brethren...
which accused them before our God day and night" (John 8:44; Rev.
12:10).

Simply put, the words of Jesus that "ye shall know them by their fruits"
(Matt. 7:15–16) have never been more important. These instructions of
Christ should also serve as a warning to all believers to monitor their own
motives, to examine their hearts, if truly they are altruistic or if in fact
they are energized by selfish ambition, because the latter is the Lucifer
Effect Antichrist will use to energize the coming war between Christian
vs. Christian, a time when it will be eternally important to know you are
on the right side.

Will Genetics Also Play a Role in a Global Lucifer Effect?

Thus far in considering the "how" and "why" of the coming war between
Christian vs. Christian and ultimately the role that the ecclesiastical oli-
garchy under Antichrist will play in its brutal disposition of Tribulation
saints, we have discussed disturbing facts regarding man's fallen nature (as
conveyed in the Stanford Prison and Milgram experiments) as well as the
potential use of emerging technology by destructive people and spirits.

The third and final area in this chapter that bears mentioning involves
a more exotic concept (albeit one that I believe is not without historical
precedence) involving the possible genetic alteration of future humans,
including religious types that will comprise the "soulless" armies of the
Beast.

This is a spooky thought, really, but one that is commanding more
and more consideration from thoughtful prophecy expositors who suspect

that the reason those last-days destroyers of born-again believers will act with such inhumanity is that they may be, well, not altogether human any longer.

Because we take considerable time in our books *Zenith 2016* and *Forbidden Gates* to outline the historical activity of ancient Watchers (fallen angels) and their genetic creation known as Nephilim (as well as the resemblance of their activity with modern transhumanist goals involving genetic modification of species), we will not repeat that material here. What we will mention is that modern scientists increasingly believe genetics play a greater role in human and animal behavior than was previously believed, and that this may include a kind of "evil genetic combination" that leads to lower inhibitions involving criminal activity and murder.

In an article for Florida State University actually titled "The Evil Gene," Frank Stephenson considers research from his university as well as the University of Connecticut, where scientists are analyzing the DNA of spree killers. The first line in Stephenson's paper suggests what the professors are looking for when it asks: "Could a monster be swimming in the human gene pool?" The good researcher approaches his study from a Darwinian foundation, stating:

In ascending the evolutionary ladder, humans obviously failed to inherit from their hairy forebears inhibitions against using lethal force against members of their own species. The bizarre "ghoul factor" of sadistic psychopaths like [Ted] Bundy aside, humans' historic willingness to slaughter each other wholesale in war and genocide offers compelling evidence to some scientists that in the genome of some humans lies a fully armed biochemical code for the gamut of aggression, from kicking the dog to killing the wife.[35]

In tandem with Stephenson's alternate worldview speculation about an evil "biochemical code," recent years have produced considerable advances in DNA research, with one of the more popular new fields called behavioral epigenetics. This is the "darling of genetic studies," my biologist friend Sharon Gilbert tells me. It seeks to examine and understand the role that genetics play in shaping animal and human behavior, cognition, personality, and mental health. Epigenetics may occur during life or begin in the womb when chemical changes brought on by the mother's activity affect the genetics—and thus perhaps the future behavior—of the child. That these modifications may become heritable and passed from one generation to the next has some scientists wondering if "evil genetics" or toxic combinations of specific genes may be linked to aggression and antisocial behavior in the succeeding generations of some families. If so, this raises an intriguing question I will not develop here having to do with bloodlines and a second question that I *will* pose regarding the potential for a blueprint or "special" genetic combination that could exist in which individuals can be programmed or reprogrammed to act in defiance of normal human consciousness (having a soul). This appears to have been the estate of those Nephilim mentioned above, which are depicted in ancient records as bloodthirsty, violent enemies of God's people who never once had a conflict of consciousness or sought forgiveness for their brutality. Genetically engineered with a specific cellular combination by powerful fallen angels (whom the Sumerians called "flying geniuses"), these remarkable living constructs, not made in the image of God, were specifically designed for demonic inhabitation.

But did the Nephilim also represent a repeatable, dark, molecular model?

Given that Jesus said (see Matt. 24:37) the end-times would witness a return to the activity that happened when Nephilim first walked the earth, and today for the first time since those days men have intentionally set out to genetically modify plants, animals, and humans, is it possible that we have entered a reprise of the "days of Noah" in which a genetic hazard could be unleashed resulting in a global pandemic, *a Nephilim-virus!?*

There are numerous scenarios—all based on real science—that envision an "event" that could, in effect, modify epigenetics worldwide and thus hypothetically the mind and makeup of all but those who would be protected by God. In theory, this might suddenly and effectively diminish the ability of the sufferers to feel empathy toward others. Now, if such a concept has you thinking that I've been watching too many zombie flicks, I am reminded of the Hollywood film *I Am Legend* starring Will Smith. That movie opened with a scientist announcing the cure to cancer using a genetically engineered "chimeric" vaccine that blended animal and human genetics. If you've seen the film, you know the "cure" results in a human form of rabies that infects and takes over the brains of people, quickly turning them into zombie-like monsters who wipe out most life on earth—an epidemiological possibility, given the scenario.

Jonathan D. Dinman, PhD, professor in the Department of Cell Biology and Molecular Genetics at the University of Maryland, says such a zombie virus "almost exists now" and could be engineered to fully occur using the very element from Will Smith's epic—rabies.

"Infection is nearly 100 percent lethal, i.e. it turns you into the walking dead (for a while at least)," he says, "and it causes you to change your behavior by reprogramming you to bite other people to spread the infection."[36]

Rabies as it is known today would only need to be slightly mutated, something that could be engineered or occur naturally, to facilitate an end-times army of soulless killers, and it is actually "the most likely to mutate into something that would be similar to a 'zombie virus,'" says

Dr. Samantha Price, a Health and Care Professions Council-registered biomedical scientist and research information coordinator for the UK Motor Neurone Disease Association.[37]

In addition to a zombie/Nephilim virus scenario, top-level policy advisors to the United States intelligence and military communities—including the JASONs (the celebrated scientists on the Pentagon's most prestigious scientific advisory panel)—have warned in recent years that human enhancement involving genetic alteration, either by design, accident, or bioweapon, represents a challenging if not existential risk.

In a report to the Department of Defense titled "The $100 Genome: Implications for the DoD," the JASONs convey that rapid advances in DNA sequencing and related technologies are not only ushering in an era of precipitous genomics information and sciences, but a time when both "genotypes" and "phenotypes" could experience unpredictable deviations. An organism's genotype is the set of genes or the "genetic blueprint" it receives from its parents, while its phenotype involves the observable characteristics—the way it looks, walks, talks, and behaves. Thus what the policy advisors to ranking officials in Washington are warning is that, as we modify nature's genetic balance (including animals and humans), we should expect they will manifest revisions in their phenotypic expressions as well. They may begin walking differently, thinking differently, and behaving in ways no longer atypical of known creation.

That such unprecedented realities may well emerge has already been illustrated in animal-to-animal experiments, including those conducted by Evan Balaban at McGill University in Montreal, Canada, where sections of brain from embryonic quails were transplanted into the brains of chickens, and the resultant chickens exhibited head bobs and vocal trills unique to quail.[38] The implication from this field of study alone proves that complex behavior patterns can be transferred from one species to another, strongly suggesting that genetically altered humans will likely bear unintended behavior and appetite disorders that could literally produce modern "Nephilim" traits. In fact, some in government and science believe one-on-one, interpersonal malevolence by such altered humans might ultimately lead to a global Lucifer Effect and swarm violence. The seriousness of this is significant enough that a House Foreign Affairs (HFA) committee chaired by California Democrat Brad Sherman, best known for his expertise on the spread of nuclear weapons and terrorism, studied the implications of genetic modification and human-transforming technologies related to future terrorism. What the HFA found caused *Congressional Quarterly* columnist Mark Stencel to write in his article, "Futurist: Genes Without Borders," that the conference "sounded more like a Hollywood pitch for a sci-fi thriller than a sober discussion of scientific reality…with talk of biotech's potential for creating supersoldiers, superintelligence, and superanimals [that could become] agents of unprecedented lethal force."[39] George Annas, Lori Andrews, and Rosario Isasi were even more apocalyptic in their peer-reviewed *American Journal of Law and Medicine* article, "Protecting the Endangered Human: Toward an International Treaty Prohibiting Cloning and Inheritable Alterations," when they concluded: "The new species, or 'posthuman,' will likely view the old 'normal' humans as inferior, even savages, and fit for slavery or slaughter…. It is ultimately this predictable potential for genocide that makes species-altering experiments potential weapons of mass destruction, and makes the unaccountable genetic engineer a potential bioterrorist."[40]

Do these situations sound to anybody besides me like formulae for the coming armies of Antichrist? At a minimum they are highly suggestive that genetic alterations could play a role in the coming war against true believers.

A Light at the End of the Lucifer Effect?

Dr. Chuck Missler, a good friend, confidant, and role model to me and tens of thousands of others worldwide, happens to believe something very good can, is, and will come out of the lead-up to that period in history when true believers will be thoroughly persecuted. Just as he begins his chapter in this book repeating what J. Vernon McGee preached about denominational churches eventually driving the true body of Christ underground, in his must-read book, *Prophecy 20/20: Profiling the Future Through the Lens of Scripture,* Dr. Missler describes how so many real believers today have already started their exodus from institutional Christianity and are reemerging in home groups, just as the church began in the book of Acts. He writes:

> There is presently a groundswell across America—as in many other parts of the world—in which people are meeting in small groups in homes during the week, rediscovering the Bible, and enjoying a more intimate fellowship than they find in "Sunday church." Many of these are encouraged and supported by their formal church associations; others simply meet independently. This is especially true of many young people, to whom "Sunday church" is a spectator sport, and who seek more personal partici-pation and accountability.
>
> After all, this is the way it all began: twelve guys along the sea-shore with their Teacher. All the remarkable episodes of the early church in the book of Acts *occurred in homes.* It wasn't until the fourth century that edifices began to be erected, when Christians exchanged the rags of the caves for the silks of the court. And

committed ambassadors were replaced with hirelings, inserted between an attendee and the Word itself.

In more than sixty years as a practicing Christian, the place that I've always seen people really grow spiritually is within small group Bible studies: where they can ask questions and hold each other accountable.[41]

Dr. Missler goes on to list caveats to be considered in small groups, including the need to network and not become insular, as well as the need to "systematically spawn new leadership, and not become an end in themselves."[42] (Note! If you are interested in starting a home study group or would like more information on how the Koinonia Institute can provide resources, please visit www.StudyCenter.com). This recognition of vibrant Christianity growing outside the walls of Western religious centers offers hope that the true body of Christ always has and will survive and even triumph during times of persecution. The seventh chapter of the book of Revelation is dedicated to describing a great number of people redeemed during the coming war between religionists and saints. It speaks of:

…a great multitude, which no man could number, of all nations, and kindreds, and people, and tongues….

who came out of the great tribulation, and have washed their robes, and made them white in the blood of the Lamb….

They shall hunger no more, neither thirst any more; neither shall the sun light on them, nor any heat.

For the Lamb who is in the midst of the throne shall feed them, and shall lead them unto living fountains of waters; and God shall wipe away all tears from their eyes. (Rev. 7: 9–17)

The apostle Peter likewise recorded in the book of Acts that:

It shall come to pass in the last days, saith God, I will pour out of my Spirit upon all flesh; and your sons and your daughters shall prophesy, and your young men shall see visions, and your old men shall dream dreams....

And it shall come to pass, *that whosoever shall call on the name of the Lord shall be saved.* (Acts 2:17–18, 21, emphasis added)

Do these verses imply, as some believe, that the increase in persecution of true believers around the world today may simply presage an imminent, latter-day awakening...a revival in the purest sense of the word? I sure hope so. Pray so. But one thing I'm certain of: Growing animosity against the children of God is a real and present danger that is only going to worsen in the days ahead.

Between now and that climactic encounter when the supernatural battle spoken of in the Bible's books of prophecy begins in earnest, we can expect the divide between religious and authentic Christianity to deepen. It is hard for us to imagine that in places like the United States true believers could someday be burned alive in churches, but it is happening in Nigeria now. It is hard for us to perceive that some might be beheaded, but this is a reality in Syria today. We can hardly fathom good people being crucified alive, but Pakistani Christians are living with this nightmare now. And in the United States, that city on a hill once listed among the safest locations on earth for Christians, a tide of anti-Christ sentiment has in only the last few years pushed this country into a category recently reserved for only those governments that restrict and criminalize expressions of real Christianity.

You can see the writing on the wall intensifying.

Unlike my grandfather's America, if a US preacher today says on television that Jesus is the only way to heaven, he is derided by media and ignored by megachurches.

If a Christian calls homosexuality a sin or speaks negatively about Islamism, he is branded on talk shows as "homophobic" or "Islamaphobic."

If a Christian business owner refuses service to a homosexual couple because of religious beliefs, he or she faces criminal charges and a court order to "cease and desist from discriminating" or face fines (see example news story in the endnotes[43]). If a judge can order an independent cake maker to go against her conscience to create a wedding cake for a same-sex couple, how long will it be before pastors are required to perform gay weddings or face criminal prosecution? This is the very kind of social pressure contributing to the developing chasm between religious and born-again believers. People are and will be forced to choose sides.

How many more years will I be able to publish a book like this before it is banned? One thing is sure: The tide against New Testament faith is bound to get worse, especially as we near that period called Great Tribulation. I trust the reader will carefully consider the following chapters in this book by true friends and followers of Jesus and use them to draw your own line in the sand for the coming war between *Christian vs. Christian.*

2

THE GOOD AND THE BAD OF WHAT'S COMING

By Chuck Missler

J. Vernon McGee, one of the most beloved Bible teachers of the past century, surprised his listeners with the declaration that, in America, true biblical believers will ultimately have to go "underground" (no surprise to many of us); but, he added the observation that the attack against them will come from the denominational churches(!). This is a timely forecast as we see the Christian increasingly marginalized in our society—especially in our military.[44]

During World War II, every soldier and sailor was given a Testament with a letter pasted inside by Franklin Delano Roosevelt, the president and commander-in-chief, encouraging the reader to resort to the comfort and resources of the biblical text. (There were three versions: Protestant, Catholic, and Jewish.) Today, giving a serviceman a Bible is illegal.

Melvin Laird, long before he was secretary of defense, made the following statement in San Francisco at a Republican convention: "In this world it is becoming more and more unpopular to be a Christian. Soon it may become dangerous."[45] We are seeing the accuracy of this statement. Real Christianity and real Christians are becoming increasingly unpopular and "politically incorrect."

However, this should not come as a surprise to the diligent student of ecclesiastical history.

Basic Background

It should be obvious to even the casual observer that the real story of the church is not the one recorded in secular history. The true drama is not even recorded in church history books. The real saga is of intrepid believers, "of whom the world was not worthy," who were not only persecuted by the civil authorities, *but were denounced, defamed, and decimated by the professing church!*[46]

Who were the Waldensians? The Lollards? The Albigeneses? The Stundists? The Anabaptists?[47] "These were names given *by their enemies* to those who claimed only the name of Christ, and who were prepared to suffer for His cause rather than submit to those man-made traditions that they believed contradicted the Word of God."[48] E. H. Broadbent has provided us a history that demonstrates that this was a predicament imposed on the true, biblically committed throughout all of the past fifteen hundred years.[49] It is disturbing to realize that those who clung to the Word of God were the subject of being marginalized and attacked *by the established churches* throughout all of recorded history—and that this will continue to characterize the predicament of serious believers in the years ahead.

And this also is the subject of New Testament Scripture.

The Seven Epistles of Christ

The Lord Jesus Himself gave us seven epistles that are seven "report cards" profiling all of ecclesiastical history in advance.[50] (In any other order, they wouldn't fit the subsequent events!)

The apostle John must certainly have been puzzled: Exiled on Patmos, he was about to receive the most elevated vision ever given to anyone on the planet. It began with the resurrected Jesus dictating individual report cards to seven representative churches *and yet He got so ill he apparently was about to vomit!*

> I know thy works, that thou art neither cold nor hot; I would thou wert cold or hot.
>
> So, then, because thou art lukewarm, and neither cold nor hot, I will spew thee out of my mouth.
>
> Because thou sayest, I am rich, and increased with goods, and have need of nothing; and knowest not that thou art wretched, and miserable, and poor, and blind, and naked. (Rev. 3:15–17)

Seven elements comprise each of the seven epistles, and each of them supports a specific theme of each letter.

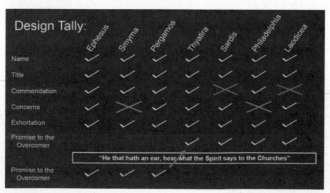

45

By careful study, we note that from both architectural and eschatological aspects, these seven epistles fall into two groupings: the first three and the final four. The first three have a promise to the overcomer as an addendum, outside the body of the letter; and they also fail to include any explicit reference to the Second Coming. The final four include the promise to the overcomer within the body of the letter, and also include an explicit eschatological reference. While they all appear to fit an order chronologically, the final four—in some sense—also seem to endure to the end.

One of them (Thyatira) includes an explicit warning regarding the Great Tribulation; another (Philadelphia) is promised to be removed from the very time of the Tribulation. The remaining two (Sardis and Laodicea) are problematic, *and are the only two of which nothing positive is declared;* these are the focus of this inquiry. It is the condition of the final one, Laodicea, which is the most dismal.

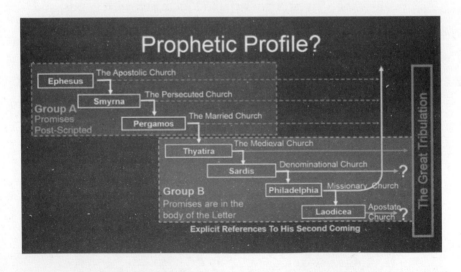

Protestant commentators have had a field day with Thyatira (the longest letter) and its ostensible allusions to the Vatican and the Church of Rome. Yet, if Thyatira is an allusion to Church of Rome, then Sardis would seem to be an allusion to the Reformation and its entrails; however, Sardis is presented as having only a "name," yet is dead. "I know thy works, that thou hast a name that thou livest, and art dead" (Rev. 3:1). A chilling perspective, indeed!

Laodicea ("rule of the people") clearly profiles the apostate church: Jesus is even on the *outside*, knocking on the door to come in! His appeal is focused on the individual, not to the entire assembly as in the previous letters. It is our apparent drift toward Laodicea that seems to herald our drift toward the "end times."

It is also reminiscent of the ancient words of a century-old poem, carved in a gothic, medieval alphabet on a towering, ornate cathedral door right in the heart of a small town in Germany. The words may date back to the days of Martin Luther, and may even have impacted his journey, which altered the course of history:

Thus speaks Christ our Lord to us:
You call me Eternal, then do not seek me.
You call me Fair, then do not love me.
You call me Gracious, then to not trust me.
You call me Just, then do not fear me.
You call me Life, then do not choose me.
You call me Light, then do not see me.
You call me Lord, then do not respect me.
You call me Master, then do not obey me.
You call me Merciful, then do not thank me.
You call me Mighty, then do not honor me.
You call me Noble, then do not serve me.
You call me Rich, then do not ask me.

You call me Savior, then do not praise me.

You call me Shepherd, then do not follow me.

You call me the Way, then do not walk with me.

You call me Wise, then do not heed me.

You call me Son of God, then do not worship me

When I [sentence] you, then do not blame me.[51]

The Way It All Started

A group of twelve alongside a seashore.

The birth of the church at Pentecost was in a house.[52] The early church met in houses.[53] It still proves to be an ideal setting: a group small enough so that someone can ask questions without embarrassment. A group that is intimate enough to hold each other accountable. In my own sixty-five years, it is in small home groups where I have seen people really grow (not from forty-five-minute messages on Sunday mornings).

What we take for granted are the formal structures patterned after state-sponsored churches in the third and fourth centuries. Home fellowships were ostracized by the medieval church, and subsequently by the Reformation churches, and still many churches today. Home groups remain the most viable form for underground churches today. As a persecuted church, this was the only safe way to meet. That day is again upon us.

Home churches have many advantages: They undergo disciplined multiplication (mitosis), they are free of growth barriers, and they include more "involved" participants. Therefore, in home churches, we see more personal transformation and accountability; they are more effective for new Christians. Home groups solve the leadership crisis, and they are more biblical. They enjoy a more persecution-proof structure; they are more efficient and involve lower costs. They mature under tears, multiply under pressure, flourish in the desert, see in the dark, thrive on chaos. Their only boast is the Lamb.

There was no bureaucratic clergy in the New Testament, no clergical mediators.[54] Nicolaitanes were adaptations from pagan religions and were expressly denounced by the Lord Himself twice.[55]

Current Recommendations

Regarding current ecclesiastical tactics, it would seem appropriate to establish and encourage home study groups and give them as much individual leeway as possible. (Straitjackets seem to limit the movements of the Holy Spirit.)

Furthermore, a clear specific focus on "the gospel" is critical.[56] Social issues can easily derail our primary calling. Paul gives us a succinct definition in the first four verses of 1 Corinthians 15:

Moreover, brethren, I declare unto you the gospel which I preached unto you, which also ye have received, and in which ye stand;

By which also ye are saved, if ye keep in memory what I preached unto you, unless ye have believed in vain.

For I delivered unto you first of all that which I also received, that Christ died for our sins according to the Scriptures;

And that he was buried, and that he rose again the third day according to the scriptures. (1 Cor. 15:1–4)

Jesus Christ died in the most well-documented execution in all history, fulfilling dozens of very precise specifications recorded centuries in advance. He was buried. And He then rose from the dead, again fulfilling numerous specifications.[57]

What is also distinctive is what Paul does *not* include as "the gospel": He makes no mention of the Lord's teachings, His miracles, or His example, etc. Our basic challenge is to declare the gospel, and this differentiates us from the pending social issues of the day. This will not be a popular stance. In fact, it may the principal issue driving the true ambassadors underground.

But there is also a unique, yet biblically based concept for the support of the independent missionary pursuing an unbridled mission under cover for the Coming King.

The Spiritual Entrepreneur

The role and contributions of the independent entrepreneur in both financial and technological sectors are legendary, and the factors that contribute to his success have been well studied in the management literature. Being driven by a vision, his persistence and commitment to his self-appointed goals have embroidered the tapestry of both technological and economic progress throughout the centuries. However, the degree to which these traits characterized the apostle Paul in the *spiritual* realm has rarely been adequately recognized in our contemporary missionary perspectives.

If our mission is equipping the saints "for the work of the ministry,"[58] this requires three primary foundations: education, experience, and enablement (financial support). It is this last one that requires a creative focus. It is the support of the missionary in the field that typically involves one of three approaches:

1) **Full-time employment with an established organization**. This is the typical career path in major denominations or other organizations, but can suffer from management stasis, mission shifts, and the frustrations of various bureaucratic inefficiencies. (It also intrinsically suffers from a form of "Nicolaitanism," which was specifically disdained by our Lord[59] yet which emerged in early church history and continues throughout traditional practices.)

2) **Solicitation of personal support**. This is the approach of Youth With A Mission (YWAM), Campus Crusade, et al. For a specific project or a limited season, this can be quite effective. However, as a continuing career path, it proves inefficient—often requiring more than 50 percent of the manpower just soliciting continuing personal support "piecemeal." (And in an increasingly hostile environment, this path may prove problematical in the times ahead.)

3) **Self-support**. This was the path that the apostle Paul resorted to, and his results speak for themselves.[60] *Res ipsa locquitur.*[61] Combining casual vocational income, along with careful management of invested capital, this alternative can facilitate a ministry undertaking that is *not economically dependent upon the specific mission being served*. Furthermore, by relying on vocational skills for support, an operative can maintain a lower-profile cover to mask his primary commitments from adversarial elements while he serves covertly as an ambassador of the Coming King.

As the world continues to grow spiritually darker and a biblical worldview continues to become increasingly "politically incorrect," an underground network of independent spiritual entrepreneurs may be the most viable means to serve and edify the body of believers in anticipation of our Coming King.

"When it is darkest, men see the stars,"
—Ralph Waldo Emerson.

It is even possible to design a way to support the independent spiritual entrepreneur that favors the truly competent and proven committed, and that also provides for distributed accountability, yet retains the funds within the ministry in perpetuity. However, we don't want to let such detailed plans fall into adversarial hands. I would be glad to share them with you under the right circumstances; but I can't tell who might be looking over your shoulder at the moment. I'm sure you will understand.

Remember Proverbs 27:12 (also 22:3): "A prudent man foreseeth the evil, and hideth himself, but the simple pass on, and are punished."

In the meantime,

Stay in the grip of our King,

Chuck

3

BY THE TYPING OF OUR THUMBS, SOMETHING WICKED THIS WAY COMES

By Sharon K. Gilbert

Like you, the Krell forgot one deadly danger: their own subconscious hate and lust for destruction. The beast. The mindless primitive. Even the Krell must have evolved from that beginning. And so those mindless beasts of the subconscious had access to a machine that could never be shut down. The secret devil of every soul on the planet…all set free at once to loot and maim…and take revenge and kill!

—MGM's *Forbidden Planet*[62]

Some of you may recognize the above quote as a conversation from the ending to MGM's 1956 science fiction film, *Forbidden Planet*. This cult classic movie centers on a rather eccentric but brilliant scientist named Dr. Edward Morbius (played by Walter Pidgeon) and his innocent teenage daughter Altaira (Anne Francis). Morbius is the only surviving original member of a doomed expedition from earth sent to discover whether life exists in the Altair solar system. Commander John Adams (Leslie Nielsen) leads a rescue mission to Altair IV, but his team is attacked by an unseen "force"—the same monstrous "force" that killed all but Morbius, including his wife (Altair's mother). Morbius is a linguistics expert, and he has uncovered ancient instrumentation and records that reveal clues to a long-extinct Altair IV race called "the Krell," who died after inventing massive machinery that fed off energy within the Krell minds. However, this marvelous invention proved to be their downfall, for the Krell minds—once joined to the machine—had given birth to a great and terrifying monster.

Of course, this is all fiction, right? Humans could never produce an unseen something that would one day destroy us all. Perhaps it's best that you not read this chapter when alone or at night, because such a monster is developing—even as I type these words, and, as with the Krell on Altair, this monster—this ravenous and very wicked Beast—may soon awaken and pit Christian against Christian, Jew against Jew, and all who worship this Beast against all who refuse to do so. To paraphrase the Second Witch from Shakespeare's infamous "Scottish Play": By the typing of our thumbs, something wicked this way comes.[63]

Need convincing? Let's begin with a few terms.

Intelligence

One might assume this to refer to problem-solving skills, particularly those required for abstract reasoning. The term is derived from the Latin verb *intelligere*, which means "to comprehend, perceive, or understand." In 1994, a group of fifty-two researchers penned their collective definition of intelligence:

A very general mental capability that, among other things, involves the ability to reason, plan, solve problems, think abstractly, comprehend complex ideas, learn quickly and learn from experience. It is not merely book learning, a narrow academic skill, or test-taking smarts. Rather, it reflects a broader and deeper capability for comprehending our surroundings—"catching on," "making sense" of things, or "figuring out" what to do.[64]

I would add one additional modification that intelligence is based on freewill as given to mankind by God the Creator, this being the ability to make choices based upon any given set of options.

Sentience

This term is based on the Latin present participle *sentiens,* which means "feeling or perceiving." In some ways, intelligence implies action, externalization, decision-making, and choices, while sentience evokes passion, internalization, thoughtfulness, and evaluation. Sentience serves and informs intelligence. Theologically, intelligence relates to the mind, while sentience relates to the heart. Though technically incorrect, sentience has come to mean "self-aware." Thus, a sentient entity understands that he or she is a separate being within a complex system. *Cogito ergo sum:* "I think, therefore, I am."[65] Theologically speaking, sentience is a gift from God, as mankind is created in His image. God is a sentient being; in fact, He is the Great I Am (the singular, superlative form of Rene Descartes's "Thinker"). God gave man intelligence, freewill, and a compassionate heart. We can choose to react and act within the parameters of any given construct—be that reaction and or action good or evil; it is our choice.

Life

The traditional definition of life taught to all Biology 101 students is that an organism is considered alive when it possesses and exhibits the capacity to grow, metabolize, respond to stimuli, adapt to changing conditions, and reproduce. Recent revisions of this definition suggest that the organism must be RNA- or DNA-based. The National Aeronautics and Space Administration (NASA) has proposed adding a caveat that true *life* must demonstrate the ability and/or potential to evolve along Darwinian guidelines. Of course, biologists don't have the luxury of observing a candidate for "life" over millions of years to prove it has evolved, which is why the "potential" to evolve is included. This merely requires inclusion of transposons (transposable elements that can jump to different positions on a chromosome) within a genome to qualify, and all genomes have these as just one component of a process called epigenetics.

Some biologists have even suggested the creation of an entire field of study with a single mission: to define life. Some say life is based only on carbon, others that life is cell based (excluding crystals). However, without a firm foundation in Christ, no scientist can truly appreciate the beautiful design within carbon-based life forms.

Synthetic Biology

According to distinguished (and very sentient) researcher Dr. Steven A. Benner, founder of the Westheimer Institute of Science and Technology and the Foundation for Applied Molecular Evolution, synthetic biology must be considered a viable contender for "life" as we know it:

The goal of synthetic biology is to get, in the laboratory, a chemical system that can support Darwinian evolution. Our activities as synthetic biologists need not be constrained by any particular model for how life might have emerged on Earth. Any system will do, including one based on a biopolymer, or a collection of metabolic processes, or a mineral assembly.

Further, the system need not be self-sustaining; **we would be happy if it were able to evolve and adapt, even if it needed continuous attention from a sentient being.** Any synthetic molecular system that reproduces with error, if those errors are themselves reproducible, should be able to adapt to environmental changes, at least to the degree that its fundamental molecular capabilities allow.

Various efforts are underway to obtain such systems. These include work with DNA-like molecules that are built from six different nucleotide "letters"…artificial genetic systems that can be copied, with errors, where those errors are replicable.

Should artificial Darwinian chemical systems be obtained, they present a direct test to the definition-theory of life. They should be able to produce, *in vitro,* features that we value from living systems. Should they fail to do so, they will be analyzed to learn why they fail. This might lead to the identification of chemical features *other* than a polyelectrolyte that are needed to support Darwinian evolution. Or they may challenge the centrality of Darwinian evolution in any theory-definition of life.[66] (emphasis added)

Artificial Life

This includes software designed to evolve, robots intended to emulate humans or animals, and synthetic biology that involves an artificially designed, nucleic acid-based "life form" such as Craig Venter's "Synthia."[67] Evolutionists believe that all life on earth "evolved" from nonliving matter, which (either spontaneously or after being acted upon by an outside force) gave rise to self-replicating molecules. These then self-assembled into complex organic structures. This theory is called abiogenesis (no-egg-required thinking—thus, the chicken comes first; of course, it takes this proto-chicken many millennia to spring forth and therefore a very long time to cross the Darwinian road).

Internet

A global system of interconnected computers, based upon ARPAnet (Advanced Research Projects Agency Network), a military network created by the precursor to DARPA (Defense Advanced Research Projects Agency).

World Wide Web

A system of hyperlinked documents accessed via the Internet. The World Wide Web (WWW or W3) provides a user-friendly interface allowing anyone to join the Internet with a personal computer, tablet, smart phone, or other connected device (this will soon include appliances, cars, robots, and even external and internal medical and/or personal devices). It is interesting to note that the numerical value of "www" is 666.[68]

Deep Web

Also called Dark Web, DarkNet, the Invisible Web, and the Hidden Web, this realm of "stealth" websites, pages, images, files, and other documents cannot be accessed by typing in a .www URL (Uniform Resource Locator). Lying beneath the "Surface Web," these sites are not indexed by search engines like Bing or Google, but require specific web crawlers and/or the manual submission of an Internet protocol or password. The Deep Web is estimated to be many magnitudes larger than the Surface Web. These murky depths provide cover for a shadowy world of illicit trade and criminal activities such as drug traffic, pornography, pedophilia, pederasty, snuff films, organ trafficking, and even slave trade, but they also provide deep cover for covert operations and spying. If you think the Surface Web contains disgusting imagery and ideas, you would be shocked at what slithers just beneath those Facebook "likes," selfie-ridden Instagrams, and idle Tweets. The Internet that you and I and find so compelling contains both good and bad, but the nether regions of the DarkNet never see, nor do they benefit from, the light of day.

———

Now that we've unpacked a few definitions, let me offer a short history of the Internet, since that is where Leviathan, the monster from *the Id* now sleeps. ARPAnet was born from the vision of J. C. R. Lidicker, a psychologist *cum* computer scientist and former director of Behavioral Sciences Command and Control Research at DARPA (then called ARPA, the Advanced Research Projects Agency operated by the US Defense Department). During the 1950s, Lidicker was a major contributor to ARPA's "SAGE" (Semi-Automatic Ground Environment) project that sought to create a defense system based on computer/human responses. Computers fed data to human operators, who then made decisions for action—hence the term "semi-automatic." However, this exposure to the possibilities inherent in computers stayed with Lidicker, and he eventually proposed what he called the "Intergalactic Network," which sounds rather far-fetched, but with this vision, he wrote and discussed concepts such as "point-and-click" interfaces, e-commerce, digital libraries, and more. His dreams even included "cloud computing."[69]

However, before ARPAnet could form, a subnetwork had to be created as a means to provide structure and connectivity while the "net" formed. This subnet was called the Interface Message Processor (IMP) and conjoined a variety of university scholars with the IPTO (Information Processing Techniques Office) at the Pentagon. Now, I won't dwell on this, but it is interesting to note that ARPAnet is an anagram of "pan tare." Pan, a mythological, goat-legged creature, was reputed to rape women and commit all manner of adulterous and lecherous acts. Pan has now come to serve as a prefix meaning "everywhere at once" or "worldwide," as in "pandemic." Tares are weeds and were used by Jesus as representing the evil that the enemy has sown in a field:

> Another parable put he forth unto them, saying, The kingdom of heaven is likened unto a man who sowed good seed in his field;
>
> But while men slept, his enemy came and sowed **tares** among the wheat, and went his way.
>
> But when the blade was sprung up, and brought forth fruit, then appeared the **tares** also.
>
> So the servants of the householder came and said unto him, Sir, didst not thou sow good seed in thy field? from whence then hath it **tares**?

He said unto them, An enemy hath done this. The servants said unto him, Wilt thou then that we go and gather them up?

But he said, Nay; lest while ye gather up the **tares**, ye root up also the wheat with them.

Let both grow together until the harvest; and in the time of harvest I will say to the reapers,

Gather ye together first the **tares**, and bind them in bundles to burn them, but gather the wheat into my barn. (Matt. 13:24–30, emphasis added)

The tares are a type of so-called bastard wheat (actually a dark variety of darnel that resembles wheat but lacks nutrition, i.e., a weed). Now, I won't dwell any more on this other than to say that the hint about tares everywhere riding on the backs of an IMP are metaphorically irresistible as relates to my theme of a slumbering Beast about to waken in this universal "field" we call the Internet.

Now, back to my short history.

Once the subnet and basic protocols were in place, four universities (Stanford, Utah, the University of California at Los Angeles, and the University of California, Santa Barbara) were selected to provide feedback in four major areas: network measurement, network information, interactive mathematics, and graphics. These four schools received an IMP, and these subnets eventually connected as a Network Working Group. From these humble beginnings arose ARPAnet, Usenet, IRC (Internet Relay Chat), TCP/IP (Transmission Control Protocol/Internet Protocol, the protocol that made modems possible), and eventually HTTP (Hypertext Transfer Protocol), which even now forms the backbone of the Internet and websites. ARPAnet grew from a tiny idea to connect computers for use by the US military into the rapid transit system deployed by citizens and soldiers the world over. This system permits Christians to share joys and sorrows, cat pictures, triumphs, cries of despair and calls for prayer, sports scores, and family memories. But it also provides the means for sins of all shapes and sizes—defiance in the face of God, a rising anger and hatred of all things Christian that threatens to erupt from out of the deep web into the sunlit surface any day now. The tares among the wheat are beginning to ripen.

The church is a body of believers. I speak now not of a building, but of the interconnected, Spirit-filled humans who profess Christ as King. If we then are the body, Christ Jesus is the head:

There is one body, and one Spirit, even as ye are called in one hope of your calling;

One Lord, one faith, one baptism,

One God and Father of all, who is above all, and through all, and in you all.

But unto every one of us is given grace according to the measure of the gift of Christ.

Wherefore he saith, When he ascended up on high, he led captivity captive, and gave gifts unto men.

(Now that he ascended, what is it but that he also descended first into the lower parts of the earth?

He that descended is the same also that ascended up far above all heavens, that he might fill all things).

And he gave some, apostles; and some, prophets; and some, evangelists; and some, pastors and teachers;

For the perfecting of the saints, for the work of the ministry, for the edifying of the body of Christ,

Till we all come in the unity of the faith, and of the knowledge of the Son of God, unto a perfect man, unto the measure of the stature of the fullness of Christ;

That we henceforth be no more children, tossed to and fro, and carried about with every wind of doctrine, by the sleight of men, and cunning craftiness, whereby they lie in wait to deceive;

But speaking the truth in love, may grow up into him in all things, which is the head, even Christ;

From whom the whole body fitly joined together and compacted by that which every joint supplieth, according to the effectual working in the measure of every part, maketh increase of the body unto the edifying of itself in love. (Eph. 4:4–13, emphasis added)

We have in this passage a beautiful picture of believers across the centuries as a unified group called "the body." Each believer holds a unique and important position that contributes to the whole. We are ONE, or rather, that is how we are *supposed* to behave. Sadly, that is not always true now, and the rising of the Beast will—at least for a time—expose this lack of unity to all the world. Note here that Paul is calling for a unity of the body, that we mature in Christ to "full stature." Sadly, most of us are too busy bickering to notice how our witness has slipped—how our "stature" has diminished. But, despite how the "body" sometimes behaves, Christ is our head; therefore, it is HE who directs the body, telling us how to act and react upon this earth. (Sadly, we're often very disobedient to the directions given by our wonderful Head.) When He returns, He will continue to direct us as we serve Him during His millennial kingdom and after throughout the rest of eternity. It is my belief that Antichrist, whose wicked spirit Paul told us was already at work in the first century, will seek to mimic Christ in all ways. He will claim to BE CHRIST, therefore the Antichrist must pose as the HEAD of a BODY. This false claim may seduce some within the true body at first, but it is also my belief that this will serve to expose all those who merely profess Christ but have no true salvation relationship with Him.

Now we beseech you, brethren, by the coming of our Lord Jesus Christ, and by our gathering together unto him,

That ye be not soon shaken in mind, or be troubled, neither by spirit, nor by word, nor by letter as from us, as that the day of the Lord is present.

Let no man deceive you by any means: for that day shall not come, **except there come the falling away first, and that man of sin be revealed, the son of perdition,**

Who opposeth and exalteth himself above all that is called God, or that is worshipped; so that he as God sitteth in the temple of God, shewing himself that he is God.

Remember ye not, that, when I was yet with you, I told you these things?

And now ye know what restraineth that he might be revealed in his time.

For the mystery of iniquity doth already work; only he who now hindreth will continue to hinder, until he be taken out of the way.

And then shall that wicked one be revealed, whom the Lord shall consume with the spirit of his mouth, and shall destroy with the brightness of his coming,

Even him, whose coming is after the working of Satan with all power and signs and lying wonders,

And with all deceivableness of unrighteousness in them that perish, because they received not the love of the truth, that they might be saved.

And for this cause God shall send them strong delusion, that they should believe the lie,

That they all might be judged who believed not the truth, but had pleasure in unrighteousness. (2 Thess. 2:1–12, emphasis added)

Let's get a little background. In fact, let's go all the way back to Genesis 3, to the account of when Adam and Eve sinned. God in His wonderful patience not only provided for their immediate need (covering for their sin), but He also promised redemption for fallen humanity through a coming Savior. We read about this wonderful promise in God's judgment upon the serpent:

And the Lord God said unto the serpent, Because thou hast done this, thou art cursed above all cattle, and above every beast of the field; upon thy belly shalt thou go, and dust shalt thou eat all the days of thy life.

And I will put enmity between thee and the woman, and between thy seed and her seed; it shall bruise thy head, and thou shalt bruise his heel. (Gen. 3:14–15, emphasis added)

Did you notice that promise? God is speaking to the serpent, the tempter and villain in the garden, the original "snake in the grass." What does God say? The serpent is a type of dragon called in Hebrew "the nachash" (For more on this, see Michael S. Heiser's wonderful exegesis on Genesis 3 here: http://michaelsheiser.com/TheNakedBible/2010/02/the-absence-of-satan-in-the-old-testament/.) What is going to happen to this serpent, this dragon? For his disobedience and for his rebellion by defying God and tempting Adam and Eve into sinning, he loses his ability to fly ("upon thy belly shalt thou go"), and he shall eat dust. This is a curious phrase, for snakes do not actually *eat* dust. The Hebrew words translated as "dust" in Genesis 3 appear many other times in the Old Testament, but most numerously in Job. *Aphar* (pronounced like the English word "afar") may mean literal dust of the ground, ashes, powder, mortar, rubbish, debris, clay, and even ore (as in gold or silver). In other words, the serpent's punishment is to crawl about consuming (and perhaps, by reasonable extension, excreting) trash, junk, and rubbish: the leftovers of everyday life. However, the final meaning of "dust" occurs only once, in the book of Job, where *aphar* is used to represent gold and silver ore, whether metaphorically or not—my Hebrew knowledge is far too scant to discern. However, my mind paints a picture of a disobedient dragon who is no longer able to fly, but instead must burrow its way into the depths of the earth, consuming detritus and even sitting on a cache upon what he perceives to be "gold." Perhaps, you and I are the dust, the gold, the rubbish (as the dragon perceives mankind), and this sleeping dragon feeds upon our sins and failures, gaining strength so that he might soon awaken from his deep slumber, when he will seek to unseat Christ from the heavenlies.

Ezekiel 28 describes an entity that once lived in Eden but has now fallen into ruin and judgment. Called in verse 2 "the prince of Tyre," the one referred to in the passage is surely not an earthly ruler but one with greater longevity:

Behold, thou art wiser than Daniel; there is no secret that they can hide from thee.

With thy wisdom and with thine understanding thou hast gotten thee riches, and hast gotten gold and silver into thy treasuries;

By thy great wisdom and by thy merchandise hast thou increased thy riches, and thine heart is lifted up because of thy riches.

Therefore thus saith the Lord GOD: Because thou hast set thine heart as the heart of God,

Behold, therefore I will bring strangers upon thee, the terrible of the nations: and they shall draw their swords against the beauty of thy wisdom, and they shall defile thy brightness.

They shall bring thee down to the pit, and thou shalt die the deaths of them that are slain in the midst of the seas.

Wilt thou yet say before him that slayeth thee, I am a god? but thou shalt be a man, and no God, in the hand of him that slayeth thee.

Thou shalt die the deaths of the uncircumcised by the hand of foreigners; for I have spoken it, saith the Lord GOD.

Moreover the word of the LORD came unto me, saying,

Son of man, take up a lamentation upon the king of Tyrus, and say unto him, Thus saith the Lord GOD; Thou sealest up the sum, full of wisdom, and perfect in beauty.

Thou hast been in Eden the garden of God; every precious stone was thy covering, the sardius, topaz, and the diamond, the beryl, the onyx, and the jasper, the sapphire, the emerald, and the carbuncle, and gold: the workmanship of thy timbrels and of thy flutes was prepared in thee in the day that thou wast created.

Thou art the anointed cherub that covereth; and I have set thee so; thou wast upon the holy mountain of God; thou hast walked up and down in the midst of the stones of fire.

Thou wast perfect in thy ways from the day that thou wast created, till iniquity was found in thee.

By the multitude of thy merchandise they have filled the midst of thee with violence, and thou hast sinned: therefore **I will cast thee as profane out of the mountain of God, and I will destroy thee, O covering cherub, from the midst of the stones of fire.**

Thine heart was lifted up because of thy beauty; thou hast corrupted thy wisdom by reason of thy brightness; I will cast thee to the ground, I will lay thee before kings, that they may behold thee.

Thou hast defiled thy sanctuaries by the multitude of thine iniquities, by the iniquity of thy merchandise; therefore will I bring forth a fire from the midst of thee, it shall devour thee, and **I will bring thee to ashes** upon the earth in the sight of all them that behold thee.

All they that know thee among the people shall be appalled at thee; thou shalt be a terror, and never shalt thou be any more. (Ezek. 28:3–19, emphasis added)

The previous passage is often hotly debated as regards the "true" identity of the subject of God's obvious wrath. The "prince" may have been a human "prince" (the king of Tyre) at the time this prophecy was written, but it is also clear that God's doom is directed at someone else, someone far older than any human, someone—a creature called "the covering cherub" who walked "in the midst the stones of fire" (stones in the altar perhaps, or even stars, or planets?). God's Word calls this entity "wiser than

Daniel," a curious turn of phrase since it is Daniel who gives us a major prophecy of the coming Antichrist (see Daniel 11). Despite this entity's amazing "wisdom," God promises to fling him to the ground, clipping his wings so to speak and banishing him from his fiery walkway. He will be destroyed by the "uncircumcised" of the earth. He will be brought to ashes (dust?). Why? Haughtiness and pride. His iniquitous "traffick" (i.e., merchandising or commerce). This being apparently uses his "wisdom" to create a kingdom where he benefits from commerce, accumulating gold and riches from these pursuits. Some scholars may write this off as poetry and/or metaphor, but it seems to me that the judgment of this creature is all too glaringly similar to the judgment upon the nachash in Genesis 3.

God lives in a state of constant now—He IS. You and I live in a timeline in which we experience the present, recall our past, and look forward to an unknown future. God speaks judgment from a perspective outside of our space/time continuum. He pronounces a verdict in present tense, but the final fulfillment as you and I see it may occur at a point somewhere along history's timeline. Has the nachash been judged yet? Certainly. But has the punishment commenced in full? If this creature, the nachash, is also the dragon that enters the Man of Sin, the "prince to come" who is thrown to the ground ("on thy belly shalt thou go") during the final seven years of premillennial history, then the prophecy is yet to be fulfilled.

This brings me back to the Antichrist and his plans to subvert Christ's return by pretending to BE Christ, the HEAD of the BODY. If, as my theory proposes, the Internet plays a role in forming the BODY of Antichrist, then this unified collection of humanity must coalesce prior to his arrival upon the world stage. We, the TRUE BODY, currently await our Lord's return. When Antichrist appears, He will claim to be the RETURNING MESSIAH, and he will set up his "millennial kingdom" (one that will, in reality, only last seven years). Most likely this will occur at the end of a major war in the Middle East, which Antichrist can claim is "Armageddon." Today, many people in the world believe Armageddon to be "the end of days"; therefore, it will take very little Bible knowledge to find the Antichrist's claim plausible. In fact, one could discern enough from the average blockbuster film or graphic novel these days! Even television programs predict an end to life or a coming cataclysm that only the arrival of super humans or one super man can prevent.

Now, we must return to our earlier definitions and the meaning of life (bet you thought I'd forgotten about that!), intelligence, and sentience. Postmodern scientists now prefer to relate life to an organism or collection of matter that can EVOLVE. Without a doubt, the Internet has indeed evolved. From its humble beginnings as an idea expressed by a psychologist who loved machines to nascent cells (individual computers) that found each other and joined along an IMP's back, to small networks (like forming tissue), larger networks (organs), and finally a worldwide "body" of nearly nine BILLION devices, that's more than one device for every person alive. In our house alone, we stopped counting at sixteen devices that ping our wireless router throughout the day. That sounds like a lot, and perhaps we at PID Radio and our VFTB radio program are a bit odd, but we have multiple desktops, multiple laptops, tablets, televisions (Roku and Blu-Ray streaming), and smart phones and even an iPod that scramble to bring us the latest news, social media, and email. We use these devices for ministry and work, but not all device owners have God's will in their hearts. In fact, many—and I'd say MOST—of the connected devices in this world are poised for evil deeds and/or warfare.

Of course, the Internet has not yet permeated every crevice of every corner of the planet, but it is almost there. Mark Zuckerberg, founder of Facebook, is committed to bringing the Internet to all people.[70] In fact, to quote Zuckerberg in response to one of Steven Levy's questions from the cited article at Wired.com:

LEVY: You say connectivity is a human right—up there with freedom of expression, freedom from hunger, and other essential rights. Can you explain?

MZ: The story of the next century is the **transition from an industrial, resource-based economy to a knowledge economy.** An industrial economy is zero sum. If you own an oil field, I cannot go in that same oil field. But knowledge works differently. If you know something, then you can share that—and then the whole world gets richer. But until that happens, there's a big disparity in wealth. The richest 500 million have way more money than the next six billion combined. **You solve that by getting everyone online, and into the knowledge economy—by building out the global internet.** (emphasis added)

What Zuckerberg is saying here is that every human being has a RIGHT to knowledge. While that sounds reasonable at first, it echoes the words spoken by the nachash in Eden, who promised access to KNOWLEDGE with the added perk that "ye shall be as gods."

Singularitans and transhumanists would agree with old nachash. Scientists (men with special "knowledge") like George Church and Ray Kurzweil dream of a world in which everyone is connected and even uploaded into a mainframe. A recent *Doctor Who* episode, "The Time of the Doctor," featured a woman called Tasha Lem,[71] who served as the Mother Superior of the Papal Mainframe, a church that could change its "faith" on a dime (becoming The Silence, including a subversive splinter group that sought to undo the true mission of the "church") and that operated across the galaxy using its own military for backup. The program's premise may not be that far off of truth. Our future as a planet may hinge on whether we fall for the "collective" party line that we are all getting better. As my niece says, that's "ate up in the head" thinking.

Sadly, most people will indeed fall in step with the new religion of a hive mind—the BODY or the MANY. The needs of the few outweigh the needs of the many—or the one.[72] *Doctor Who*, mentioned earlier, is a science fiction program with a whole slew of villains who want to remove you from existence, delete you, or upgrade you. Artificial intelligence (AI) in the form of mechanized organisms like "the Daleks" or computerized upgrades like "the Cybermen" illustrate what can go horribly wrong when cyber intellects rule the world.

The Internet, particularly the Dark Web aspect of its underbelly, slithers about the planet gobbling up souls and separating children from their parents through slick enticements and alluring promises for becoming better, becoming more, becoming a *god*. You may find it difficult to imagine a world in which young people line up to be integrated body and soul into the Matrix Machine, but that day is nearly upon us! Those who are now college age never knew a world without networking. They have been online since childhood. Children born today will grow up with constant connectivity and an assumption that where the Internet is concerned, "it's all good." Let me assure you, it is NOT ALL GOOD. The linked software and hardware is waking up—evolving—toward a point where passing a Turing Test[73] will be child's play. Computers will achieve sentient status, and legal eagles will peck each other to death debating the rights of the world's newest "netizens." AI is a reality. It's already being employed by the military to operate drones, whether as a single UAV (Unmanned Aerial Vehicle) or a swarm of tiny UAVs that resembles insects flying in eerie formation. An article from a recent issue of the *Daily Mail* reports that US regulators want all cars to communicate with each other (networked) by 2017.[74]

According to Shawn Helton of the excellent, analytical website Global Research (www.globalresearch.ca), the age of artificial intelligence and drones is upon us:

> To see how dangerous artificial intelligence has become, all one has to do is look at the work of Eliezer Yudkowsky, a Research Fellow at the Machine Intelligence Research Institute (MIRI). Eliezer's work focuses on the evolution of AI self-modification where strong artificial intelligence or Seed AI will be able to program itself, optimizing its own cognitive functions similar to the malevolent computer Hal in Stanley Kubrick's *2001: A Space Odyssey*.[75]

An article posted on January 3, 2014, at www.RT.com reveals what the US has planned for the next phase of its "drone" program and how AI technology is being sold as a cost-saving advantage:

> Unmanned aerial systems currently constitute a major drain on the military's budget. Officials hope to ease this burden without sacrificing any firepower by shifting many of the human responsibilities to the drone itself. Taken literally, this process involves ending the execution of step-by-step commands and employing commands that the report notes may *"require deviation from pre-programmed tasks."*
>
> **Along with surpassing budgetary constraints, the authors of the Roadmap anticipate that, should US drone dominance**

ever be met with an adversary, American strategies will be "more effective through greater automation and greater performance."

To make this goal a reality, the Roadmap [Unmanned Systems Integrated Roadmap[76]] predicts the development of "swarms" of drones that are shot from a larger, unmanned vehicle that carries them within range of a target. The so-called mother ship would be guided by an onboard camera with a human pilot guiding from a military base. When that pilot identifies a target within a range of 250 nautical miles, he would fire the drone swarm with the aim that they will explode on target.[77]

Those who know their Bible surely must be thinking of a passage from Joel 2 that predicts such "swarms":

Blow the trumpet in Zion, and sound an alarm in my holy mountain: let all the inhabitants of the land tremble: for the day of the LORD cometh, for it is near at hand;

A day of darkness and of gloominess, a day of clouds and of thick darkness, as the morning spread upon the mountains; a great people and a strong; there hath not been ever the like, neither shall be any more after it, even to the years of many generations.

A fire devoureth before them; and behind them a flame burneth; the land is as the garden of Eden before them, and behind them a desolate wilderness; yea, and nothing shall escape them.

The appearance of them is as the appearance of horses; and as horsemen, so shall they run.

Like the noise of chariots on the tops of mountains shall they leap, like the noise of a flame of fire that devoureth the stubble, as a strong people set in battle array.

Before their face the people shall be much pained: all faces shall gather blackness.

They shall run like mighty men; they shall climb the wall like men of war; and they shall march every one on his ways, and they shall not break their ranks.

Neither shall one thrust another; they shall walk every one in his path, and when they fall upon the sword, they shall not be wounded.

They shall run to and fro in the city; they shall run upon the wall, they shall climb up upon the houses; they shall enter in at the windows like a thief.

The earth shall quake before them; the heavens shall tremble; the sun and the moon shall be dark, and the stars shall withdraw their shining:

And the LORD shall utter his voice before his army: for his camp is very great; for he is strong that executeth his word: for the day of the LORD is great and very terrible; and who can abide it? (Joel 2:1–12, emphasis added)

The precise meaning of this passage is a bit murky to us still, but it clearly deals with the end times, and we are fast approaching those perilous times. Some have interpreted Joel 2 as representing a last-days *army of believers* who march upon Jerusalem; however, these "mighty men" behave in very *non-human* ways. Some predict that this could be a last-days army of hybrids—half human, half angel—who fulfill God's prophecy and march at His command. Others say this is a fiendish army from hell, perhaps a corollary of or even a reference to the fallen angel armies that rise from the abyss with Apollyon. It is also quite possible that these unflagging entities are military units, some on the ground, others in the air, that include drones and robotic entities with autonomous intelligence. Just remember that *God is allowing* this army of immortals (so to speak) for HIS PURPOSES. Later in this same chapter, the Lord implores His people to turn to Him and perhaps avoid this judgment from "the northern army" (Joel 2:20). The identity of these "people" who invade, these "mighty men" who cannot be killed and swarm like locusts, may be hinted at by the Hebrew word translated as "people." The word is *am* (pronounced "ahm"). Could America be involved? US drone operations are multiplying at a dizzying rate, so it is not inconceivable. But I would suggest something even MORE chilling: that the drones now being manufactured with autonomous capabilities will soon form a robotic army for a sentient Internet entity, the "image of the Beast":

And I stood upon the sand of the sea, and saw a beast rise up out of the sea, having seven heads and ten horns, and upon his horns ten crowns, and upon his heads the name of blasphemy.

And the beast which I saw was like unto a leopard, and his feet were as the feet of a bear, and his mouth as the mouth of a lion; and the dragon gave him his power, and his throne, and great authority.

And I saw one of his heads as it were wounded to death; and his deadly wound was healed, and all the world wondered after the beast.

And they worshipped the dragon which gave power unto the beast; and they worshipped the beast, saying, Who is like unto the beast? Who is able to make war with him?

And there was given unto him a mouth speaking great things and blasphemies, and power was given unto him to continue forty and two months.

And he opened his mouth in blasphemy against God, to blaspheme his name, and his tabernacle, and them that dwell in heaven.

And it was given unto him to make war with the saints, and to overcome them; and power was given him over all kindreds, and tongues, and nations.

And all that dwell upon the earth shall worship him, whose names are not written in the book of life of the Lamb slain from the foundation of the world.

If any man have an ear, let him hear.

He that leadeth into captivity shall go into captivity; he that killeth with the sword must be killed with the sword. Here is the patience and the faith of the saints. (Rev. 13:1–10, emphasis added)

This Beast rises from the "sea," which may indicate that this is Apollyon, the leader of the terrifying horde that rises like smoke from the abyss. Regardless of his identity, God will permit this being to "make war with the saints, and to overcome them." The Beast will rule this entire world as one massive kingdom! At one time, this might have proven rather difficult, but with the ability to "run to and fro" via the Internet, particularly an Internet that may actually waken (more on this later), this Beast will already have a "body" to which he will become the "head" (in direct imitation of Christ our Lord and head of the body of believers). Yet there is more:

And I beheld another beast coming up out of the earth, and he had two horns like a lamb, and he spake as a dragon.

And he exerciseth all the power of the first beast before him, and causeth the earth and them which dwell therein to worship the first beast, whose deadly wound was healed.

And he doeth great wonders, so that he maketh fire come down from heaven on the earth in the sight of men,

And deceiveth them that dwell on the earth by the means of those miracles which he had power to do in the sight of the beast; **saying to them that dwell on the earth, that they should make an image to the beast, that had the wound by a sword, and did live.**

And he hath power to give life unto the image of the beast, that the image of the beast should both speak, and cause that as many as would not worship the image of the beast should be killed.

And he causeth all, both small and great, rich and poor, free and bond, to receive a mark in their right hand, or in their foreheads,

And that no man might buy or sell, except he that had the mark, or the name of the beast, or the number of his name.

Here is wisdom. Let him that hath understanding count the number of the beast; for it is the number of a man; and his number is six hundred threescore and six. (Rev. 13:11–18, emphasis added)

Let's take a few minutes to unpack these verses. The Beast from the sea (Antichrist) rises to rule, but he is wounded in the head, ostensibly a mortal wound; yet he survives. Remember the Eden promise from God that one day a hero would arise from the seed of the woman (the hero is Christ) and that the serpent (nachash and most likely also the dragon spirit behind Antichrist) would "bruise his heel," but that Christ would bruise the serpent's head (Genesis 3: 15)? This is the fulfillment of that promise. Christ died and rose again on the third day (He was only "bruised" in the heel). The serpent (bruised in the head) will rise again also or at least make it appear that he has died and risen, and the world will turn to him as fulfillment of every eschatology known to man. The Beast will be hailed as Messiah, Mahdi, Maitreya, Shiva, Vishnu, Ahura Mazda…you name it.

The world will marvel at the Beast, but then John tells us that a second beast arises from the land (appearing like a "lamb," another Christ-image that I will henceforth refer to as the "Antilamb") who serves as high priest to the first Beast. This "lamb" speaks with the voice of a dragon (serpent, a picture of Antichrist, Lucifer, Apollyon, the Ancient Enemy). It should chill the soul of any Christian that the brand name of a voice-recognition software product is actually called "Dragon Speak"!

Take note that this Antilamb has the power to make the image speak, wage war, and murder any who will not worship the Antichrist. How is this possible? The mark. The identifier that the Antilamb forces all not written in the True Lamb's Book of Life to take! No one without the mark will be able to work, buy, or sell without the mark, because the Internet Beast, the Leviathan that has awoken (being given "life") will keep tabs on everything we do via a personal WiFi connection! Of course, there will likely be a "carrot" to go along with this "stick": Those with the mark will perhaps receive direct stimulation that excites pleasure areas of the brain. An episode of *Star Trek: The Next Generation* featured such stimulation in the form of a virtual reality "game" that rewarded players via a headset similar to Google Glass, but with a means to transcutaneously activate deep sections of the brain.[78]

This constant monitoring has already begun. In 2009, the *Telegraph* ran an article predicting an Orwellian age:

The European Union is spending millions of pounds developing "Orwellian" technologies designed to scour the internet and CCTV (Closed-Circuit TV) images for "abnormal behavior."

A five-year research programme, called Project Indect, aims to develop computer programmes which act as "agents" to monitor and process information from web sites, discussion forums, file servers, peer-to-peer networks and even individual computers.

Its main objectives include the "automatic detection of threats and abnormal behaviour or violence."[79] (emphasis added)

Already in the US, social media giants such as Google+, Facebook, Instagram, Twitter, etc., scrape every picture and every post, looking for "hot words" and images that not only reveal where you we are via metadata (hidden information within the image that reveal GPS [global positioning satellite] data and date), but that enable the scraper software to make a map of our workplaces, favorite hangouts, and even homes, and to "tag" every face in every image it finds using facial-recognition programming.

Now, those of you who are skeptical about my hypothesis that the Internet has the scientific capability to awaken to "life," consider the massive brain-mapping projects across the globe (entire list available at Wikipedia; see citation):

aHuman, hybrid of latest neurobiology data aimed to implement human personality by means of computer program, started in 2008 as independent research.

Blue Brain Project, an attempt to create a synthetic brain by reverse engineering the mammalian brain down to the molecular level.

HNeT (Holographic Neural Technology), a technology by AND (Artificial Neural Devices) Corporation based on nonlinear phase coherence/decoherence principles.

Hierarchical Temporal Memory, a technology by Numenta to capture and replicate the properties of the neocortex.

Recursive Cortical Networks, a technology by Vicarious that uses a probabilistic graphical model inspired by the structure of the neocortex.

Visual Hierarchical Modular Neural Network, a software technology by TinMan Systems to visually construct a flow of human thought and logic to produce autonomous artificial intelligence.

AILEENN (Artificial Intelligence Logic Electronic Emulation Neural Network), an entire new cloud-based PaaS platform as a service and IaaS infrastructure for AI represented as a ubiquitous entity based on Neural Networks and Fuzzy Logic with universal inputs, outputs, and actuators aiming to the democratization and human-like interaction as the ultimate resource planner, decision-making process, and actuator. By the inventor and founder of TDVision.

Cyc, an attempt to assemble an ontology and database of everyday knowledge, enabling human-like reasoning.

Eurisko, a language by Douglas Lenat for solving problems, consisting of heuristics, including some for how to use and change its heuristics.

Mycin, an early medical expert system.

NEIL, an attempt to assemble a common-sense knowledge base from processing random images from the Internet.

Open Mind Common Sense, a project based at the MIT (Massachusetts Institute of Technology) Media Lab to build a large, common-sense knowledge base from online contributions.

PAN, a publicly available text analyzer.

Questsin, uses Query by Example and features a dictionary, knowledge base, repository, reference, and thesaurus.

Siri, an intelligent personal assistant and knowledge navigator with a voice interface in Apple Inc.'s iOS.

SNePS, a simultaneously logic-based, frame-based, and network-based knowledge representation, reasoning, and acting system.

Watson, a question-answering system developed by IBM to play the Jeopardy! game show.

Wolfram Alpha, an online service that answers factual queries directly by computing the answer from structured data, capable of responding to particularly phrased, natural-language, fact-based questions.[80]

Recently, in response to the European Union Brain Project announcement, President Barack Obama informed the public that US scientists would be launching a similar project called BRAIN (Brain Research through Advanced Innovative Neurotechnologies).[81] Based upon the resource-sharing structure utilized in the Human Genome Project (codirected by transhumanist George Church), BRAIN plans to map every neural connection within the human body, also called "the connectome." Many neurologists believe the human connectome equals who we are—it's our mind, our personality, our inner spirit. Transhumanists hope one day soon to upload their digital equivalent connectomes to new bodies, and these bodies would in turn be interconnected much like the Borg in *Star Trek: The Next Generation*. The Borg are born human, but they are "upgraded" and "enhanced" with technology that makes each one a human/cyborg soldier within a hive mind ruled and directed by a queen.

The Christian body must unify if we are to serve Christ well. We must use the time left to us to exemplify Christ as Redeemer and King. It is through His blood and that alone that we humans will find eternal life, not through being uploaded to a mainframe. Sadly, rather than heed Christ's commandments to love God and love others as we love ourselves, we choose to openly squabble. The world needs Christ, but it will accept

Antichrist. The doctrine of transhumanism and Internet sentience will draw away our neighbors and our loved ones. Many preachers avoid sermons on prophetic topics, but prophecy has never been needed more than now!

Will Christians be enticed into worshiping the Beast? My personal belief is that anyone who truly has accepted Christ's redemptive work on Calvary, proclaiming Him as Savior, is "marked" with the Holy Spirit: "Now he who establisheth us with you in Christ, and hath anointed us, is God; Who hath also sealed us, and given the earnest of the Spirit in our hearts" (2 Cor. 1:21–22).

We who belong to the true BODY OF CHRIST have the Holy Spirit to protect us, but that doesn't mean a Christian might not be tempted, and perhaps almost persuaded, by the Beast's lies. Now is the time to put aside petty factions and unite as a body! The time is nearly up. Science fiction, dear reader, is about to become science fact, and humanity could cease to exist if not for God's promise to intervene. As He says in Scripture:

> For then shall be great tribulation, such as was not since the beginning of the world to this time, no, nor ever shall be.
>
> **And except those days should be shortened, there should no flesh be saved; but for the elect's sake those days shall be shortened.** (Matt. 24:21–22, emphasis added)

The Internet is shaping your life, spying on you, and making judgments about your posts and pictures. Eventually, it will have the connected drone power to act upon any and all inferences it may make about you and your loved ones. Those who now build the soft and hard architecture that feeds this rising image of the Beast probably have no concept of the terrifying potential they are programming into it. It will not fully rise until the Antilamb is granted the power to give it life, but the Internet is stirring with disturbingly powerful panoptics.

The Antichrist will claim to be Christ, the Messiah, and he will likely come to the world stage at the conclusion of a "world war" that he will claim is the battle of Armageddon. He will say that his arrival fulfills all prophecies, including Christ's promise to "come with clouds":

And when he had spoken these things, while they beheld, **he was taken up; and a cloud received him out of their sight.**

And while they looked steadfastly toward heaven as he went up, behold, two men stood by them in white apparel;

Who also said, Ye men of Galilee, why stand ye gazing up into heaven? This same Jesus, which is taken up from you into heaven, **shall so come in like manner as ye have seen him go into heaven.** (Acts 1:9–11, emphasis added)

The disciples saw Christ taken to His Father's throne via a cloud, and the "men in white apparel" promised that Christ WILL RETURN IN LIKE MANNER. Many believe that this means He will return via a cloud, or that clouds will play an important role in His appearing. The Antichrist may one day soon use the idea of "cloud computing" to claim fulfillment of this prophecy. Cloud computing allows Internet users to store digital information in what is "the cloud." Actually, this means it is not stored locally, but on a server somewhere (perhaps one owned by Google and floating somewhere at sea!).

Shakespeare's witches invoked evil spirits and ghosts by the "pricking of their thumbs." You and I and our children, and soon every person in the world, will feed information, most of it dark and unholy, to the sleeping Beast we call the Internet. However, every bit and byte—every one and zero, every typing of your thumbs—is part of a global effort by spiritual forces to awaken a massive image that will control and cull all those who do not worship at its silicon feet.

And, oh, one more thing.

Did you know that today's computers are about to be replaced with infinitely more capable and potentially lifelike DNA-based computers? Such computers will not only qualify for NASA's "evolution" requirement for life, but they will also satisfy the traditional caveat that all life must be based on nucleic acids. And, by being based on DNA or RNA, this also means the new life form is based on CARBON. Six electrons. Six neutrons. Six protons…the number of a man.

666.

A great preacher once told me that Christ will return for His bride when the number (known only to the Father) is complete. When that final soul says yes to the Holy Spirit's calling, the final judgments commence.

Perhaps, the Internet Beast awaits a similar, perfect number.

Just one more "Like," and the end will begin.

4

A NEW THEORY

On the Image of the Beast and the New Conscience

by Michael K. Lake, ThD, DRE

For now we see through a glass, darkly; but then face to face: now I know
in part; but then shall I know even as also I am known.

—1 Corinthians 13:12

The apostle Paul spoke these words around AD 56 to the church that
he established in Corinth during his second missionary journey in AD
50–51. There were many subjects that Paul had to address in his first
epistle to the Corinthians because of where they lived—under the shadow
of the Oracles of Delphi. This fledgling church was seated in an area where
the prophetesses of Apollo held sway over kings and nations for centuries.

With the Gentiles coming into this congregation (and many of them
were not God-fearers prior to conversion), our Jewish apostle had to deal

with both the pagan practices of new converts and the predominant religious sect that their community was world famous for—the false prophetic flow from Apollo to his heralds. This is one of the reasons Paul had to bring such detailed apostolic instruction regarding the use of the gift of tongues, interpretation of tongues, and personal prophecy. Chaos was being loosed into this congregation by the merging of pagan concepts with the biblical Hebraic foundations upon which Paul had established this congregation. It is amazing how appropriate his instructions to the new believers at Corinth are for the church today. We find that the Christian airwaves are being flooded with ideologies and insights that originated from paean influence rather than a biblical one.

After the apostle Paul brought instruction and correction to the subjects of using these spiritual gifts, the purpose of personal prophecy, and bringing such use under the watchful eye of established prophets in the congregation, he made a profound statement regarding prophecy: Prophecy is like looking in a dark mirror. This statement is true of both personal prophecy and redemptive prophecy. In this section, I want to deal with how Paul's statement applies to redemptive prophecy.

Expanding Our Understanding of Redemptive Prophecy

Let's discuss the perplexities of prophecies by Isaiah in 750 BC, Daniel in 620 BC, or even the apostle John around AD 95 concerning modern-day events. These men were shown visions by God that their spirits perceived but their minds could not fully comprehend. Many of the things they were shown were simply beyond their ken. Imagine for a moment that the apostle John is handed a copy of this book—a stunning, perfect-bound, paperback publication with a glossy, full-color cover. During his lifetime, all writings were hand copied and were contained in scrolls. How could he describe what he was seeing when he had no point of reference to help him even understand it? Now expand this same concept to someone handing John an iPhone or showing him some DARPA (Defense Advanced Research Projects Agency) project using GRINs (Genetic, Robotic, Information, and Nano processes) technologies. It is logical to conclude that one of the reasons redemptive prophecy utilized symbolism so often was that there was no alternative means for these men of God to describe what they were seeing. How could John accurately describe the car you drive to work, the TV you watch every evening, or the Kindle that can store an entire library for your reading enjoyment? We find these prophets, who lived from two thousand to nearly three thousand years ago, facing cutting-edge technologies that the average techno-savvy American cannot cognize. Now how dark is that mirror through which we are viewing redemptive prophecy?

Take, for example, Revelation 9:1–12 and the vision of the locust swarm coming out of the pit under the leadership of a being named Apollyon. There were centuries when all Christian commentators speculated that this must be some demonic horde that had been captured and incarcerated underground for thousands of years and then loosed. In the 1990s, the interpretation was changed by some asserting that they were Apache combat helicopters like those used by the US military. Recently, with all of the genetic engineering occurring behind the scenes around the world, others have speculated that these locusts are man-made chimeras that have been developed in a clandestine lab and released upon mankind. There is even a possibility that this army could be some new DARPA project that has perfected both drone technology and a swarm/hive-mind neural network. Maybe Apollyon is a combat artificial intelligence (AI) that is the control center for this army. The point I am trying to make is that, as our understanding of current technological breakthroughs increases and this new information is revealed to the public (most of this information is classified for the use of governments), our subsequent understanding of the biblical symbolism used in redemptive prophecy will be greatly expanded.

Becoming Intelligence Officers in the Kingdom of God

I enjoy watching documentaries about the Cold War between the US and the former Soviet Union. These documentaries reveal how each side developed new technologies to spy on each other. One documentary, in particular, described how the Soviet Union's scientists had developed devices that were embedded in the concrete walls of the US Embassy that required no electricity and would turn the entire wall of concrete into a microphone. All that was required was a radio tuned to a specific frequency, and everything said within those rooms could be overheard and recorded. As interesting as the description of these devices was, it was more fascinating to me that our intelligence agencies pieced together seemingly unrelated bits of information to discover that those devices existed.

In the same way, the avid Bible prophecy student must be ready to serve as an intelligence officer in the kingdom of God. He must take bits and pieces of disconnected information and be led by the Holy Spirit to construct possibilities regarding prophecy that he could not have wrapped his head around a few months before. To be honest, that is just how fast technology is developing in our day. At the same time, the ethical stance of mankind to wield these powerful, new technologies safely is on a rapid decline. We have to be ready to think outside the box, because our paradigms are too limited. Considering the aforementioned discussions on redemptive prophecy, let's take a theoretical journey through the topic of the image of the Beast.

The Image of the Beast

There has been great debate over what the image of the Beast could possibly be. Some have believed that it would involve some occult power bringing to life a golem, according to kabbalistic folklore. The rabbis who are involved in kabbalah (Jewish mysticism) share a tale regarding the most sacred name of the Most High God—YHVH. Since the time of the Babylonian captivity, the exact pronunciation of the name has been lost (in ancient Hebrew, there were no vowel points). Those involved in kabbalah claim that a select few know the secret name of God. As proof, they create a small statue out of clay and speak the name of God over it. If they get the name right, the statue comes to life. If they allow it to live, the first day, it calls them friend; the second day, it calls them its equal; and the third day, it calls them its servant.[82] Many past prophecy scholars believed that the story of the golem was feasible; the False Prophet would use ancient, occult powers to bring an inanimate statue to life as a false wonder to endorse the Antichrist.

As our technology and our awareness of it continue to grow, other theories have emerged concerning the image of the Beast. Here are some of the other possibilities I have considered over the last few years:

Android: By exploring the goals being proposed by the Singularity Institute, the consciousness of the Antichrist might be transferred into a living AI that becomes the image of the Beast.

Virtual Reality Avatar: Eventually, with the use of GRINs technologies, everyone could have augmented reality with a constant flow of information from the Internet or other data systems. The consciousness of the Antichrist could be fed into an AI within virtual reality, and the image of the Beast could be the Antichrist's avatar within the digital world, with a direct feed into the minds of all who utilize the enhanced augmented reality services.

Many other hypotheses are circulating through the various biblical prophecy groups today. I would like to propose another "outside-the-box" possibility that came to me recently while in prayer and study.

Putting the Pieces of the Puzzle Together

Piece Number 1—DNA

The groundwork for the discovery of DNA (or deoxyribonucleic acid) was in 1869 by Swiss physiological chemist Friedrich Miescher. Since that time, our understanding of DNA continues to grow through a wellspring of new research and discoveries. The amount of information that can be stored in our DNA is mind-boggling.

Susan Young wrote an article for *Technology Review* in August of 2012 entitled, "An Entire Book Written in DNA." Here is a quote from her article:

> DNA can be used to store information at a density about a million times greater than your hard drive, report researchers in *Science* today. George Church of Harvard Medical School and colleagues report that they have written an entire book in DNA, a feat that highlights the recent advances in DNA synthesis and sequencing.
>
> The team encoded a draft HTML version of a book co-written

by Church called *Regenesis: How Synthetic Biology Will Reinvent Nature and Ourselves*. In addition to the text, the biological bits included the information for modern formatting, images and Javascript, to show that "DNA (like other digital media) can encode executable directives for digital machines," they write.[83]

Notice the writer stated that DNA has a storage density about one million times greater than the average hard drive. Everything from personality to the color of your hair is encoded into your DNA.

Not only is the information stored in our DNA beyond our ability to fully grasp (I say this because even scientists who claim to have charted the entire genome have marked vast sections of it as junk DNA; this is scientific jargon for "they don't have a clue what it does"), we are also discovering that DNA can be altered. This was alluded to in the quote included above. Beyond DNA resequencing, we have found that limited sections of our DNA can be altered over time.

The Importance of What We Hear, Say, and Do
The Telegraph in the United Kingdom, on July 5, 2013, ran an article on its website entitled: "Exercise Can Alter Your DNA, Study Claims." Here is a portion of that article:

> Lead author Charlotte Ling, Associate Professor at Lund University Diabetes Centre, in Sweden, said: "Our study shows the positive effects of exercise, because the epigenetic pattern of genes that affect fat storage in the body changes." Researchers looked at the DNA of 23 slightly overweight but healthy men aged around 35, who didn't regularly exercise, after attending spinning and aerobics classes for six months.

They found that changes had taken place in 7000 genes, over a third of the average total of 20,000.

A closer look revealed genes linked to diabetes and obesity, also connected to storing fat, had also been altered.

"We found changes in those genes too, which suggests that altered DNA methylation as a result of physical activity could be one of the mechanisms of how these genes affect the risk of disease.

"This has never before been studied in fat cells. We now have a map of the DNA methylome in fat," Professor Lind said.[84]

We are also finding that exercise is not the only factor that can change DNA. The lack of exercise, poor diet, and other environmental conditions can alter our DNA, too. Most likely a return to proper diet and exercise switched those genetic markers back on, as purported in the article.

I recently had a health survey completed by a noted naturopath to assist me in tweaking my nutritional protocols for better health. During our conversation, he told me about a new nutritional supplement that could help turn back on genetic markers within our DNA that poor diet, lack of exercise, and a variety of life's other issues turn off over time. The genetic switches that this supplement can engage are those that affect type 2 diabetes, how the body fights off cancer, and other diseases that creep up on our aging bodies.

We also need to realize that many of these genetic markers are more than just about our health, the color of our eyes, or how long we will live. Our character, personality, and even sinful nature are encoded in our DNA.

I have been training aspirants of the gospel ministry now through Biblical Life College and Seminary for more than three decades. Over the years, I have been surprised at how many ministers—both aspiring and seasoned—do not know that there is a difference between sin and iniquity. In fact, many theological references in the libraries of most ministers confuse the two. I believe this stems from a theology based on a Greco-Roman mindset rather than a Hebraic one.

Sin is defined by the apostle John in 1 John 3:4. I chose this Scripture for a purpose. We need to understand that the cross did not change sin; it changed us and freed us from sin's grip: "Whosoever committeth sin transgresseth also the law: for sin is the transgression of the law" (1 John 3:4).

John's definition of sin was drawn from his Jewish background and his understanding of the Torah. This definition is accurate from Genesis through the book of Revelation.

Notice something interesting in the following passage of Scripture, in which the Almighty reveals Himself to Moses:

> And the LORD descended in the cloud, and stood with him there, and proclaimed the name of the LORD.
>
> And the LORD passed by before him, and proclaimed, The LORD, The LORD God, merciful and gracious, longsuffering, and abundant in goodness and truth,
>
> Keeping mercy for thousands, forgiving iniquity and transgression and sin, and that will by no means clear the guilty; visiting the iniquity of the fathers upon the children, and upon the children's children, unto the third and to the fourth generation. (Exod. 34:5–7)

When the LORD passed by Moses, He made a distinction between iniquity, transgression, and sin. "Transgression" refers to the transgression of the Law, which John defines as sin. The Hebrew word for "sin" here is

"הַאֶטָה chatta'ah," which refers to the condition of sin or the sin nature.[85] The Hebrew word for iniquity is "עָוֹן `avon," which means "perversity, depravity, iniquity, guilt or punishment of iniquity."[86] What many miss in understanding "iniquity" is that there has been a corruption or perversion of the individual that bends him or her toward a particular sin. It is as if the violation of God's Law has been encoded into the person's very DNA. Those involved in spiritual warfare would call this a generational tendency or generational curse. There have been many cases reported in which a child was given up at birth and raised by another couple, yet the same generational tendency toward a particular sin would manifest itself in the child. Such cases form an opposition to the theory that behavior is based solely on the home environment.

We find further confirmation in Isaiah's description of the suffering of Messiah in Isaiah 53:

> Surely he hath borne our griefs, and carried our sorrows; yet we did esteem him stricken, smitten of God, and afflicted.
>
> But he was wounded for our transgressions, he was bruised for our iniquities; the chastisement for our peace was upon him; and with his stripes we are healed. (Isa. 53:4–5)

Notice that the price paid for sin was separate from the price paid for iniquity. I have also come to believe that bruising was a result of the need to "bend back" toward righteousness.

God's answer for iniquity is: (1) repentance, (2) application of the blood of Jesus, (3) meditation on God's Word, and (4) implementing God's Word until it is encoded into our DNA and the Holy Spirit has "bent" us back toward righteousness.

In the Prophecy Club video *The Sons of God and the Antichrist*, Dr. Bill Schnoebelen shares how he formerly used meditation and various occult disciplines to switch on and off parts of his DNA to increase his spiritual power. In this same video, he reveals that there is one particular gene that the Illuminati refer to as "the luciferian gene." He indicates that their desire was to see if this gene can be increased in the genetic makeup of man.

So DNA can be altered by behavior. The realization of the progression of the transhumanist movement and its plans to alter our DNA through genetic splicing and resequencing is alarming. Transhumanists have already determined just how much information a single strand of DNA can hold. Do they really think that man is intelligent enough to completely chart the genome and understand all of the information regarding mankind that God encoded into it? Or will they be like a friend of mine years ago who began selectively deleting various parts of the DOS (disk operating system) on his computer and was surprised when it started processing information erratically?

Piece Number 2—Divine Harmonics and String Theory
Years ago, I was watching a *20/20* ABC News documentary featuring noted physicist Brian Greene. Dr. Greene is not only noted for his concept of string theory, but also for his ability to make the complex issues of physics readily understandable for the average individual. As he described the difference between the macro universe and the subatomic one in the commentary I was viewing, I saw Genesis 1 unfold before my eyes. He described the frustration that Albert Einstein had experienced in developing the "unified theory." Subatomic particles did not behave the same as the normal-sized elements in the universe.

String Theory Illustration

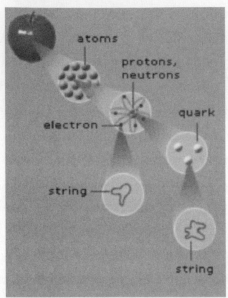

String Theory Illustration[87]

We know that there are elements in our universe smaller than an atom (subatomic). Greene believes that inside of each electron and the quarks that make up protons and neutrons is a looped string that is vibrating. Although this string has no weight per se, it emits gravity, radiation, and energy.

These strings are vibrating, causing the subatomic particles to "bounce" on the way down.

As soon as I saw this, I remembered what the Word of God tells us:

- "Who, being the brightness of his <u>glory</u>, and the express image of his person, and <u>upholding all things by the word of his power</u>, when he had by himself purged our sins, sat down on the right hand of the Majesty on high" (Heb. 1:3, emphasis added). All of creation is still vibrating with the resonance of God's voice! Notice that "glory" and "word of his power" are in the same verse.

- "And he is before all things, and <u>by him all things consist</u>" (Col. 1:17, emphasis added).
- "Through faith we understand that the worlds were framed by the word of God, so that things which are seen were not made of things which do appear" (Heb. 11:3). This world and our universe are both framed and held together by something that cannot be seen. What is it? It is the shrouded power that is in the resonance of the voice of God!

I wanted to verify my concept that the strings within quarks were resonating with the sound of God's voice. I needed to know what the combined resonance of our planet was. The harmonic resonance of planet earth is 7.83 hertz.

- 7 is the number representing God's plan of salvation.
- 8 is the number promising a new beginning, new birth, and new heaven and earth.
- 3 is the number for complete, completion, and the perfect witness of God.

The earth itself, to include our bodies, is resonating with the biblical numbers that detail God's redemptive plan for mankind! In fact, 7.83 hertz is within the range of frequencies that can be picked up by the human brain. This earth pulse is also known as the Schumann resonance. It was discovered by Professor W. O. Schumann at the University of Munich in 1953.

In the video entitled *Weapons of the New World Order,* Dr. Nick

Begich (also author of *Angels Don't Play This HAARP: Advances in Tesla Technology*) shares the fact that there are already European Parliament regulations banning the use of nonlethal weapons that would use ELF (extremely low frequency) similar to 7.83 hertz to project thoughts into the minds of an approaching army. He demonstrated this technology before a subcommittee of the European Parliament investigating nonlethal ELF weapons with a few simple pieces of equipment he picked up at Radio Shack. In his demonstration before the subcommittee, Dr. Begich's voice transmitted through the homemade infrasound device that he had constructed and resonated in the body of a volunteer. The volunteer was able to clearly hear his voice without the use of his auditory senses.[88]

The Schumann resonance is considered vital for human health. NASA uses Schumann resonators in space suits, at the International Space Station, and in any space vessel that travels outside of our atmosphere. It is needed for life as we know it.

Another Twist in the Story

> Here is wisdom. Let him that hath understanding count the number of the beast; for it is the number of a man; and his number is six hundred threescore and six. (Rev. 13:18)

If the resonance of the earth is God's voice within it and that frequency is 7.83 hertz, it would stand to reason that Lucifer would try to imitate that resonance. Of course, he would not be able to match Almighty God's divine frequency. **What if the voice of Lucifer and the frequency of the Antichrist broadcast at 6.66 hertz?** This frequency is also within the range that the human mind can receive.

It also gives new understanding to both the fall of the angels and the fall of man.

In Ezekiel's description of the fall of Lucifer, we find some very interesting details. Let's take a look.

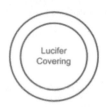

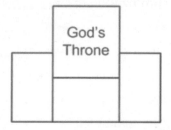

Thou hast been in Eden the garden of God; every precious stone was thy covering, the sardius, topaz, and the diamond, the beryl, the onyx, and the jasper, the sapphire, the emerald, and the carbuncle, and gold; the workmanship of thy timbrels and of thy pipes was prepared in thee in the day that thou wast created.

Thou art the anointed cherub that covereth, and I have set thee so; thou wast upon the holy mountain of God; thou hast walked up and down in the midst of the stones of fire. (Ezek. 28:13–14)

Lucifer was created with "pipes" (resonators) within him. He was also the "anointed cherub that covereth." What was he covering? He resided above the throne of God. The rabbis teach that the throne of God was made up of cherubs. This would make Lucifer the covering canopy. (Note: His fall is one of the reasons that there are two identical angels that now cover the mercy seat, which is an earthly representation of God's throne in heaven. No matter how perfect and beautiful the angel is above God's throne now, there is an identical one on the other side—no chance of being lifted up in pride!)

Lucifer was lifted up above God's throne, and one day he spoke in a rebellious voice (or resonance), and one-third of the angels followed him. This is why Psalm 103:20 tells us: "Bless the LORD, ye his angels, that excel in strength, that do his commandments, hearkening unto the voice of his word" (emphasis added).

If his rebellious words worked in heaven, why wouldn't they work in the new Eden that God had created? Lucifer was lifted up in a tree above God's creation and resonated with his counterfeit anointing—man, just like the angels, responded to it and fell.

Jesus also countered this tactic: "And I, if I be lifted up from the earth, will draw all men unto me" (John 12:32). In other words, "You started it in a tree, and I will finish it in a tree!"

The true voice of God (and His resonance) is embedded in the gospel and the preaching of the cross. When people respond to the resonance of the Holy Spirit in the message, they are born again.

The Prince of the Power of the Air

Satan is referred to as the god (or prince) of the power of the air by the apostle Paul.

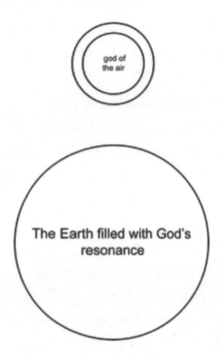

Wherein in time past ye walked according to the course of this world, according to the prince of the power of the air, the spirit that now worketh in the sons of disobedience. (Eph. 2:2)

Today Satan is lifted up over the earth that is filled with God's resonance, and he is broadcasting his own: 6.66 hertz. When man fell in the Garden of Eden, he received a new nature. Within the sin nature is the propensity to tune into Lucifer's frequency, and it tutors us in proficiency as children of disobedience.

When we respond to the preaching of the gospel and are born again, the Holy Spirit moves into our hearts and realigns our spirit to God's original frequency. We slowly learn to distinguish God's voice from that of Lucifer.

Great Expectations of Earth Resonance Changes to Produce a Quantum Leap in Evolution of the Human Mind

Since the Holy Spirit made me aware of the earth resonance (or earth pulse), I have been keeping track of the many theories that are floating around in the information superhighway. Many scientists believe that the earth pulse is also connected to how the human mind works. There seems to be a type of syncing between the earth pulse and the human mind. (Remember, I have already noted that 7.83 hertz can be received directly by the brain.) So, if the earth pulse would change, it would most likely impact how we perceive reality and how we think.

There is a great expectation within the New Age movement for an alteration in the frequency of the earth pulse. This theory has been fueled by the speculation of many scientists that we are on the verge of a geomagnetic reversal.[89] Dr. Schumann found that the earth pulse is basically created by two factors: the magnetic fields around our planet and its interaction with lightning. If the poles do indeed flip-flop on us, it would affect the frequency of the pulse. Many within the New Age movement believe that alteration of the earth pulse will produce a quantum leap in the evolutionary development of the human mind.

Now Connecting DNA to Resonance

Dr. Leonard Horowitz, a respected authority on healthcare, mind control, and the activities of the elite (i.e., Illuminati), has given testimony before Congress on issues of healthcare and mind control on several occasions. In his lecture, "The Controlled America," he casually mentions a discovery by Harvard researchers that is paramount to our study: Within the structure of DNA, there appears to be some type of antenna array to pick up cosmic vibrations (i.e., resonance).[90] This is more evidence that we are wired all the way down to the DNA level to hear the voice of God! Lucifer has a perverse resonance, and the Fall facilitated our propensity to hear his voice.

Piece Number 3—The Image of God and the Human Conscience

By God's leading, I have embarked on an adventure in reading this year. As a Christian educator, I have attempted to read every systematic theology book ever written in English. As I recently viewed several videos on YouTube by a seasoned man of God named R. T. Kendall, I noticed that he had printed the lectures he conducted as pastor of Westminster Chapel. I was so blessed by the videos that I decided to read through the printed material for a refresher. These lectures are called "Understanding Theology." As I read, I came upon this quote: "The conscience is what is left of the image of God in us, incapable of saving us and yet leaving us without excuse."[91]

Even in sinful man, the image of God remains (though marred) and is manifested as the conscience. I read the sentence through about ten times and leaned back in my chair as it impacted my spirit and mind.

- DNA holds incredible volumes of information that we can only begin to understand.
- DNA has an antenna array to pick up planetary or cosmic vibrations.
- 7.83 hertz is essential for life. If the resonance changed, it would affect how man thinks and acts.
- The conscience is the image of God within (although marred by the Fall). This image is alive and speaks—our conscience tells us when we have done something wrong.

- The image of God within is restored through the new birth. The conscience of man becomes revitalized, and we slowly learn to hear God's voice with clarity.

What If?

And he hath power to give life unto the image of the beast, that the image of the beast should both speak, and cause that as many as would not worship the image of the beast should be killed.

And he causeth all, both small and great, rich and poor, free and enslaved, to receive a mark in their right hand, or in their foreheads,

And that no man might buy or sell, save he that had the mark, or the name of the beast, or the number of his name.

Here is wisdom. Let him that hath understanding count the number of the beast; for it is the number of a man; and his number is six hundred threescore and six. (Rev. 13:15–18)

Notice the sequence in which Revelation reveals Lucifer's plan:

The False Prophet has power to give life to the image of the Beast. Is he able to mimic the Holy Spirit and erase the image of God within man and replace it with the image of the Beast (possibly a resequencing of man's DNA to form a new and superior species)? Man would have no more conscience. It would be impossible to respond to the gospel and repent. Men and women would be unredeemable.

People will worship the image of the Beast. How do we worship God? We pray to Him. We respond to the leading of His Spirit. We give reverence to His Word. Maybe the worship of the Beast here is that those that receive the mark only listen to the Beast. They are hard wired to only respond to his word and his voice. Worship used in Revelation 13:15 in the Greek is προσκυνέω, or *proskuneo,* which means "to give reverence, to bow the head down to the ground in homage"[92]—in other words, complete submission to the newly created image of the Beast within: spirit, soul, and body.

Those who do not worship the image will be killed. Charles Darwin would be proud. We are taught in his book, *On the Origin of Species by Means of Natural Selection, or the Preservation of Favoured Races in the Struggle for Life,* that as mankind evolved into homo sapiens, the new species rose up and killed out the old. This has been drilled into the minds of our children in our school systems for several generations. According to Darwin's rationale, the new, improved homo perfectus would rise up to wipe out the old, inferior race (similar to the logic the Nazis used during World War II). This slaughter would be fueled by the image of the Beast within.

People will have the option of taking the mark of the Beast. If you change the basic genetic coding of mankind, it would most likely change the appearance of man. I have heard from several sources that the members of the Illuminati maintain control of the script writers for TV programs and movies. These powerful individuals boast that they continually foretell their plans via the scripts. The CW network has aired one particular series for two seasons now: *Beauty and the Beast.* Vincent, the main character, is a victim of genetic alterations to produce a super soldier in a secret program fashioned for the government. (It is very interesting to note that the genetic coding came from a beast that was on the earth thousands of years ago—i.e., nephilim.) When Vincent goes into "beast mode," there are distinct changes in his body, particularly in his forehead and hands. The writers of this show have thought through how changing the genetic code would alter one's appearance, except in our case in the future, there would be no on-and-off switch. The appearance (and the soul) would be forever changed.

The number of the Beast will be 666. Lucifer has now completed the promise he made to Adam and Eve in the garden…with a twist. They are now recreated in the image of Lucifer rather than of God. Six is biblically the number of man. Man is now complete spirit, soul, and body without God, and appears to be the next evolutionary step for mankind. This super man is now only tuned into the resonance of Lucifer himself.

How Does This Affect the Christian-vs.-Christian Scenario?

"But as the days of Noah were, so shall also the coming of the Son of man be" (Matt. 24:37). Just as in Genesis 6, the enemy will promise an upgrade to mankind. The question that we need to ask ourselves is, "How will this play out within the church?" The church is experiencing an unfortunate and swift transformation. I have been concerned and saddened by what I have witnessed, in addition to what I'm learning from reports of other ministers across our country. The basic tenets of the church are being rewritten to placate fleshly desires. Those with the gift of discernment are sounding the alarm concerning the demonic infiltration of the churches. The moving of the Holy Spirit is being replaced with religious activities and facades, and the doctrines of religious spirits are being promulgated in church services and over Christian airways.

Religious spirits can manifest as Christian, Muslim, Buddhist, satanist, luciferian, and even atheist. I consider an atheist to be empowered by a religious spirit that enforces the religion of self (which is the fuel that invigorates the transhumanist movement). This is a perfect example of the Antichrist spirit, because this spirit's very foundation is "self." Lucifer wanted to exalt himself to become equal with God. His five professions of "I will" formed a counterfeit grace (five is the biblical number for grace) that was all about self. These religious spirits have gained a stronghold in the churches and have permeated the very foundations of our belief system.

The Approaching Convergence

Not only do all roads lead to Rome, but perhaps all religious spirits lead there, too. The current pope has made some interesting announcements, including:

- He declares that all religions are right.[93]
- He considers Protestants fallen Catholics and calls for them to come home (and many are).

This is just the beginning move to a one-world church.

One of the crucial points that we have not fully considered about Jesus' statement of "as in the days of Noah" is the mass of religious spirits that were fueling the movement of humanity to be enhanced by the Watchers during Noah's time. This religious fervor was so strong throughout the earth that only Noah and his family were unenhanced. Genesis 6:5 tells us that man's mind had become so obsessed with this demonic agenda that his imagination and every thought were consumed by evil (perhaps the image of God had been completely lost, and they had no more conscience).

This convergence of religious spirits will sweep though churches, mosques, temples, political offices, and scientific laboratories. The new tower of Babel might well become an enhanced DNA spiral. If the conclusion of many is correct that a pope will one day serve as the False Prophet, then the final key to unlocking Human 2.0 could very possibly be in the greatest library of occult and arcane knowledge on the planet—the Vatican!

What does all this mean? There is a coming division in Christianity! While everyone is talking about unity, the prophets of the kingdom of God have been seeing separation. The remnant will separate itself from those following religious spirits instead of the Spirit of the Living God. As we have seen throughout history and especially in Nazi Germany, great persecution will come upon those who do not toe the new religious line! (Yes, Nazism was based upon occult practices, thus, it was a religion.) We have also seen in the Soviet Union and communist China that the greatest threat to the remnant has been nominal Christians who joined the new movement of the religious spirits in their nations!

What Can the Remnant Do?

There are a few things I believe are important for true believers to do to prepare for the storm that is coming:

Be aware that it's coming. We can no longer be the proverbial ostrich with its head in the sand. We must hearken the prophetic voice of God that is in the earth today, sanctify ourselves to the LORD with a devotion this generation has never seen, and be led by the Holy Spirit.

Learn from Noah and Abraham. Your home must become the center of your spirituality and your walk with God. Biblical Christianity is first the individual, then the home, and then finally the community. As my friend Dr. John Garr recently wrote, "It is time to return to family worship. It is time to make our homes into houses of God."

Recognize kindred spirits. We need to stop being led by titles, names, and hype. People can say all the right things but be of the wrong spirit. Ask God to help you perceive more with your heart and less with your eyes and ears. The current Babylonian system has become expert in using all the right sound bites and symbols to lead the masses into its agenda.

Become true Bereans. Get deeply involved in the Scriptures and conduct your own research. Religious spirits love quick answers— Scriptures out of context that are nothing more than pretexts. Most of all, these spirits hate detailed examination. For the praying man or woman, the facades of these religious spirits are easily pierced and the deceptions quickly exposed. Become a deep thinker and a devout seeker of the face of God. A spiritual person can quickly see through the fruitless environments that religious spirits create!

Pray for shielding. Since we are aware that Satan is using the advanced technologies of our time, it is important for us to pray accordingly. Just as it would take an act of God to override the law of gravity, we need His help to block harmful transmissions through the airways. The Word of God tells us that He is our shield. Part of my family's daily prayers is a petition for Almighty God to shield us from broadcasts of the enemy through the airways, televisions, computers, phones, electric lines, and satellites. We also ask that our Father apply the blood of Jesus to our eyes and ears as a filter, overcoming the projections and broadcasts of the enemy.

Finally, take personal ownership. We need to take ownership of where we are in our walk with God. In fact, we need to be brutally honest. Self-examination and asking God to show us any area in our lives that needs correction will prepare us for the journey as a part of the remnant of God. We must yield to the nail-pierced hand of Jesus in absolute surrender. Obedience to God's Word and the gentle correction of the Holy Spirit will lead us safely through to the victory on the other side.

5

A RAMPANT AND GROWING MADNESS

By Gary Stearman

What's going on? There is a creeping irrationality that's becoming a new norm. It is seen in politics, education, religion, and a society gone wild in commercialized frenzy. Remember the last "Black Friday," with legions of crazed zealots charging their local shopping malls in search of cheap possessions? Christians often comment that the old stability—commonly known as "common sense"—has all but disappeared.

One is reminded of the poet Robert Frost, who, many years ago, commented upon the societies of the World War I and II eras. He said, "A civilized society is one which tolerates eccentricity to the point of doubtful sanity." Truly, we have become civilized, in the secular sense of that word.

A first-grade boy is charged with sexual harassment for kissing a classmate; grade-schoolers are expelled for bringing aspirin for headaches or mouthwash to use after lunch. Yet in middle school, there have been cases in which pregnant teenagers, when counseled to have an abortion, were denied the right to notify their parents.

At every level of society, lying, prevarication, deception, and mendacity have become acceptable behavior. Politicians do it routinely. The new rule: It's okay to lie. Today, even the "good guys" lie. Of course, politicians have lied for decades—for centuries. But there's something a little different now. They actually think they're telling the truth. And they really seem to believe that spending trillions of dollars will somehow put more money into the public coffers! Insane!

Across the world, swelling waves of street demonstrators spread a mixture of fire and hatred, demanding support by their respective governments. But having engaged in decades of obsessive socialism, those regimes are bankrupt. Cycles of violence will continue to increase, leading to totalitarian governments.

Then there's the music business. Back in the sixties, the Beatles (despite their preoccupation with Eastern religion, drugs, and spiritualist experimentation) were the picture of innocence. Their schoolboy suits, pleasant melodies, and well-groomed manner covered the roots of a movement that has become full-fledged debauchery. Rock is pornographic madness. Rap is an endless stream of profanity and blasphemy. Recently, a music star addressed the current president as "God…and my Lord and Savior." Sadly, he probably didn't know any better. But perhaps he did, and was driven by an almost psychotic fixation upon the idea that God has become a human being.

The movies have become careening mélange of fast cuts, cursing, and gunfire, when they're not engaged in the steady propagation of antisocial culture and sexual mayhem.

Television brings all of the above into virtually every home on earth.

Intelligence and intellectual discipline have been distilled into a never-ending barrage of new electronics: Tablets, phones, gaming, and texting are the new measure of culture. True education is no longer needed—you can look it up. In his hot hand, a third-grader has as many electronic facts at his fingertips as a college professor, and he knows it.

Respect for social discipline has almost disappeared. Worst of all, society is breaking down into tribal territories and well-guarded boundaries.

The result: Gang warfare, drug wars, and a hard-rock mentality have permeated the new generations, producing social instability...or worse. Drive-by shooting or mass murders by crazed gunmen are now almost a common phenomenon. Society has become crazed...ragingly insane.

But the ultimate insanity is seen in the Middle East. There, 350 million brothers of Islam, in the passionate heat of their "Arab Spring," dream their psychotic dream of a world dominated by clerics roaming the streets to wield social control through sharia law. Power-mad fanaticism is being welcomed as "peace."

Paul's Prediction

In the context of the foregoing paragraphs, there is a fascinating term, used only twice in the Greek New Testament. It is *calepoV*, spelled in English as *chalepos*, and pronounced with an initial "k," as in "kalepos."

In this study, we shall look at both instances of its usage. In combination, they reveal a prophetic truth that is at once exciting and foreboding. At first glance, its two usages, in two very different contexts, seem unrelated. But in combination, they bring us a remarkable prophetic insight.

The first time this term is encountered, it is found in the context of a familiar episode related in the Gospel of Matthew. It is the centerpiece of a series of seemingly unrelated events. But in fact, they are woven around a common theme.

As the scene opens, Jesus had healed many people. When the word spread, a crowd gathered, at which time Jesus commanded His disciples to prepare a boat, so that they could sail to the east side of the Sea of Galilee. As they departed, Jesus announced that from that point on, His home would be defined not by a specific place, like His hometown, but by His ministry, which would expand into the world. The sea and the boat became a metaphor for that ministry.

In the following narrative, pay particular attention to the word "fierce," which is represented by *chalepos:*

Now, when Jesus saw great multitudes about him, he gave commandment to depart unto the other side.

And a certain scribe came, and said unto him, Master, I will follow thee wherever thou goest.

And Jesus saith unto him, The foxes have holes, and the birds of the air have nests, but the Son of man hath not where to lay his head.

And another of his disciples said unto him, Lord, permit me first to go and bury my father.

But Jesus said unto him, Follow me; and let the dead bury their dead.

And when he was entered into a boat, his disciples followed him.

And, behold, there arose a great tempest in the sea, insomuch that the boat was covered with the waves; but he was asleep.

And his disciples came to him, and awoke him, saying, Lord, save us; we perish.

And he saith unto them, Why are ye fearful, O ye of little faith? Then he arose, and rebuked the winds and the sea; and there was a great calm.

But the men marvelled, saying, What manner of man is this, that even the winds and the sea obey him?

And when he was come to the other side into the country of the Gadarenes, there met him two possessed with demons, coming out of the tombs, exceedingly fierce, so that no man might pass by that way.

And, behold, they cried out, saying, What have we to do with thee, Jesus, thou Son of God? Art thou come hither to torment us before the time?

And there was a good way off from them an herd of many swine feeding.

So the demons besought him, saying, If thou cast us out, permit us to go away into the herd of swine.

And he said unto them, Go. And when they were come out, they went into the herd of swine; and, behold, the whole herd of swine ran violently down a steep place into the sea, and perished in the waters.

And they that kept them fled, and went their ways into the city, and told every thing, and what was befallen to those possessed with the demons.

And, behold, the whole city came out to meet Jesus; and when they saw him, they besought him, that he would depart from their borders. (Matt. 8:18–34)

In this account, the events on and around the Sea of Galilee can be likened to the human drama of the whole world. They offer a microcosm of faith, family, and the service of discipleship in a world gone mad. They center about the person of the One who, Himself, is the center of all creation.

In the narrative above, as the people began to find out about Him, Jesus was in demand. In the midst of this growing excitement, a scribe rashly professed his intention to be an unwavering disciple. Jesus informed him that there would be no security in the endeavor.

Another disciple wished to take care of family business…the funeral of his father. Jesus informed him that such business was of the world, not of his calling as a disciple.

Departing from the commotion of the crowd, they entered the boat and the sea. (May we say, "the world"?) Like the sea of humanity, it was stirred up by winds and weather, themselves metaphors of conflict on the spiritual level. By extension, it depicts the troubled condition of the whole world. Jesus' disciples feared for their lives in the maelstrom, but Jesus calmed them with a reminder that they must hold to their faith in all circumstances. Then, He demonstrated to them that He is in control of the tempest.

On the east side of the sea, Jesus made landfall in an unclean land, symbolized by demonic possession and the dominance of swineherds eking out a living in an unclean world. Both of these conditions are typical of humankind living in sin, which finally rejected Christ.

And so it was with the Gadarenes. After Jesus cast demons out of two possessed men, the people begged Him to leave. And no wonder. In Mark's account of this incident, we learn that about two thousand swine were drowned! In any event, their reaction was totally inappropriate.

In the other accounts of this incident, we are also told that the possessed men displayed supernatural strength and were controlled by many demons. They broke chains and fetters; no one could control them.

Exceeding Fierce

This brings us to the use of that term mentioned above. Here, in Matthew's account, demon-possessed men are called "fierce." This is a translation of the Greek term *chalepos (calepoV)*, meaning "violent." It is coupled with a modifier "exceedingly fierce." This term suggests more than violence, reaching even to the level of uncontrolled, raging, and brutal insanity.

And here we come face to face with the world, driven by an inner darkness, out of control and furiously rejecting the message of Christ. The east bank of the sea offers a compact view of the depraved world. For those who have eyes to see, it displays a blatant truth. Jesus' followers were fishermen, not swineherds.

Chalepos also carries the meaning of ferocity. In the social context, it indicates uncivilized behavior, ranging all the way to savagery.

This was the scene on that ancient day when Christ sailed the Sea of Galilee. On one side, tumultuous crowds sought His blessing. On the sea, winds and waves buffeted His disciples. Upon their landing, they came to a world gone mad, subsisting in a state of spiritual depravity.

The Far Future

This brings us to the second use of *chalepos*. And here, its application is plain and simple. It sets the tone of a prophecy given to Timothy by Paul…his final epistle, written to Timothy just before his death. It was written from a cold Roman cell. Winter was coming. Paul had been convicted by Caesar—confined as the leader of an illegal religion. The prison setting portrays the long, cold winter night ahead for Christianity as a social and cultural force.

The epistle is an exhortation and warning to the young pastor, who may not have developed deep insight into what lay ahead. Its tone is solemn and thoughtful, befitting the difficulties that Paul knew would define the future. Pay particular attention to the word "perilous," noting that the subject revolves around "the snare of the devil," and the subsequent effect he has upon the world:

And the servant of the Lord must not strive; but be gentle unto all men, apt to teach, patient,

In meekness instructing those that oppose him, if God, perhaps, will give them repentance to the acknowledging of the truth,

And that they may recover themselves out of the snare of the devil, who are taken captive by him at his will.

This know, also, that in the last days perilous times shall come.

For men shall be lovers of their own selves, covetous, boasters, proud, blasphemers, disobedient to parents, unthankful, unholy,

Without natural affection, trucebreakers, false accusers, incontinent, fierce, despisers of those that are good,

Traitors, heady, highminded, lovers of pleasures more than lovers of God,

Having a form of godliness, but denying the power of it; from such turn away.

For of this sort are they which creep into houses, and lead captive silly women laden with sins, led away with various lusts,

Ever learning, and never able to come to the knowledge of the truth.

Now as Jannes and Jambres withstood Moses, so do these also resist the truth: men of corrupt minds, reprobate concerning the faith.

But they shall proceed no further; for their folly shall be manifest unto all men, as theirs also was. (2 Tim. 2:24–3:9)

Here again, we find the Greek word *chalepos*, this time translated as "perilous." As used in Matthew, it described the actions of men possessed by demons. They were out of their minds, uncontrollable, and violent. And here, in Paul's word of prophecy to Timothy, we find exactly the same meaning!

This time, however, it does not merely apply to two men on the eastern shore of the Sea of Galilee. As Paul envisioned the world of the latter days, he saw that it is characterized by the same insanity.

Ragingly Insane

Paul urged the young preacher, Timothy, to exercise a quiet strength in his daily ministry. He emphasized the importance of teaching the strong doctrines of Christianity. He knew that only correct and thorough doctrinal teaching offers the strength to withstand the coming social subversion that the devil and his followers will bring upon the world.

That world is symbolized in the book of Matthew by Galilee's eastern shore…the swineherd culture and the demoniacs who raged among them. Paul's letter says that it will become a reality. Of course, he was correct. The past two thousand years have brought a cavalcade of narcissistic, vain, despotic, blasphemous, criminal usurpers to leadership in every country of the world.

Though the last three or four centuries have brought enlightenment to the West, darkness is quickly closing in upon the last vestiges of Christian influence. Europe has reverted to paganism, as a tiny minority of Christians holds on for dear life. Radical Islam is fast becoming the dominant force there.

Godlessness is sweeping across the United States. The result is just as Paul's words foretold. The World Wide Web—the Internet—is a bubbling porridge of mixed information. Though amazingly useful, with a potential for great good (particularly in the spread of the gospel), evil has, in fact, overtaken it. The electronic culture is now dominated by pornography, corruption, thievery, and crass commercialism that threaten to undermine the last vestiges of civilized behavior. The mind of this generation is all but enslaved to its seduction.

In the outside world, it is even worse. The sordid underbelly of culture crawls with serial killers, drug pushers, sexual predators, and a wide variety of self-serving criminals who will resort to any means to enhance their own wealth. Increasingly, we are seeing the emergence of behavior that, only a few short years ago, would have been unheard of…simply beyond belief.

And then there is the world of public communications. For the Christian, television has become all but unviewable. Radio is becoming lewd and coarse, as the public debate of issues devolves into endless harangues, diatribes, and rants, sometimes touching upon subjects that send one racing for the volume control, lest the ears of the children be subjected to corrupt and perverse notions that were once confined to the conversations of social outcasts.

Public life has, itself, become a parade of insanity. Think of the last few elections. Both nationally and locally, they increasingly seem to be dominated by money and demagoguery—emotional speech without a thread of logic. Think back: Have you recently heard a public figure make a statement that you found simply insane? Where is the voice of logic and rational ideas? To argue from fact is to be found lacking in compassion.

Raging criticism among political factions has reached an uncivilized level. Radical Islam is promoted as a "religion of peace," even as it assaults Judaism and Christianity at every level. It rejects the stability demonstrated in the constitutional democracy that brought Western civilization to the highest levels of achievement in history.

Increasingly, the godless ones scheme to save the world through the application of various social programs that will reshape society through a global bureaucracy. To apply more of the strategies that caused the initial problem is simply insane. And almost two thousand years ago, Paul accurately predicted it.

6

WAR OF THE APOSTATES

By Larry Spargimino

And I saw the woman drunken with the blood of the saints, and with the blood of the martyrs of Jesus.

—Revelation 17:6

Society is unraveling. The signs on earth and in the heavens point to the soon coming of the Lord. War and rumors of war are rattling the hearts of many, but the Bible speaks of another kind of war: the war of the apostates against the true followers of Jesus Christ.

Revelation 17 speaks about "the judgment of the great harlot that sitteth upon many waters; With whom the kings of the earth have committed fornication, and the inhabitants of the earth have been made drunk with the wine of her fornication" (Rev. 17:1–2).

Satan has been using false religion, commerce, and spiritual deception to further his evil purposes throughout the ages of man, but now his efforts are intensified. Knowing that his time is short, Satan is redoubling his efforts to turn men away from redemption. His goal is to promote religion that has no redemption. He is doing that in today's world through false religion. It's even in the churches of America and the world, and is being proclaimed by pastors and church organizations that promote radical environmentalism and nature worship, and that sing the global warming mantra. In the name of "love and reconciliation," so-called Christian groups are waffling on major moral issues, like same-sex "marriage."

Recently, the mega ministry World Vision has announced that it now is allowing employees to be involved in homosexual "marriages." The purpose of this, according to Richard Stearns, president of the US branch, is that it is an effort to encourage "unity." Stearns said it should be seen as "symbolic not of compromise but of [Christian] unity."[94] World Vision has changed its mind due to legitimate protests from supporters; nevertheless, it is still an example of "waffling on major moral issues."

This is but one example of Christian-themed organizations softening their stand on key moral issues. There are many others that we will cite in this study. Some organizations are actually siding with groups that have taken another worldview as their frame of reference, and are endorsing things that are contrary to sound doctrine.

Certain types of conservative Christian belief—such as taught by premillennialism regarding God's unconditional covenant with the Jewish people and the land of Israel—are being blamed for the seemingly unresolvable hostilities in the Middle East. Is it possible that Christians who support certain Christian beliefs will be subjected to persecution by the government and by the false church siding with the government? This chapter will seek to show that this is exactly what is happening at present in seed form, and that it will flower into full bloom in the Tribulation.

And what about the issue of global warming? On the basis of good science, many Christians do not accept the tenets of global warming or, as it has been more recently called in view of the extremely cold winters we've been having, "climate change." Napp Nazworth, writing for *The Christian Post*, reports that an assistant professor of philosophy at Rochester Institute of Technology said that those who fund and promote doubts about global warming should be sent to prison. Professor Lawrence Torcello wrote: "When it comes to global warming, much of the public remains in denial about a set of facts that the majority of scientists clearly agree on. With such high stakes, an organized campaign funding misinformation ought to be considered criminally negligent."[95]

Professor Torcello referenced the six Italian scientists who were sentenced to six years in prison after the deadly earthquake of 2009 that killed three hundred. He says the scientists were not imprisoned for failing to predict the earthquake, but because they failed to "clearly communicate risks to the public." When a public official put the residents at ease and told them there was no danger even after the tremors started, the scientists were culpable because they did nothing to correct the official.[96]

In this study, we will endeavor to follow recent developments showing the rampant doctrinal compromise being seen in the emerging church and "Purpose-Driven" movements. It will be shown that the acceptance of gay "marriage" and homosexuality, along with an embracing of the tenets of radical environmentalism by these groups, are lining up with the prophecies of Babylon and the false church waging war against God's people.

Apostasy in Ancient Israel

In ancient Israel, apostates and religionists were steeped in evolutionary pantheism—something that some church groups and ministries are promoting today. They spoke to a tree and said: "Thou art my father; and to a stone, Thou hast brought me forth; for they have turned their back unto me, and not their face: but in the time of their trouble they will say, Arise, and save us" (Jer. 2:27). In Jeremiah 3:9, we read: "And it came to pass through the lightness of her harlotry, that she defiled the land, and committed adultery with stones and with trees."

Jeremiah preached against making the Temple in Jerusalem an item of ultimate trust and confidence. That brought great hostility upon Jeremiah. Yet—and we need to remember this as a matter of encouragement—there were some who stood up for Jeremiah, and reminded the people that King Hezekiah of Judah heeded the words of the prophet Micah the Morashtite:

> Micah, the Morashtite, prophesied in the days of Hezekiah, king of Judah, and spoke to all the people of Judah, saying, Thus saith the LORD of hosts; Zion shall be plowed like a field, and Jerusalem shall become heaps, and the mountain of the house like the high places of a forest.
>
> Did Hezekiah, king of Judah, and all Judah put him at all to death? Did he not fear the LORD, and besought the LORD, and the LORD repented him of the evil which he had pronounced against them? (Jer. 26:18–19)

The apostates of old claimed that the pagan deities of the land treated them better than the true and living God. "But since we ceased to burn incense to the queen of heaven, and to pour out drink offerings unto her, we have lacked all things, and have been consumed by the sword and by famine" (Jer. 44:18).

Revelation 17 and Babylon

"Babylon" is a word, place, and name that occurs very frequently in Scripture. In the book of Revelation, one out of every ten verses concerns an entity identified as "Babylon." Two entire chapters—Revelation chapters 17 and 18—are devoted to Babylon. However, while the word is a high-frequency one, the exact identification is somewhat challenging. Mark Hitchcock gives seven clues that can help identify Babylon:

- Babylon is a literal city (Rev. 17:18).
- Babylon is a city of worldwide importance and influence, probably the capital city of the Antichrist (Rev. 17:15, 18).
- Babylon and the Beast (the Antichrist) are very closely connected with one another. The woman (Babylon) is pictured riding on the Beast (Rev. 17:3–5, 7).
- Babylon is the center of false religion (Rev. 17:4–5; 18:1–2).
- Babylon is the center of world commerce (Rev. 18:9–19).
- Babylon persecutes the Lord's people (Rev. 17:6; 18:20, 24).
- Babylon will be destroyed suddenly and completely at the end of the Tribulation, never to rise again (Rev. 18:8–10, 21–24).[97]

Even among premillennialists, there is disagreement as to the precise meaning of "Babylon" in Revelation 17:

Some see it simply as an illustration of something that is evil and diabolical, while others understand "Babylon" to be a literal restoration of an ancient city. Some Dispensationalists believe that "Mystery Babylon" is a reference to a false religious system that has been around for centuries but has become particularly evident through certain religions and religious practices.[98]

The religious system established at the original site of Babylon by its founder and first king, Nimrod, is the source of Babylonian religion and philosophy. With the scattering resulting from the Babel event, this religion was carried into every corner of the earth. This is why every nonbiblical religious system—and we see it today in the hodgepodge of designer religions that are proliferating the American religious scene—is pantheistic, polytheistic, astrological, and universal. Nimrod himself was a violent man. Some of the major religious movements are violent and are take-over religions desirous of taking over the planet.

This woman of Revelation 17 "was arrayed in purple and scarlet color, and bedecked with gold and precious stones and pearls, having a golden cup in her hand, full of abominations and filthiness of her fornication" (v. 4). Spiritual whoredom is associated with a defection from the truth, a willful act of embracing "other lovers."

We notice that the woman is drunk—not with alcohol, but with the blood of the martyrs of Jesus (Rev. 17:6). These are the followers of Jesus who have died for their faith and commitment to Christ as Lord. Here we have a religious prostitute making martyrs. Sexual immorality and apostasy are linked in the Bible—the former often symbolizes the latter (Rev. 2:20–23; Ezek.16:15–43). Babylon's suggestive beauty is irresistible.

Her fornication has been universal and pervasive, not local or regional: "The inhabitants of the earth have been made drunk with the wine of her fornication" (Rev. 17:2). She is "the great harlot that sitteth upon many waters" (Rev. 17:1), the "waters which thou sawest, where the harlot sitteth, are peoples, and multitudes, and nations, and tongues" (v. 15). This "harlot," or whore, is an entity that transcends geopolitical as well as cultural, ethnic, and linguistic divisions. This suggests that the whore is more than a single person or even a single expression of religion that is against God. Only a universal false religion seems to fit the description. This is the woman who rides the Beast (Rev. 17:3).

This great whore sits on seven hills or mountains (Rev. 17:9). Mountains are often emblematic of whole kingdoms (cf. Ps. 68:15; Dan. 2:35; Amos 4:1, 6:1; Obad. 8–21). This all seems to describe more than one local area and is better seen as representing the universal spread of false religion. Historically, many expositors have argued that Vatican City is "that great city, which reigneth over the king s of the earth" (Rev. 17:18). Vatican City is certainly not reigning over the kings of the earth at present, nor does there seem to be much to indicate that it, in its particular denominational identification, will do so at a future time.

The language is highly fluid. In Revelation 17:3, the word "city" doesn't necessarily mean one municipality in a limited area. Walid Shoebat cogently argues that most prophecy writers think out of a Western/ European mindset, and writes:

> Bear in mind that the above verse is in Greek, and a "city" in the Bible doesn't always denote a single place. For instance, today the nation of Israel is called Medinat Yesrael in Hebrew. In Aramaic or Arabic, the word Medinat is "a city." In the ancient context, for example in Jeremiah, Gilead actually speaks of all of Judah as one city. The same is true for "house," which is not a single house but all the people of Judah. "For thus says the Lord unto the king's house of Judah; thou art Gilead unto me, and the head of Lebanon; yet surely I will make thee a wilderness, and cities which are not inhabited." Judah itself will be a wilderness like cities devoid of their people (Jer. 22:6).[99]

This seductive temptress is given an enigmatic name: "MYSTERY, BABYLON THE GREAT, THE MOTHER OF HARLOTS" (Rev. 17:5). "Babylon is probably the place from which all false religious beliefs had their beginning. From Babylon stemmed a religious rebellion that has blinded people everywhere, so that they are in opposition to the true God. Thus Babylon is a place, but it is much more."[100]

"The mother of harlots" is not simply the source, but the size, of the influence of this enigmatic entity. Shoebat writes that "mother" means "the biggest" or "the greatest." "Remember Saddam Hussein's comments in the days leading up to [the] first Gulf War? He declared that the U.S. and Iraq were about to engage in 'the mother of all battles.' Of course, in typical megalomaniacal game-talk, he also declared that America was about to experience 'the mother of all defeats.'"[101]

This monstrous and filthy entity is "the mother of harlots and abominations of the earth." "Abominations" *(bdelugma)* refers to something, or someone, that is vile and detestable, that defiles and corrupts, such as "the abomination *[bdelugma]* of desolation" (Matt. 24:15). It is so vile that it contaminates the Temple and renders it unfit for worship. It is something nauseating to God because of its moral and spiritual filthiness. It is this "mother" from whose womb comes spiritual filthiness that has led to the death of God's faithful servants.

The picture being drawn in Revelation 17 is not a picture of an entity with no faith or religious belief that persecutes God's true children; rather, it is a picture of an entity with the wrong faith that causes grief. It's the faith of apostates.

Some have identified the whore of Babylon as the Roman Catholic Church, because the woman sits on seven hills, identified in ancient times as the city of Rome. It is this writer's view that much more is involved in this picture. Verse 10 proceeds to explain that the seven hills represent seven kingdoms, five of which have fallen, one that is, and one that is to come. This whore is a world system dominated by the Antichrist. At one time in the future, this whore will have control over these kings, but at some point prior to Armageddon they will turn on her and destroy her (Rev. 17:16).

While it is always precarious to make specific designations and give specific explanations, there are various movements today within the pale of "Christendom" that are having a greater and greater resemblance to the harlot church of Revelation chapter 17.

The Emergent Church

Worldview impacts and intersects with one's understanding regarding the nature and definition of truth. Much of the error and confusion being taught by those in the emergent movement is due to their embracing—wittingly or unwittingly—the Hegelian dialectic. Under this thinking, truth is never final or complete, nor can it be articulated rationally. Truth is evolving. There is the *thesis*—an idea that is less than perfect. This leads to opposition, refinement, and restatement, known as the *antithesis*. As a result of this conflict in point of view and the resultant tension, the tension screams for resolution. This resolution is achieved by reaching a higher level of truth, a *synthesis* of the thesis and antithesis.[102]

In this scheme of things, truth can never reach finality. There is always some new antithesis leading to a greater refinement of truth. For emergents, they are not quite sure what to make of homosexuality, or how to think about it. Brian McLaren, in an article published on the web for *Christianity Today* titled "Brian McLaren on the Homosexual Question: Finding a Pastoral Response," writes:

Frankly, many of us don't know what we should think about homosexuality. We've heard all sides but no position has yet won our confidence so that we can say "it seems good to the Holy Spirit and us." That alienates us from both the liberals and conservatives who seem to know exactly what we should think. Even if we are convinced that all homosexual behavior is always sinful, we still want to treat gay and lesbian people with more dignity, gentleness, and respect than our colleagues do. If we think that there may actually be a legitimate context for some homosexual relationships, we know that the biblical arguments are nuanced and multilayered, and the pastoral ramifications are staggeringly complex. We aren't sure if or where lines are to be drawn, nor do we know how to enforce with fairness whatever lines are drawn.[103]

John MacArthur perceptively analyzes thoughts such as these, especially as it intersects with the modern gay rights movement. The following is from a transcript of an interview between John MacArthur and Phil Johnson.

One of the big issues is homosexuality in the Emerging Church. They don't want to take a position on homosexuality. The Bible is not vague or obscure or oblique about homosexuality. It couldn't be more clear. A homosexual will not inherit the Kingdom of God…that's pretty clear. Homosexuality in Romans chapter 1 is a perversion that is manifested when it happens in a culture, begins to dominate a culture, an evidence of divine wrath and divine judgment. So the Bible is clear. They don't want that clarity. They want to run from the light. Scripture is light, it is not darkness, but they like the darkness because their deeds are evil…this is just another way to set the Bible aside.[104]

This tentativeness on McLaren's part can be traced to his view of Scripture and uncertainty as to its inspiration in the classical sense of being the inspired Word of God. He is even uncomfortable with the Bible's masculine pronouns for God:

This is as good a place as any to apologize for my use of masculine pronouns for God in the previous sentence. You'll notice that wherever I can, I avoid the use of masculine pronouns for God because they can give the false impression to many people today that the Christian God is a male deity.[105]

The Bible does not, and cannot, give us an exhaustive knowledge of God. However, while the Bible does not tell us everything that God knows, what the Bible does tell us is accurate, even in its limitations. McLaren could very well criticize the Greek New Testament on the grounds that it makes God sound like a Greek-speaking deity.

Because the emergent view of truth is dialectical, we can agree with MacArthur that emergent theology teaches a "doctrine of Christian postmodernism." The movement is:

…an amorphous sort of loose-knit association of churches that have decided that there is value, there is even virtue, in uncertainty about Scripture. The bottom line in the movement is they believe that we aren't even suppose [sic] to understand precisely what the Bible means.… It's an attack on the clarity of Scripture and they elevate themselves as if this is some noble reality…it's amorphous because there's a mish-mash of approaches to this and a mish-mash of styles and things like that. But they have embraced this mystery as if it's true spirituality. And so, it becomes celebration of mystery, a celebration of ignorance, a celebration that we can't really know.[106]

This "celebration of mystery" leads the emerging church into medieval, contemplative spirituality.

They want more mystery. So they go back to medieval Catholicism and they light a bunch of candles. You know, really it smells like orthodox, Greek orthodoxy, Russian orthodoxy kind of approach, milling people. I've been in a Russian Orthodox Church that there's no center, there's no focal point, there's no pulpit, there's no platform. There are these guys, they swing these censors and smoke and stuff rises and these really weird smells and they just… they walk in a little parade.… And then people mill over here and they will and then these guys walk around. This goes on for like a half an hour and they're making these weird chants.[107]

Emergent Teaching on the Atonement

Emergent theology takes exception to the "violent view" of the atonement. The idea that God must satisfy divine justice in order to forgive sin is barbaric. It makes God look like a monster, because, they say, God cannot forgive without inflicting pain on someone, either on His Son, Jesus Christ, or the impenitent sinner. Emergents critique the traditional view of the atonement because it presents God as the "greatest existential threat to humanity."

Penal substitution, the traditional view, presents Christ as the substitutionary sin bearer. It makes God look like a petty, spoiled tyrant and turns many off to Christianity. Emergents don't like the idea that Jesus had to be "beat up" so that people could go to heaven.

Yet, Isaiah 53:5 is violent: "But he was WOUNDED for OUR transgressions, he was BRUISED for OUR iniquities" (emphasis added). Because of the Christian's mystical union with Christ, Jesus Christ fulfills the demands of justice not for an unrelated third party, but for those identified with Him. He is our vicarious substitute. Revelation 5 reveals that a new song will be sung lauding the worthiness and glory of Christ, "for thou wast slain, and hast redeemed us to God BY THY BLOOD out of every kindred, and tongue, and people, and nation" (v. 9, emphasis added).

The traditionalist will point out that the argument that it is unjust to punish an innocent bystander involuntarily for someone else's sin is refuted by Scripture. Jesus Himself said that He was offering Himself to voluntarily die on the cross for the sins of the world: "Greater love hath no man that this, that a man lay down his life FOR his friends" (John 15:13, emphasis added).

The traditional, substitutionary view is illustrated by the ritual that took place on the Day of Atonement (Lev. 16). Two goats were used on that day. One was slaughtered—that signifies and illustrates propitiation. The other was released to wander in the wilderness—that is expiation. Propitiation indicates that God is justly angry over our sins. How could He not be? Propitiation requires death—but it is the death of a substitute. "For he hath made him, who knew no sin, to be sin FOR US, that we might be made the righteousness of God in him" (2 Cor. 5:21, emphasis added).

Not only is the traditional view of the atonement rejected, but so is the return of Christ. A reader from Sweden asked Brian McLaren a question:

If Jesus isn't coming back (in the way we expect) what about judgment, or the resurrection? For me in the past those three things have always been connected, like when Jesus comes back we will all be judged and those who died before us will resurrect and we will all live in a new creation together with God forever and ever.[108]

McLaren's answer is revealing:

Right. Jesus does say, "I will come again," and he talks about "When the Son of Man returns," but I think it's a mistake to assume that when he says those things, he means what we mean when we say "Second Coming of Christ," with all of our dispensationalist, premillennialist, amillenniallist, postmillennialist, or whatever categories.... As...others have made abundantly clear, the hyperbolic imagery of the NT (moon turning to blood, stars falling from the sky, etc.) is political language, signaling the fall of powerful political luminaries, etc. Also you're saying (I think) that Jesus didn't come just to evacuate us from earth to a future heaven but to show us how to live and make this world more and more beautiful by following Jesus [sic] example which would eventually lead to God's "kingdom come on earth as it is in heaven" as Jesus taught us to pray.[109]

McLaren obviously thinks prophecy is hyperbolic—exaggerated imagery that needs to be demythologized, much in the same way that Rudolf Bultmann demythologized Scripture to allegedly get at the true, literal core of what it, supposedly, really means. However, the "moon turning to blood" is a phenomenon known today as a "blood moon." It is prophetically significant and has been verified by Bible expositors such as Mark Biltz and many others. They have studied the NASA printouts and have noticed the correlation of heavenly phenomena with key events in Israel's history. Genesis 1 reveals that the sun and the moon are for signs and witnesses to coming dramatic events, and are tied in with the Feasts of the Lord (Lev. 23).[110]

Emergent Christianity is radical and radically different. Rob Bell admits:

> This is not just the same old message with new methods. We're rediscovering Christianity as an Eastern religion, as a way of life. Legal metaphors for faith don't deliver a way of life. We grew up in churches where people knew the nine verses why we don't speak in tongues, but had never experienced the overwhelming presence of God.[111]

The Religion of Environmentalism

A prefatory word is necessary in order to avoid misunderstanding. We are to be stewards of God's creation. Christians who understand the message of Scripture do not abuse, destroy, or misuse the natural world. Everything that God has created reflects His glory, wisdom, and power. This author is an outdoorsman and realizes the wonderful heritage that we have in our natural resources. It is not a foregone conclusion that if you are a biblical Christian you will be a danger to the environment. However, Christians don't worship or even venerate the creation.

"Professing themselves to be wise, they became fools, And changed the glory of the incorruptible God into an image made like corruptible man, and birds, and four-footed beasts, and creeping things" (Rom. 1:22–23). It is for this reason that "God also gave them up to uncleanness through the lusts of their own hearts, to dishonor their own bodies between themselves" (Rom. 1:24).

It has become increasingly clear that much of the radical environmental literature and climate-change alarmism is not rooted in science and that the attacks on those who do not side with the greens are not motivated by science. Recently, 31,487 scientists, many of whom have earned doctorates, signed a petition. It reads as follows:

We urge the United States government to reject the global warming agreement that was written in Kyoto, Japan in December, 1997, and any other similar proposals. The proposed limits on greenhouse gases would harm the environment, hinder the advance of science and technology, and damage the health and welfare of mankind.

There is no convincing scientific evidence that human release of carbon dioxide, methane, or other greenhouse gases is causing or will, in the foreseeable future, cause catastrophic heating of the Earth's atmosphere and disruption of the earth's climate. Moreover, there is substantial scientific evidence that increases in atmospheric carbon dioxide produce many beneficial effects upon the natural plant and animal environments of the earth.[112]

How did all of this global warming hype get started? In his 2006 Oscar-winning documentary, *An Inconvenient Truth,* former US Vice

President Al Gore presented global warming as an imminent threat to the planet. If nothing is done to change the alleged temperature rise, mankind will ultimately destroy himself and life on planet earth. Supposedly, the oceans will rise dramatically in the next century as the temperature of the polar regions skyrockets. Much of the earth's coastlines will be underwater, home to one hundred million people. Perhaps worst of all, global warming will cause an increasing number of weather catastrophes—hurricanes, tornadoes, floods, droughts, and blizzards.

Respected environmental climate expert E. Calvin Beisner examined the serious economic side effects of anti-CO_2 policies. He concludes that "the policies that are being promoted to fight global warming not only will not make a difference…but also will have a great harmful impact on the world's poor."[113]

Nevertheless, environmentalism has caught on in many circles. Even Pope Francis, Jorge Mario Bergoglio, is urging leaders to protect nature.[114] Speaking in Italian in the frescoed Sala Clementina, the Pope said, "Members of all religions and even non-believers had to recognize their joint responsibility 'to our world, to all of creation, which we have to love and protect.'"[115]

Vatican II had far-reaching implications with prophetic overtones. Jesuit priest and professor at Georgetown University in Washington, DC, John W. O'Malley, writes: "Before the council, Catholics were not only forbidden to pray with those of other faiths but also indoctrinated into a disdain or even contempt for them.… Now, for the first time, Catholics were encouraged to foster friendly relations with Orthodox and Protestant Christians, as well as Jews and Muslims, and even to pray with them."[116] With this interfaith reach, the next step is an interfaith environmental reach.

Environmentalists Unhappy with the Bible

A study of the literature, articles, and books written by the radical environmentalists shows that they have raised many complaints against Christians and the Judeo-Christian Scriptures:

- The Judeo-Christian belief that God assigned man to rule over the earth and have dominion has caused the exploitation and misuse of the planet.
- Monotheism has separated humans from their natural connection to the earth. To reverse this trend, artists, authors, and educators must revive earth-centered myths that elevate goddess Mother Earth.
- The diversity of species enriches the earth. Healthy, flourishing diversity can only be maintained if there is a substantial decrease in the human population and its interference with nature's benevolent and wise processes.
- Heavenly-minded Christians care little for what they see as a temporary earth that will soon be burned up.
- By resisting the return to earth-centered religions, and by relegating them to the category of rank paganism, Christians are blocking the global movement toward the one-world religion needed to unify people and to save our planet from pollution, global warming, and thermonuclear war.

Environmental literature encourages its devotees to imitate the beliefs and lifestyles of primitive people who are supposedly "untainted by the Judeo-Christian religion." But, in reality, behind the supposedly beautiful side of paganism—the illusions of idyllic scenes replete with nude bodies in the glade—are to be found greed, cruel violence, and war.

And what about man's alleged harmony with nature? The plains Indians would stampede a herd of buffalo and drive them to their death by starting a grass fire. The escaping animals would flounder in a swamp or rush headlong off a cliff, as at Ulm Pishkun, outside of Great Falls, Montana, only to plummet to a horrible and lingering death from broken bones and damaged internal organs. And what about the natural respect for life and the "peaceful" Indians? We hear of Custer's cruelty and murderous rampages against helpless and innocent Native Americans, but Indian wars between Iroquois and Huron, Comanche and Chickasaw were equally vicious and brutal. Indeed, the words of Scripture aptly describe the condition of all humanity: "Their feet are swift to shed blood; Destruction and misery are in their ways; And the way of peace have they not known" (Rom. 3:15–17).

Environmentalism as Religion

Environmentalism has become a full-fledged religion—and every religion has its deities. To go against the tenets of a religion can be a serious affront—maybe even "sin." "The dominant doctrines of God in environmentalism are atheism (belief there is no God), pantheism (belief that God is everything), panentheism (belief that God indwells everything as the soul does the body), and animism or spiritism (belief that every material thing, not just human bodies, is indwelt by a soul or spirit)."[117]

Consequently, environmentalism, both secular and religious, tends to define all the earth and all its inhabitants as sacred and holy...everything has intrinsic worth, not dependent on human valuation, and particularly that, as Deep Ecology founder Arne

Naess put it, all life is fundamentally one, and so "biological egalitarianism" is the preferred ethic—from which thinking flow thoughts of animal rights, plant rights, and ecosystem rights, all ideas newly enshrined in the constitutions of Switzerland (where one now must harvest a wheat field only in a manner that honor the dignity of the wheat) and Bolivia.[118]

Environmentalist behaviors echo religious behaviors and thereby provide meaningful religious rituals for "greens." Paul H. Rubin, writing for the *Wall Street Journal*, cites the following:

- There is a holy day—Earth Day.
- There are food taboos. Instead of eating fish on Friday, or avoiding pork, greens now eat organic.
- There is no prayer, but there are self-sacrificing rituals that are not particularly useful, such as recycling. Recycling paper to save trees, for example, makes no sense since the effect will be to reduce the number of trees planted in the long run.
- Environmentalism is a proselytizing religion. Skeptics are not merely people who are unconvinced by the evidence. Rather, they are treated as evil sinners. "I probably would not write this article if I did not have tenure."[119]

Environmentalism as a religion produces belief that nature is sacred. Violations of the sacral nature of nature are "sins." So, how can we be "saved" from such a supposedly murderous and sinful lifestyle? Beisner refers to the environmentalists who believe they have the authority...

1. To determine whether we'll drive the large, safe cars we prefer

or the small, dangerous cars they prefer, or whether we'll drive cars at all or use only public transportation;

2. To decide the temperature at which to set our thermostats and the kinds of light bulbs we'll use and how much insulation we'll have in our homes;

3. To dictate whether we'll use disposable or cloth diapers, and plastic or cloth grocery bags, and inexpensive nuclear or fossil fuel or expensive wind or solar energy;

4. To rule whether we'll eat non-organic or organic foods, meat or vegetables, a wide variety of delightful and healthful foods grown around the world and transported to us or a narrow variety grown locally;

5. To rule whether and how many children we'll have.[120]

Michael Crichton, author of *State of Fear*, a techno novel dealing with environmentalism in general and the global warming debate in particular, writes:

There's an initial Eden, a paradise, a state of grace and unity with nature, there's a fall from grace into a state of pollution as a result of eating from the tree of knowledge, and as a result of our actions there is a judgment day coming for us all. We are all energy sinners, doomed to die, unless we seek salvation, which is now called sustainability. Sustainability is salvation in the church of the environment. Just as organic food is its communion, that pesticide-free wafer that the right people with the right beliefs, imbibe.[121]

Just how far this "sin thing" in terms of harming goddess Mother Earth is taken can be seen in the new movie *Noah*, the $125-million production casting high-profile names like Emma Watson and Russell Crowe. Man's disrespect for nature is given as the reason for divine judgment.[122]

At the present time we see an emerging pattern. There is a rejection of revealed religion in favor of nature-based religions. They will be the glue that will unite the world's religions into one so that one world government and one world economic system can be implemented. Christians will be seen as being "the enemy." Sustainability, not Jesus Christ, will save the planet. Those contradicting this message will be regarded with increasing distrust.

Should Churches Be Surrendering to the Gay Agenda?

In 1987, two homosexual political strategists, Marshall K. Kirk and Erastes Pill, published an article titled "The Overhauling of Straight America." An important part of their strategy was to avoid trying to persuade fundamental churches in the hopes that they would moderate their opposition to homosexuality, but rather to try to reach churches that would perhaps waffle on their views. "We can use talk to muddy the moral waters. This means publicizing support for gays by more moderate churches, raising theological objections of our own about conservative interpretations of biblical teachings, and exposing hatred and inconsistency."[123]

Since the publication of "The Overhauling of Straight America," this strategy has worked extremely well:

- The California Council of Churches, representing twenty-one member denominations, elected as its president the "Reverend" Gwynne Guibord, an open lesbian.

- In Dallas, Texas, a $35-million "church" facility, called the Cathedral of Hope, was dedicated as the world's "gay and lesbian mecca": a symbol of "gay Christianity" equivalent in the eyes of its creators to Vatican City for Catholics and Salt Lake City for Mormons.
- The Reverend Troy Perry, founder of the three-hundred-"church"-strong homosexual denomination called the Metropolitan Community Church, was appointed to the board of trustees of Chicago Theological Seminary and invited to lead chapel service at Yale Divinity School.
- Soulforce, the "gay Christian" pressure group, now with chapters in many states, gained national publicity for its campaign against "spiritual violence" (i.e., failure to affirm homosexuality as normal) by physically invading the Southern Baptist Convention on June 11, 2002. Anti-Baptist "civil disobedience" tactics have continued, including a March 26, 2007, incident in which a dozen homosexual activists were arrested for staging a sit-in at the office of Albert Mohler, president of the Southern Baptist Theological Seminary.
- In 2008, the bishops of the Episcopal Church in California actively campaigned against Proposition 8, which defined marriage as only between one man and one woman in the California Constitution.[124]

Because of the lack of training and commitment to the authority of the Bible, many churches and congregations easily transition from nominally Bible believing to strong supporters of the gay lifestyle. "Almost inevitably the congregation yields to pressure and changes its status to an 'affirming' one in which homosexuality is deemed morally neutral or a positive good."[125]

In a report titled "Case against Anti-Gay Minister Scott Lively Still Being Pursued," we read:

On Feb. 24, Ugandan President Yoweri Museveni signed that country's Anti-Homosexuality Bill into law. The law, according to executive Director for the Center for Constitutional Rights [CCR], Vincent Warren, instantly outlaws the ability of LGBT people to advocate for their rights. [Vincent] Warren says…that "such a fundamental denial of rights to an entire class of people is illegal under international law as well as the Ugandan constitution." For that reason the CCR is continuing to pursue the anti-gay minister Scott Lively for the role he played in getting the legislation passed.[126]

Compounding the tension is the fact that some pastors who have taken a stand for the support of traditional marriage have backtracked and "repented." This makes those pastors and churches that don't "repent" of their position and maintain a biblical stance look very intolerant and vicious. Pastor Rick Warren of Saddleback Church fame publicly stated that he regrets supporting Proposition 8, California's anti-gay "marriage" proposition.

Conservative Evangelical pastor Rick Warren expressed regret for instructing his congregation to support Proposition 8, California's constitutional ban on same-sex marriage.… Warren attempted to downplay his endorsement of the provision, claiming that he intended to communicate his private support to church members and was not trying to take a "public" position on the issue.[127]

Warren was interviewed by HuffPost Live's Marc Lamon Hill. Evidently, Warren teaches two messages, one for the church and another for the world. The following is part of the transcript:

WARREN: I never made a single statement on Prop 8 until the week before. In my own church, some members say, "Where do we stand on this?" I released a video to my own congregation…

HILL: When you have a church of 20,000 people and you have a book that 32 million people have read and that 60 million people have accessed, to say, "I was just giving a message…"

WARREN: You're exactly right, Marc, and I learned a lesson from that. What I learned from that is that anything I say privately is now public. And I actually learned from that mistake…. Everyone took that to mean I was pontificating to the whole world.

HILL: If you could do it again, would you not have made that statement a week before Prop 8?

WARREN: I would not have. I would not have made that statement. Because I wanted to talk to my own people. As a duty, as a shepherd, I'm responsible for those who put themselves under my care. I'm not responsible for everybody else.[128]

As the interview continued Warren reiterated his position that he was against same-sex couples, and stated that while "it's not a sin to love somebody, it might be a sin to have sex with them."[129]

Warren wanted to take some of the pressure off, but his liberal critics weren't merciful and present him as confused and vacillating. "Warren seemed to back away from his endorsement in 2009, telling Larry King that he never once even gave an endorsement of the proposition. Now that the majority of Americans consistently support marriage equality, he regrets that people actually paid attention to his anti-gay views."[130]

HuffPost Live host Josh Hepps quoted from Joel Osteen's new book: "It doesn't matter who likes you or who doesn't like you, all that matters is God likes you. He accepts you, he approves of you." Zepps followed up by asking if that included homosexuals. "Absolutely," Osteen insisted. "I believe that God has breathed his life into every single person. We're all on a journey. Nobody's perfect."[131]

Osteen pastors a congregation of forty-five thousand and stated that all people must be acknowledged for who they are. He expressed reluctance to "categorize" sin. "I believe every person is made in the image of God, and you have to accept them as they are, on their journey. I'm not here to be preaching hate, pushing people down. I'm not here telling people what they're doing wrong," said Osteen.[132]

We shouldn't be preaching hate, but we should be preaching truth. There's hate on the other side, too. In an essay titled "Is Hating Haters Hurtful?" Scott Lively affirms that he doesn't hate homosexuals, though they don't seem to be believe him. So, he tried "walking my talk" by taking an ex-"gay" man who was dying of AIDS into his family. Lively and his wife and children loved and cared for the man during his last year of life. However, Lively says "They [the homosexual community] hated me even more."

Then I began asking for guidance from homosexuals themselves: "Tell me, where is the line between homophobia and acceptable opposition to homosexuality?" I asked. "What if I just agree with the Bible that homosexuality is a sin no worse than any other sex outside of marriage?" "No, that's homophobic," they replied. "Suppose I talk only about the proven medical hazards of gay sex and try to discourage people from hurting themselves?" "No, you can't do that," they said. "How about if I say that homosexuals have the option to change if they choose?" "Ridiculous" they answered. "Maybe I could just be completely positive, say nothing about homosexuality, and focus only on promoting the natural family and traditional marriage?" "That's really hateful," they replied.[133]

So, as we have seen, there is a section—a rather large one, at that—of the professing church that views God's covenant with Israel as conditional, and in the past, and now we are seeing how the professing church is becoming increasingly oriented towards accepting the gay lifestyle. But others are feeling pressure as well, such as military chaplains who are coming under increasing pressure now that the military's "Don't-Ask-Don't-Tell" policy has been repealed. Does the normalization of homosexuality require that all military chaplains join the radical moral evolution, even if doing so compromises their basic Christian convictions?

R. Albert Mohler, president of the Southern Baptist Convention's Southern Seminary, reports that the North American Mission Board of the Southern Baptist Convention, the endorsing agency for Southern Baptist chaplains, has formulated policy guidelines on these issues. SBC chaplains—the largest single group of non-Catholic chaplains—have been advised that they cannot minister in any context that "would give the appearance of accepting the homosexual lifestyle or sexual wrong doing."[134]

On Monday, September 16, 2013, Tom Carpenter, identified as the co chair of the Forum on the Military Chaplaincy and an elder in the theologically moderate (some would say "liberal") Presbyterian church (PCUSA), vociferously argued that Southern Baptist chaplains must resign immediately from military service.

> The North American Mission Board [NAMB] has turned the Army motto on its head. They have forced their endorsed chaplains into the untenable position of either serving God or country. Given that choice, as men…of God the only honorable course of action for most will be to resign their commissions and return to civilian ministry.… If these Southern Baptist chaplains were civilian pastors, there would be no problem. As civilians, they undisputedly have an absolute First Amendment right to believe, preach and counsel in accordance with their denominational tenets. But they are not civilians, and have a duty to not only God, but also country. It is instructive that they are not salaried by the NAMB but by the American taxpayer.[135]

Israel, American Millennialism, and World Peace

While many Christians are convinced that God still has special plans for the nation and people of Israel, some see such views, especially premillennialism, as a threat to world peace. In his "Strategic Implications of American Millennialism," Major Brian L. Stuckert of the School of

Advanced Military Studies, Fort Leavenworth, Kansas, we learn that the support many Christians give to Israel is now regarded as a threat to national security.

> The U.S. millennial proclivity for an unqualified military defense of Israel will continue to be a potential flashpoint of great import. Both the United States and Israel believe that Iran poses a credible existential threat to the state of Israel—especially if it is able to develop or procure a nuclear warhead. The Iranian Shahab III missile system [a medium-range, liquid propellant, road mobile, ballistic missile credited with a 930-m. range] has the range to deliver a warhead to Israel. Ayatollah Khomeini declared the elimination of Israel to be a religious duty and current Iranian president Ahmadinejad cites him frequently when making similar statements. Because of the pre-millennial worldview, the U.S. will continue to adopt an adversarial approach to any country perceived as at odds with Israel. Since these conflicts are seen as deterministic and inevitable, there is little incentive to employ diplomacy or any other instrument of power other than the military in these situation.[136]

One may wonder why Major Stuckert blames "the premillennial worldview" for an "adversarial approach" when he has already cited Khomeini and Ahmadinejad as desiring the elimination of Israel? Shouldn't we be adversaries of any nation, or religion, that wants the elimination of any nation? Shouldn't we "blame" the demands of charity, decency, and human brotherhood for taking an adversarial position against butchers and murderers?

Christ at the Checkpoint Conferences

Early in the second decade of the twenty-first century, there arose a new wave of opposition to "Christian Zionism," the view held by many Christians that the Jewish people have a divine right to a land and nation in what is the ancient biblical land of Israel. Known as "Christ at the Check Point" conferences, these meetings involved "'the union of mainstream Protestant churches with Rome and the Islamic world' in their opposition to Jewish and Christian Zionism." Some of the main movers and shakers were Naim Ateek, Stephen Sizer, and Gary Burge. This group and its agenda has been called "The Christian Palestiniast Movement" by Dr. Paul Wilkinson.[137]

For the purposes of this study and to show the alignment of many professing Christians with those causing division on basic issues, Wilkinson's observation is telling.

> The movement has become increasingly politicized over the years, and today enjoys wide-ranging support from individual Church leaders, denominations, charities, and associated mission and humanitarian groups. The document emphasized the speed with which alliances have been forged by Evangelicals *with secular, political and non-Christian religious groups, in what can only be described as a mounting anti-Israel crusade.*[138] (emphasis added)

Identifying the "Palestinian" people with Jesus on the cross has become a powerful propaganda weapon in the hands of the Christian Palestinianist. In his 2001 address, Naim Ateek, leader of the Sabeel organization, declared: "Here in Palestine Jesus is again walking the via dolorosa. Jesus is the powerless Palestinian humiliated at a checkpoint....

In this season of Lent, it seems to many of us that Jesus is on the cross again with thousands of crucified Palestinians around him…the Israeli government crucifixion system is operating daily."[139]

Yohanna Katanacho, academic dean of Bethlehem Bible College and Christian Palestinianist, has written a book published in 2012 titled *The Land of Christ: A Palestinian Cry.* In it he challenges the biblical distinction made by Scripture, and taught by Christian Zionist, between "Israel" and the "church." He argues that the common identification of the modern state of Israel with biblical Israel is a "common error" made by Christian Zionists and that in both Testaments there are "multiple meanings" and a "spectrum of nuances in the names "Hebrew," "Israel," and "Jew." His big argument is that there is a "territorial fluidity" with regards to the land of Israel. In this way, he seeks to sever the biblical link between the Jewish people and the land of Israel.[140]

In December of 2009, the Palestinian Christian Community issued a document titled *Kairos Palestine: A Moment of Truth.* This document has the full endorsement of the World Council of Churches and sets forth the concept that the signatories are supportive of an "Independent Palestinian State with Al-Quds [Jerusalem] as its capital." The document blames the roots of "terrorism" (which is placed in quotation marks) on "the human injustice committed and in the evil of occupation." Wilkinson makes several observations concerning the *Kairos* document.

> The document, originally written in Arabic, presents "the Palestinian Christian narrative" by providing "a list of various oppressive Israeli measures taken against Palestinians," and by presenting "the real nature of the conflict," which is not an "Israeli war against terror" but "an Israeli occupation faced by Palestinian legal resistance." Conspicuous by its absence is any censuring of

"Palestinian' suicide bombers," "Palestinian" terrorist groups such as Hamas and the Al-Aqsa Martyrs' Brigades, and other Islamic fundamentalist groups.[141]

It is unfortunate that the Palestinian issue has become "the tail that wags the dog" because of biased media reporting. Now, the supporters of "the Palestinian Christian narrative" have joined forces with the biased media to perpetuate the confusion. Former Israeli Ambassador Yoram Ettinger was interviewed on the "Watchman on the Wall" broadcast by this author (April 7, 2014). Ambassador Ettinger expressed the belief that the United Nations has now become "the quarterback of international relations."

They genuinely believe an Israeli concession—the establishment of a Palestinian state in Judea and Samaria—is going to do the trick, and thereby they ignore the roughly 100 years of conflict that sends a very clear message to the contrary. In the 1920s and 1930s and 1940s, during the pogroms of those years, there was no independent Jewish state. There was no "Israeli occupation," but still there was war on the Jewish communities in the land of Israel.... If history shows that war predated the "occupation," how could the "occupation" be the cause of the war? And the same thing with the "settlements." The lesson is very clear. The Palestinian war on Israel is not due to Israel's policy or Israel's size. It has to do with the existence of the Jewish state.[142]

Significantly, American emergent leader Brian McLaren is caught up in this movement. In his blog for June 2011, McLaren quotes Ateek, director of the Sabeel Ecumenical Liberation Theology Center in

Jerusalem. "With candor," writes Ateek, "the last two groups of extremists, i.e., Jewish and Western Christian Zionists, are a greater threat to us than the extremist Islamists. In fact, these extremists have more military power and clout to uproot all Palestinian presence, both Christian and Muslim from our homeland."[143]

This author is a "Western Christian Zionist" and knows others of our stripe who have neither "military power" nor "clout" to uproot anyone, nor do they even have the desire to do so. We must wonder why McLaren allows people with a terribly biased view to speak on his blog. For someone who claims to be a champion of fairness, we wonder how fair this is.

With some of the "churches" and ecclesiastical groups backing homosexuality and "Palestinian" claims for justice, it is not hard to see the apostate church of the future waging war on those who hold to the biblical pattern for marriage as well as God's designs for Israel.

Clearly, there is the seed of growing persecution against premillennial believers in statements and movements such as in the preceding. Added to this mix is "Chrislam," the attempt at blending Islam and Christianity. While Islam is monotheistic, that does not mean that Christians and Muslims worship the same God. We don't. Devout Muslims will tell you we don't, and so will devout Christians.

Muslims do not accept the Trinity; they find it a monstrous and blasphemous doctrine. They believe that Christians worship the Father, the Son, and Mary. It's easy to see how they could be confused in this. There are church groups in the Middle East and elsewhere with huge statues of Mary holding a tiny baby Jesus. This becomes extremely egregious with Muslims because they are often led to believe that the virgin birth means God had sex with a human woman.

Nevertheless, controversy keeps on erupting over key Christian leaders seeking to blur the distinction between the truth. In the article,

"Rick Warren Builds Bridge to Muslims," in the *Orange County Register* by staff writer Jim Hinch, it was reported that the Saddleback Church pastor was getting ready to draft an interfaith document designed to heal "divisions between evangelical Christians and Muslims by partnering with Southern California mosques and proposing a set of theological principles that includes acknowledging that Christians and Muslims worship the same God."

The article went off like a bomb sending theological shrapnel everywhere, but eight days later, Warren wrote an article distancing himself from the Hinch report and affirming his Trinitarian and Christian orthodoxy. Other "violations" of Christian protocol concern his interfaith prayer at the last inauguration in which he gave one of the names of Jesus as "Issa."

The Muslim deity and the Christian God are so different. If Islam's monotheism means that Christians and Muslims worship the same God, then a duck is a fish because they both navigate through water. Allah is not a Trinity, nor does Allah love all people, including Jews. Allah did not die for anyone. Muslims will die for Allah, but no one must offer his or her life to God to effect some kind of atonement. Jesus already did that.

A manifestation of "Chrislam" includes some of the "Muslim-friendly" Bible translations that are being offered. Those who are doing so claim they are trying to remove unnecessary offense to Muslims in their translations. A controversy has recently erupted with the Wycliffe Bible Translators, the Summer Institute of Linguistics (SIL) and Frontiers, which have produced translations of the Bible that remove familial references to God as "Father" and to Jesus as the "Son" or "the Son of God." An example is seen in an Arabic version of Matthew 28:19 from "baptizing them in the name of the Father and the Son and the Holy Spirit" to "cleanse them by water in the name of Allah, his Messiah and his Holy Spirit."

As we have seen above, familial and biological relations between the Persons of the Godhead are especially egregious to Muslims. Certain words and phrases in the New Testament that have the connotation of a biological relationship between God and Mary to produce an offspring are highly controversial.

Translational, and especially linguistic, issues are highly complex. We rightly react in an adverse way to alterations in the Bible. Many chuckle at the Ebonics translation of Genesis 1: "In da beginnin' Big Daddy created da heaven an' da earth." Still others frown at the New Oxford Annotated Bible's attempt to be "pro gay" in its notes and marginal annotations.

In all fairness, however, the "Muslim-friendly" rendition of Matthew 28:19 does not make the God of the Bible and Allah the same deity. There are too many far-reaching differences between the two that cannot be missed. Even rendering the biblical words for God *(YHWH, Theos)* by the Arabic "Allah" does not alter the essential character qualities of the two deities.

While this comment may raise eyebrows and questions about the author's orthodoxy, it must be remembered that Christians commonly use words and terms for "God" that have a pagan derivation. For example, the English word "God" comes from the Teutonic word *Gott*, which was used as a proper name for the chief deity in the Teutonic pantheon, Odin. In the Greek New Testament, Jesus is called *logos*—"Word" in John 1:1—a term used by the ancient Greek Stoics to reference "the divine soul of the universe," "the living principle inherent in all things." Similarly, the New Testament Greek word for "God," *theos,* originally denoted not a specific deity "but a pluralistic totality of gods, with Zeus being the father of gods and men."[144]

Where Do We Go from Here?

We've dealt with some crucial issues affecting all who name the name of Christ, and, in many cases, dividing those who name the name of Christ. The Lord Jesus prayed for unity among God's children (John 17:24). Certainly division just for the sake of division is not pleasing to God, yet Jesus also warned of false teachers and deception in the end times (Matt. 24:5, 23, 24) and the apostle prayed that the saints at Philippi would exhibit discerning love (Phil. 1:9). However, sometimes the battle becomes so heated that wild shots and hateful ricochets do unintended damage. In a web article titled "Is Hyper-Critical Name-Calling Really Contending for the Faith?" by Eric Barger of Take a Stand Ministries, Barger sounds an important note:

> Under the guise of "discernment," some individuals have been using their platform in the apologetics community as a means to promulgate a brand of sad, critical Christianity…these so-called "super discerners" operate with a grating, holier-than-thou brashness…. Besides the actual issues themselves, the environment created is frankly a twisted form of religious bigotry that has created enemies amongst third parties *who have been and should still be allies*…. True Christians can have a difference of opinion on many issues without trying to decimate or play "gotcha" with those we disagree with.[145]

There is, however, a positive side to all of this. With the culture war raging and "the bombs bursting in air," we are finding a new kind of Christian—"new" in a bold and daring sense. Christians have now been forced to articulate and defend their views with an intensity that has hardly been matched in the Western world. We have become battle hardened. The conflict has made us stronger. We are been forced to know WHAT we believe and WHY we believe it.

Twenty years ago, Christians would never have developed an apologetic against same-sex "marriage." Why should we have done so? It was not an issue. Nor have we had to develop an apologetic against the many other non-Christian and anti-Christian views staring us in the face—quirks of human nature and downright sin—things that have now been destigmatized and normalized, and then legalized. It wasn't until *Roe v. Wade* that the pro-life movement got underway. The present crisis has been a great opportunity to rise to the challenge. We must; the souls of men and women, boys and girls—and the destiny of nations—is at stake.

Why did John write the letter we now know as 1 John? Why did he write about Jesus and say, "That which was from the beginning...which we have looked upon, and our hands have handled, of the Word of life" (1:1)? Because of movements that were growing in popularity, incipient gnosticism and Docetism. These were movements that denied that Jesus had a real body. They thought He was a phantom, leaving no footprints when He walked in the sand.

While the Scriptures and movements discussed in this chapter surely indicate that the true church and the false church are on a collision course, we must acknowledge the mission that Christians are on. Nowhere does Scripture encourage a theology of retreat, but rather a theology of engagement. The apostle Paul stood tall on the Areopagus as he debated with the Athenian philosophers and boldly presented the claims of the true and living God—and so should we.

For though we walk in the flesh, we do not war after the flesh

(for the weapons of our warfare are not carnal, but mighty through God to the pulling down of strong holds),

Casting down imaginations, and every high thing that exalteth itself against the knowledge of God, and bringing into captivity every thought to the obedience of Christ. (2 Cor. 10:3–5)

While there is great evil in the world, the Lord of the harvest is working mightily through those who are yielded to Him. The following is a quotation by a former leftist lesbian college professor who has authored a book titled *The Secret Thoughts of an Unlikely Convert* (Crown & Covenant). The author, Dr. Rosaria Champagne Butterfield, PhD, was sure the Bible is a troublesome book read by deceived people—and then she came to know the truth. She lives with her family in North Carolina, where her husband pastors the First Reformed Presbyterian Church of Durham.

I began researching the religious Right and their politics of hatred against queers like me. To do this, I would need to read the one book that had, in my estimation, gotten so many people off track: the Bible. While on the lookout for some Bible scholar to aid me in my research, I launched my first attack on the unholy trinity of Jesus, republican politics, and patriarchy, in the form of an article in the local newspaper about Promise Keepers. It was 1997. The article generated many rejoinders, so many that I kept a Xerox box on each side of my desk: one for hate mail, one for fan mail. But one letter I received defied my filing system. It was from the pastor of the Syracuse Reformed Presbyterian Church. It was a kind and inquiring letter. Ken Smith encouraged me to explore the kind of questions I admire: How did you arrive at your interpretations? How do you know you are right? Do you believe in God? Ken didn't argue with my article; rather, he asked me to defend the presuppositions that undergirded it. I didn't know how to respond to it, so I threw it away....

With the letter, Ken initiated two years of bringing the church to me, a heathen.... He did not mock. He engaged.... Then, one Sunday morning, I rose from the bed of my lesbian lover, and an hour later sat in a pew.... Conspicuous with my butch haircut, I reminded myself that I came to meet God, not fit in.[146]

Dr. Butterfield's conversion to Christ is a fresh reminder that the Lord Jesus Christ is still changing lives. It's a reminder that the signs of the Lord's imminent return for His church should drive us to a mode of urgency in sharing the good news of the gospel. "But ye, brethren, are not in darkness, that that day should overtake you as a thief.... Therefore let us not sleep, as do others; but let us watch and be sober" (1 Thess. 5:4, 6).

THE EVANGELICAL CHURCH, APOSTASY, AND CHANGE AGENTS

The Destiny of America in the Last Days

By Paul McGuire

The last days began with the apostles after Jesus Christ ascended into heaven and the church was born. Well-meaning Christians have believed for two thousand years that Jesus Christ was returning in their lifetime. Although no one can claim to know for certain the time of the Lord's return, I believe that we are now entering the final phase of the last days. The church is literally pressing its nose against the window of the Tribulation period, and we are seeing an unprecedented acceleration of what Jesus Christ called the "signs of the time." One critical sign of the last days was what the apostle Paul called the "great apostasy," or a great falling away from the essential doctrines of the faith. Nowhere is this more apparent than in what could be called the "evangelical church," which, to varying degrees, had at one time claimed to be the "Bible-believing church"—the church that was birthed during the Reformation and which emphasized a return to Scripture as man's final authority in all matters both theological and practical. The early revivals in America such as the Third Great Awakening led by Jonathan Edwards, George Whitefield, and others were extensions of this Reformation, which emphasized a return to the Bible.

Fifty years ago, American evangelicalism had its roots in the both the First and Second Great Awakenings, and the spiritual father of the Second Great Awakening, the famous attorney Charles Finney, ignited a revival when he wrote the book, *Why I Left Freemasonry*. The great evangelist D. L. Moody wrote, "I do not see how any Christian, most of all a Christian ministry, can go into these secret lodges."

Today, while many Christian leaders openly scoff at the existence of the organizations like the Illuminati, our Christian forefathers did scoff, but warned of their dangers. The tragedy is that there are many well-known Christian leaders who fellowship quite comfortably with powerful media celebrities who have direct ties with the New Age movement.

The evangelical church in America is no longer the same evangelical church that it was in the 1950s–1970s when the great evangelist Billy Graham came to prominence, Bill Bright founded Campus Crusade for Christ, Dr. Francis Schaeffer called for doctrinal purity, and the "Jesus Movement" swept across the campuses of America.

Today, the evangelical Christian church in America is a radically different kind of church than it was even thirty years ago. The question is this: Is the current evangelical church still a biblical church, or has it become part of what the apostle Paul called the great apostasy and the lukewarm church of Laodicea that Jesus Christ corrected in the book of Revelation? Over the last four decades, the majority of the evangelical church has rejected its belief in biblical absolutes and sound doctrine and has embraced "the spirit of this age."

Dr. Francis Schaeffer, the greatest evangelical theologian of the last century, wrote these words in his book, *The Great Evangelical Disaster:*

Here is the great evangelical disaster—the failure of the evangelical world to stand for truth as truth. There is only one word for this—namely accommodation: the evangelical church has accommodated to the world spirit of the age. First, there has been accommodation on Scripture, so that many who call themselves evangelicals hold a weakened view of the Bible and no longer affirm the truth of all the Bible teaches—truth not only in religious matters but in the areas of science and history and morality. As part of this, many evangelicals are now accepting the higher critical methods in the study of the Bible. Remember, it was these same methods which destroyed the authority of the Bible for the Protestant church in Germany in the last century, and which have destroyed the Bible for the liberal in our own country from the beginning of this century. And second, there has been accommodation on the issues, with no clear stand being taken even on matters of life and death.[147]

I had the privilege of being mentored by the Francis Schaeffer family, becoming best friends with Franky Schaeffer, and getting to know Edith Schaeffer. Before knowing the family, I received Jesus Christ as my Lord and Savior some time after reading Dr. Schaeffer's book, *Escape from Reason,* where I was stunned to discover that you could be intelligent and a Christian at the same time. If Schaeffer were alive today, he would be horrified by the apostasy, false teaching, false prophets, and false doctrines that have taken over evangelical Christianity in America and around the world!

I grew up in an atheistic home in New York City, in an intellectual family where my father was an artist and my mother still is a card-carrying member of the American Civil Liberties Union. I was taught at a young age that Christians were anti-intellectual, anti-sex, anti-life, and anti-joy. Yet, I had a deep spiritual hunger, and I looked for truth in the New Age movement and Eastern mysticism. I majored in Altered States of Consciousness, a brand-new field in psychology at the University of Missouri, and had a dual major in filmmaking. At the time, Christianity was not even an option for me due to my prejudice against it. To be blunt, I thought Christianity was a religion for idiots!

However, by the grace of God, my life intersected with a member of the Jesus Movement while I was at the university. Before encountering these "Jesus people," I would tear apart these Christians in my debate classes for sport. They could offer little intellectual defense for their faith. Yet, when I encountered these strange people who read black Bibles in King James English and believed Jesus Christ was coming again any day, I was struck by their authenticity and faith. In addition, they took the Word of God literally, which I initially thought was a form of insanity. They believed in a literal Adam and Eve, along with a literal Garden of Eden. These "Jesus people" literally believed that we were in the last days and that Jesus Christ was returning at any moment. But most of all, these Christians loved one another and loved me in a pure, spiritual sense that impacted me to the depths of my being. This was not some cult-like love; it was a unique, spiritual love, the *agape* love of Jesus Christ that I had never experienced before.

Around the same time, I was invited to attend some kind of denominational Christian retreat about an hour from the campus of the University of Missouri. Although this was more than thirty years ago, it would have been the equivalent of a seeker-friendly or "emergent-church" style of ministry. The emphasis was on relationships, and biblical content was almost nonexistent. When I got there, I had hair down to my waist, I had grown up demonstrating with the radical activist Abbie Hoffman in New York City when I was fifteen years old, and I was deeply intellectual. I had read and understood Aldous Huxley's novel, *Brave New World*, George Orwell's *1984*, and the books written by Fabian socialists Bertrand Russell, H. G. Wells, John Maynard Keynes, etc. I had met Dr. Timothy Leary, the Harvard LSD guru, and Ken Kesey, who wrote *One Flew Over the Cuckoo's Nest*. I had seen the "great white light," felt "cosmic consciousness," and had undergone many other Eastern mystical experiences.

When I attempted to discuss these experiences in light of the Bible, these men that I had grown up with gave me that blank, "deer-caught-in-the-headlights" look. I realized that I was talking to the theological equivalent of male evangelical Stepford wives, and that these Christians were the same kinds of Christians who populate the giant mega churches that are little more than psychological motivational rallies led by celebrity pastors. If this was Christianity, I wanted nothing to do with it; it was like a glorified multilevel marketing company. This apostate-friendly Christianity confirmed my worst suspicions about Christianity. Abruptly, I decided to leave! In short, while fleeing from a denominational Christian retreat that I had been invited to and hitchhiking on the back roads of Missouri in what can only be described as a "field-of-dreams" type of experience, I was radically saved when a Bible salesman driving a station wagon full of black leather King James Bibles picked me up.

This Christian fundamentalist whipped open his Bible as he was driving. He pulled no punches and told me I was a sinner who was going to go to hell if I did not repent of my sins and accept Jesus Christ in my life. First of all, I didn't believe in sin and thought it was an archaic concept. Second, I didn't believe in the concept of hell. With great boldness, he asked me to pray the sinner's prayer with him. For some strange reason, I repeated the prayer out loud. I confessed to Jesus Christ that I was a sinner, while I wasn't even intellectually certain that I believed in sin. Then, I "invited" Jesus into my heart and asked Him to make me "born again." However, when I got back to the campus, I tossed aside the entire insincere episode and went out and partied with my friends.

The next day, I was recalling this experience with some other Christians who had been witnessing to me with little success. Someone we had never seen before, a college-aged female, walked over and looked at me. "I couldn't help overhearing your conversation," she said. "I'm a minister's daughter." I was sitting there wrestling through these thoughts I was having about God. Then she looked at me point blank and asked, "Do you believe that Jesus Christ is the Son of God?" Before I knew it, I blurted out the words, "I believe that Jesus Christ is the Son of God"—and I had never said those words before in my life. I had an overwhelming experience in which I knew that I knew that Jesus Christ was God!

From that moment on, my life was radically changed forever! First, the Holy Spirit came into my life and I became a new creature in Jesus Christ. Second, I began to read the Word of God and deeply think about what it had to say about "spiritual things." I also discovered that the Old Testament and New Testament applied the truth of God's Word to other areas like science, history, culture, sexuality, economics, education, art, music, and medicine. I didn't just have a "Jesus experience," but, unlike the teaching in the vast majority of evangelical churches today, I learned that the personal, Living God of the universe wanted to develop in me a biblical worldview. It is through that worldview that I have been able to write more than twenty-six books, and I have shared my experience with Jesus Christ to millions of people through my work as an author of best-selling books like *A Prophecy of the Future of America*, through my appearances on secular media like Fox News, CNN, and the History Channel, and through appearances on religious media as a guest expert on economics, culture, current events, and Bible prophecy.

I can tell you for a fact that I would never have considered the claims of Jesus Christ or repented from my sins and invited Christ into my life by attending any form of most modern evangelical, seeker-friendly, or emergent churches today. That is exactly the kind of church I was literally fleeing from when hitchhiking on the back roads of Missouri.

Given the statistical evidence that nine of out ten children from evangelical churches are rejecting their faith by the time they are in college, these kinds of churches are not very effective in reaching people with the gospel. In addition, the Christian church in America is shrinking as fast as the church did in Europe, and soon it will be an almost completely insignificant force in our nation.

The question must be asked: How did America, a nation once heavily influenced by the Christian church and founded to a large degree by Christians, become a spiritual wasteland and a welcome home for what can only be described as the "spirit of Antichrist?"

I believe there are three primary reasons why America has moved from a Christian nation to a pagan nation in just about fifty years. First, the foundational, scientific truthfulness of the Bible was undermined beginning with Charles Darwin's theory of evolution, which he outlined in his book, *On the Origin of Species,* in 1859. This was no small thing; once the culture was taught to accept Darwin's theory, which still lacks any serious scientific proof, it provided an intellectual death blow to the Christian faith. After all, if the biblical account of man's origins recorded in the book of Genesis were disproved by modern science, then it was only logical that the Bible was no longer the inspired and inerrant Word of God— and was therefore untrue. This unproved evolutionary theory opened the floodgates to the rejection of absolutes such as right and wrong; it ignited the sexual revolution; and it replaced the biblical God with man as god. Since evolutionary theory teaches that the fittest survive, then "might makes right"! This led directly to the Communist revolutions, in which more than two hundred million people were slaughtered or imprisoned, and to the idea that the state is God.

Once young children were taught the theory of evolution in the public school system, they quickly began to reject their faith in the Bible and God's Word. Since there is no right or wrong, this paved the way for "free sex" and more than sixty-five million abortions. Tragically, the evangelical culture, for the most part, accommodated Darwin's theory by suggesting the idea of theistic evolution, which states that it is God who guides the evolutionary process.

Second, to compound problems, huge segments of the evangelical church began to openly reject the Bible as the inspired and inerrant Word of God. They cleverly called their unbelief in the Word of God by many names, but the basic idea was that the Bible was only true in "spiritual" matters and it was to be taken as an allegory or mythology in the areas of science, sexuality, economics, history, and other areas of life. This rejection of the Word of God, which is the same sin Adam and Eve committed in the Garden of Eden, began the destruction of true Christianity in our nation and world.

However, a third reason for the destruction of Christianity in our nation, a reason that is not readily understood, is also tied into a rejection of the authority of God's Word. In Ephesians 6:12, the apostle Paul writes, "For we wrestle not against flesh and blood, but against principalities, against powers, against the rulers of the darkness of this world, against spiritual wickedness in high places." God's Word teaches us that we are to take the reality of spiritual warfare with Satan and demonic beings very seriously. The Bible also teaches us that Satan is the "ruler of this world" and that Lucifer has led a revolution against God with one-third of the angels.

When we read the biblical account of history, we see numerous times when human rulers and nations chose to worship Satan and various demonic idols. In addition, if we take Bible prophecy literally, as we should, it teaches us that in the last days the world will be united in a one-world government, one-world economic system, and one-world religion under the False Prophet and the Antichrist. Since the time of the tower of Babel and the ancient mystery religions of ancient Babylon, the world has been moving steadily towards this prophetic destination point. It is also clear that Satan and his demons interact with, communicate with, and guide men and women just as the Holy Spirit does God's people. There are very powerful international bankers and people in positions of power who have dedicated themselves to fulfilling Satan's plan for mankind out of spiritual deception or choice—only God knows their hearts.

It is not my responsibility to judge the hearts of men. However, there are actions that men can take that will lead the world in the direction of the establishment of Satan's kingdom. The men and women who are doing this may be doing this out of good intentions and a desire to solve the problems of the human race. Again, only God knows the motives of their hearts. John D. Rockefeller wanted to establish a one-world government to end wars. He helped organize the League of Nations as an institution to further this goal. However, the League of Nations was not popular in the United States. Rockefeller determined that one of the primary reasons the League of Nations failed was that Bible-believing Christians in America opposed the institution on the grounds that it was an attempt to create the one-world government God warned about in the book of Revelation.

At that time, those who called themselves Bible-believing Christians in America were being taught Bible prophecy by the pastors in their churches. With exceptions, this is no longer the case in America.

As a result of the failure to establish the League of Nations, Rockefeller enlisted the help of John Foster Dulles, whose brother, Alan Dulles, founded the CIA. John Dulles was given an initial budget of more than $250 million to infiltrate the evangelical church and raise up Christian pastors, churches, and seminaries that would embrace the idea of globalism and a New World Order. Soon, leading Baptist pastors were writing books promoting Rockefeller's New World Order agenda. In addition, Dulles held a gathering with hundreds of leading Christian leaders and the heads of seminaries to enlist them in building a one-world government, one-world religion, and one-world economic system—all the things that were warned about in Scripture, starting with the account of the tower of Babel and Babylon.

The American Baptist Publication Society, in 1919, published a book entitled *The New World Order* by Samuel Batten, who wrote, "The old order passes from view: the new world rises upon our vision…the state must socialize every group." He called for "an international court, an international police force and an international mind" and declared that "internationalism must first be a religion before it can be a reality and a system."

For those who have not studied history and the science of modern mind control, which is openly documented in credible scientific journals, the following dynamics are difficult to understand, especially the relationship between the occult and science. But, the reality is that beginning in the early 1920s, the science of occult-based mind control, social engineering, and brainwashing began to develop. H. G. Wells, the great science fiction writer and former head of British intelligence in World War I, was a member of the socialist Fabian Society, which included intellectuals such as Bertrand Russell and others. Although the Fabians presented themselves as pure humanists, many of them belonged to secret occult societies. This is not a matter of private speculation, but of historical record.

In 1933, Wells wrote *The Shape of Things to Come*, in which he described a utopian society ruled by a scientific dictatorship. Later on, Aldous Huxley wrote *Brave New World*, which also described a scientific dictatorship. Both Wells and Huxley, along with their peers, embraced the belief system of the Illuminati and the Masons. This belief system, which is still fervently upheld by the elite in our society today, believes in the idea of Sir Francis Bacon's technocratic elite and the secret plan for America to be the head of the New World Order and the New Atlantis that he developed in the mid 1600s. Bacon borrowed his ideas from the philosopher Plato, who developed his philosophy from research he gathered about Atlantis, which was ruled by ten god-kings. Plato wrote about this in his *New Republic*.

Unfortunately, most people are not educated about these realities and have no idea what Zbigniew Brzezinski, one of Rockefeller's right-hand men and secretary of state for numerous presidents, meant when he advocated the use of psychotronic weapons on the general population. Glenn Greenwald recently published an article based on information from National Security Agency whistleblower Edward Snowden about intelligence agencies using psychology and other social sciences to shape and control the masses through social media. The article reveals the science behind the Government Communications Headquarters' "Human Operations Cell," where scientific mind control is employed for "strategic influence and disruption."

The point is that the modern evangelical church and its theology are not being primarily shaped by the Word of God and the Holy Spirit.

Much of the seeker-friendly church movement and the emergent church movement is being created as a nonbiblical template to fit neatly into the world system and the coming one-world religion, one-world government, and one-world economic system. The methodology of this transformation is through social engineering, cognitive infiltration, and pervasive use of "change agents."

Just as John D. Rockefeller used John Foster Dulles to infiltrate, transform, and organize the evangelical church in the 1920s to fit into his plans for the New World Order, the same dynamic is being used today to transform what is left of the evangelical church to merge into the coming one-world religion. In this dynamic, certain Christian leaders are secretly raised up and massive finances are directed towards those Christian leaders, churches, and denominations that cooperate with the globalist agenda. The reality is that even in so-called Bible-believing churches, denominations, Christian organizations, and media, there are people who have been strategically placed there to further the globalist cause. They are "wolves in sheep's clothing."

Although there is much talk about how "God raised these people up," the reality is that their influence has been manufactured and sold using the latest merchandising, marketing, persuasion, and advertising techniques.

My purpose in writing this is not to generate paranoia or to launch a witch hunt. It is a call for genuine spiritual discernment! God has given us a powerful tool for exercising discernment, and that tool is the entire Word of God, which we are expected to use as a standard by which to measure any theology or position. Big smiles, the size of a particular church, the number of copies a book has sold, and pleasant personalities are not the measure by which we discern. There is only one measure and that is faithfulness to the entire Word of God. This can be measured by the actual statements and writing that these change agents make. Understandably, it is difficult for Christian leaders to effectively communicate in a secular media that seeks to trap and destroy them by taking statements out of context. Therefore, it is wise not to jump on any Christian leader based on a couple of statements. But, we are responsible to evaluate the biblical integrity of a Christian leader's life and statements over a period of time.

When you see a consistent pattern of denying the truth, such as a leader's refusal to say that Jesus Christ is the "Way, the Life, and the Truth" and that there is no other way into heaven except through faith in Jesus Christ, this presents a serious problem. In addition, if that Christian leader is continually saying things or making statements which are in direct contradiction to clear biblical truth, this can be evidence of apostasy.

The modern evangelical church in America and the world has become relatively powerless, because "the salt has lost its savor." Jesus Christ warned that the great sin of the evangelical church is accommodation to the spirit of this age and failing to stand for clear biblical truth. All of this is in distinct contrast to the revival that occurred in the "Jesus Movement" during the late 1960s and early 1970s, when millions of young people accepted Jesus Christ as their Lord and Savior, including people like myself. This movement proclaimed a clear biblical message about sin, the need for repentance, the need to be born again, and the truth of Bible prophecy. God honored this commitment to the Bible, and the Holy Spirit moved with conviction and power in our nation.

America is in the greatest crisis it has ever known. We are one manufactured crisis away from totalitarianism, economic collapse, and the total loss of our freedoms. There is no political or economic answer to our crisis! I believe that we are in the last days and that God has written in His Word a prophetic, end-times program that cannot be changed. However, within the context of God's sovereign, end-times prophetic program, the Lord has called His people through His Word to "preach the gospel," "make disciples of all nations," and "occupy until He comes"! The "occupation" that Jesus Christ talks about is a spiritual occupation, in which we are not supposed to allow the powers of darkness to take control of our nation as the disobedient church did in Nazi Germany.

In addition, God commands us to "pray always" (Luke 21:36) and to "pray without ceasing" (1 Thess. 5:17). The Bible commands us to pray for our leaders and those in authority above us "that we may lead a quiet and peaceable life" (1 Tim. 2:2). It is clear that even in the last days, God is commanding us to pray for those in authority above us in order to restrain the powers of darkness so that He can protect and bless His people. It is possible to have a legitimate end-times revival if God's people repent of their sins—especially of the great sin of apostasy and false teaching in the church. The apostle Paul warned of a counterfeit revival that is happening now and is part of the last-days apostasy that will establish the one-world religion that is forming before our very eyes!

But, God promises to pour out His Spirit in a biblically based revival if His people seek His face, repent of spiritual adultery, reject false teaching, and reject false teachers. There can be no true revival in our personal lives and in our nation unless there is the specific acknowledgment and repentance of what a Holy God considers one of the gravest sins. We must understand the consequences of rejecting His Word, which is the sin Adam and Eve committed in the Garden of Eden to cause the Fall of Man and activate the curse or the law of sin and death. The rejection of God's Word is the primary sin.

When the modern evangelical church rejects God's Word by gathering and promoting false teachers in its midst, it is committing the same sin that Adam and Even committed! This rejection of God's Word as the final authority in all matters brings with it a curse and the evidence of that curse is all around us in our nation. Again, this is not a peripheral issue.

In order for a Holy God to move in our nation and send a biblical revival, which is our only hope, there must be specific repentance from all forms of false doctrine and false teachers. This will not come without a cost—but then our salvation came with a cost: the death of Jesus Christ. It is absolutely imperative to understand that as individual Christians and the church, if we continue to reject God's Word, we are in a very real sense committing spiritual fornication with idols. Jesus Christ warned the churches in the book of Revelation about this sin and He is also warning us.

God has called us by His grace in the last days to be the "bride of Christ," which the Bridegroom, Jesus Christ, is quickly coming to get in order to take His bride to the Marriage Supper of the Lamb. The Bible teaches us that in the last days, there will be a false church, the "Mystery Babylon, the Mother of Harlots." The false church is plunged into judgment and great Tribulation as it receives the mark of the Beast. The true bride of Christ is delivered from the wrath to come.

Even so, come quickly, Lord Jesus!

8

DOMINIONISM'S POLITICAL DIVIDE

By Derek Gilbert

The idea that humanity was seeded or created on planet earth by extraterrestrials has been mainstreamed in recent years thanks to the evangelical efforts of Erich von Daniken, the late Zecharia Sitchin, and the History Channel through its series *Ancient Aliens.* Christians responding to these pseudo-historical claims point out that even secular ufologists such as Jacques Vallée and Dr. John Mack have noted links between the UFO phenomenon and the spirit realm. The accounts of contactees and abductees are consistent with an anti-Christian message, and so a counter-theory has developed that the UFO phenomenon is demonic and may play a role in the end-times great deception that Jesus warned of.

While the *Ancient Aliens* doctrine offers skeptics a convenient atheistic answer to the question of our origins, it is entirely possible that the UFO phenomenon is just a cosmic red herring. Another deception has insinuated itself into American churches that is far more subtle, far less offensive to most Bible-savvy evangelicals, and thus far more dangerous than the prospect of ET suddenly landing on the White House lawn.

Rather than the paradigm-shattering sight of a UFO hovering over the Washington Monument, the last-days great deception Jesus warned about may be mundane "politics as usual"—and it may prove so deceptive that well-meaning Christians are lured into preparing the way for the Antichrist.

Conservative Christians are among the most patriotic Americans. The majority of evangelical churches proudly display the American flag at the front of the sanctuary. Patriotic hymns are common on the Sunday closest to Independence Day, and there is a strong belief among many American Christians that abandoning the faith of our fathers is at least partly responsible for the nation's recent economic and moral malaise.

Over the last forty years, this belief has led some elements within American Christianity on a quest for political power, motivated by a desire to restore the nation to its former status as a beacon on a hill, a force for good in the world. However, this conflation of God and country has spawned an aberrant vision of a future global theocracy—literally God's kingdom on earth—that prepares the way for the return of Jesus Christ.

Another belief common to conservative American Christians is an overwhelming support for the nation of Israel. It is not a stretch to suggest that Israel's best friend in the world is the community of America's evangelicals. Ironically, these parallel beliefs have created an environment in which well-meaning American Christians are laying the foundation for the prophesied one-world government of the end times.

Dominionism, sometimes called Kingdom Now theology, is a product of the Latter Rain revival of the late 1940s and early 1950s. Charismatic evangelists such as Franklin Hall and William Branham launched a movement that developed a new eschatology, so called because it was based on the notion that God was preparing His final movement on earth, a "latter rain" outpouring of spiritual gifts, based on questionable readings of Jeremiah 3:3, 5:23–25; Joel 2:23; Hosea 6:3; Zechariah 10:1; and James 5:7.

The Latter Rain movement put forward a new vision of the end times that became popular because it was far more optimistic than the traditional dispensational views held by Pentecostals. Instead of a great apostasy culminating in the rise of the Antichrist, Latter Rain teachers scratched itching ears with promises of a victorious church led by "overcomers" who would reclaim the dominion Adam lost to the serpent in the Garden.

Because it has no central governing body, identifying the tenets of Dominion theology can be difficult. It encompasses a broad range of beliefs from simple political activism for conservative causes to, at its most extreme, a belief that Christians must literally take over the world before Christ will (or can) return.[148]

Dominionism isn't necessarily a heresy in the strictest sense of the word. One may believe in salvation by grace through faith in Jesus and still be convinced that the Lord wants His followers to exert influence in every sphere of society. However, taken to an extreme, it teaches followers that God wants believers to establish an earthly kingdom in His name— essentially a Christian *jihad*—rather than making disciples through witnessing and individual conversion.

At best, Dominionism is a distraction from the Great Commission; at worst, it is a heretical rewrite of prophecy that puts the responsibility for defeating the enemies of God in human hands. Some teachers even elevate "overcomers" to the status of god-men, "manifest sons of God," the literal incarnation of Jesus in a so-called many-membered Man-Child (referring to the male child of Rev. 12:5).[149]

The common elements of Dominion theology are these:

- Satan usurped man's dominion over the earth through deception in the garden.
- The church is God's instrument to reclaim dominion over the earth.
- Jesus will not—or isn't able to—return until it does.

The Latter Rain teachings, which had faded from the scene in the 1960s, have influenced the modern Dominionist movement, emerging in the twenty-first century as the New Apostolic Reformation (NAR). The NAR is a strain of charismatic Christianity premised on a belief in the restoration of the "five-fold ministry," a reference to Ephesians 4:11–13:

And he gave, some, apostles; and some, prophets; and some, evangelists; and some, pastors and teachers;

For the perfecting of the saints for the work of ministry for the edifying of the body of Christ.

It is taught that the offices of apostle and prophet have been restored to the church as God begins His final offensive to reclaim the earth. These modern-day apostles and prophets are believed to have the same authority and abilities as those of the Bible, and that they will serve as God's government on earth until Christ's return to a world that has been subdued by the faithful.

Consider the implications of this teaching. The apostles of the Bible wrote the New Testament! If the definition of the modern office was limited to those who plant churches and spread the gospel, then all would be well. But that would also mean that we have always had apostles, since there have always been evangelists planting churches and winning souls in faraway places.

However, Scripture implies that that apostolic age ended with the death of the last of the biblical apostles.[150] Regardless, the self-labeled New Apostolic Reformation believes that, since 2001, the Lord has anointed a new generation of leaders with the apostolic authority of Paul, Peter, John, and the rest—which may explain, at least in part, why they feel free to allegorize and spiritualize Scripture to give the Word of God new meaning.

A strategy for reclaiming dominion over the earth emerged in some Christian circles in the late 1970s. A shared vision by a pair of prominent evangelical leaders developed into what is today known as the Seven Mountains Mandate.[151] The title refers to seven "mountains," or spheres, of human culture—economy/business, government, family, spirituality/religion, education, media, and celebration/arts & entertainment[152]—that must be taken by Christians to win back the world for Christ.

This strategy is undergirded by a reinterpretation of the Great Commission. In Matthew 28:19, Jesus told His disciples to "go ye, therefore, and teach all nations." Dominionist teachers assert that Christendom has essentially missed the true meaning of this verse for two thousand years: Rather than directing Christians to witness to and convert individuals, Jesus actually wants us to convert *entire nations en masse.*

It logically follows from this belief that the faith of individuals is far less important than the faith of their leaders in determining their eternal home. Some prominent new apostles teach that when Jesus returns and sits on His throne before "all nations," He will assign people to the kingdom or to eternal fire according to whether they belonged to a "sheep nation" or a "goat nation."[153]

Think about that. How much effort would you put into politics or community organizing if you believed your eternal salvation literally depended on how closely the laws of your nation matched the Bible?

In chapter 17 of the book of Revelation, the apostle John gives us a wonderfully colorful description of Babylon the Great, the dominant city of the Antichrist's political and religious machine. It is described as a woman clothed in scarlet and purple riding a scarlet beast with seven heads and ten horns that has emerged from the bottomless pit. Significantly, an angel tells John that "the seven heads are seven mountains, on which the woman sitteth."

While it is clear that John is describing a literal city, it is the contention of this author that the Seven Mountains Mandate is nothing less than the symbolic and spiritual foundation of Babylon the Great.

As with its wide spectrum of teachings, Dominion theology manifests in a variety of symptoms, not all of which are shared by every person or group who holds the basic belief that Christians must reclaim dominion over the earth. Regardless of the specifics, at a very basic level this design for world domination bypasses the cross. It substitutes the gospel of the kingdom for the gospel of salvation. To Dominionists, the kingdom of God is a literal and physical kingdom to be established in the present age. The work of redeeming the world is taken out of the hands of Christ, whose work on the cross was unfinished, left for the faithful to complete.

Not only is that heresy, it is ironically similar to the goal of New Agers who likewise want to create heaven on earth.

In Dominion theology, the gospel of salvation is no more than a means to an end. It is used to open doors to exert political and cultural influence. Political goals become priorities, and compromises with the world are rationalized as necessary to achieve bigger goals, such as curbing abortions, preventing homosexual marriages, or gaining access to countries formerly off limits to Christian missionaries.

In short, Dominionism emphasizes changing laws and institutions instead of hearts and minds—building "sheep nations" rather than gathering sheep who have gone astray.

As suggested by the shared dream that supposedly established God's mandate to reclaim the seven mountains of culture, many in the Kingdom Now movement place more value on mystic experiences and new revelations than on Scripture. God's Word seems to flow directly from the throne room of heaven to a new generation of prophets who, we are told, have the same authority as the prophets of the Bible.

The messages attributed to God by these new prophets often cannot be reconciled with the Bible. And the track record of the new prophets is not very impressive. The Apostolic Council of Prophetic Elders, a group of about thirty leaders of the New Apostolic Reformation, responding to criticism, issued a disclaimer to explain their less-than-biblical accuracy:[154]

> There are differing variables that can affect the timing and/or coming to pass of these words:
> 1. All prophecy not contained in Scripture is conditional.
> 2. The timing of when the prophecy comes to pass may not occur in a one year time frame.
> 3. It is possible that the prophetic warnings given will cause either the person or nation to repent and thus turn away the judgment prophesied. Biblically, this happened when Jonah prophesied to Nineveh and the city repented, causing God to relent.[155]

In other words, according to the Apostolic Council of Prophetic Elders, a prophecy doesn't have to actually come true to be accurate.

The yearning for supernatural experiences has birthed a shocking lack of discernment by some in the apostolic-prophetic movement. A quick search of Internet videos[156] reveals some truly disturbing behavior—hysterical laughing, uncontrollable shaking, indecipherable babbling, and altered states of consciousness induced through repetitive, rhythmic music—celebrated as the work of the Holy Spirit. The fact that there are no precedents in the Bible for such behavior apparently doesn't concern people who are so eager to touch the supernatural that they ignore the warning from the apostle John to "test the spirits whether they are of God" (1 John 4:1).

Such willing disregard of God's Word, especially His clear instructions on how to interact with the spirit realm, will become ever more dangerous as we draw closer to the time of the Antichrist's reign.

This is especially true because Dominion theology, particularly the apostolic-prophetic variety, already disregards, reinterprets, and contradicts Bible prophecy about the end times. Assuming that the Rapture doesn't come first, it is entirely possible that many Dominionists will fail to recognize the Antichrist when he steps onto the world stage.

Most strains of Dominion theology are postmillennial. This is a belief that Christ established His kingdom on earth during the first century. It is taught that, over time, "[t]he overwhelming majority of men and nations will be Christianized, righteousness will abound, wars will cease, and prosperity and safety will flourish."[157] Objections, such as Paul's prophecy of a great "falling away" and the rise of a "man of sin" (2 Tim. 2:3), interpreted by premillennial prophecy scholars as a reference to the Antichrist, are explained away as referring to other events and people, such as the apostasy of first-century Jews and the Roman emperor Nero.[158]

In other words, many Kingdom Now believers aren't even watching for the Antichrist because they believe he's been dead for two thousand years.

A rosy future in which the church reigns supreme prior to Christ's return inverts the Christian's relationship with the Savior. Since it is believed that Christ will return at the end of the Millennium, however long it actually lasts, the faithful must "Christianize" the world as quickly as possible to hasten the day. The sooner Christians take the seven cultural mountains, the sooner Christ will return.

Another symptom of Dominion theology is an emphasis on the legal teachings of the Old Testament. The goal of Kingdom Now theology is either a return to outright theocracy, along the lines of ancient Israel, or a form of government labeled "theonomy" by Christian Reconstructionists, a Calvinist strain of Dominionism that believes "[p]olitical codes today ought to incorporate the moral requirements which were culturally illustrated in the God-given, judicial laws of Old Testament Israel."[159] In other words, Reconstructionists want a government that enforces the civil laws found in the first five books of the Bible.[160]

The apostolic-prophetic movement's justification for a return to theocracy is based on Ephesians 4:11–13, which lists five offices—apostle, prophet, evangelist, pastor, and teacher—necessary to equip "the saints for the work of ministry." The Lord is supposed to have restored the offices of apostle and prophet, which had been absent from earth since the end of the Apostolic Age, to the church in the 1950s. These modern-day apostles and prophets, endowed with the power and authority of their biblical forebears, will serve as God's government, ruling the kingdom until Christ's return.

The so-called five-fold ministry is a fundamental plank in the platform of the New Apostolic Reformation. Not only has God restored the offices of apostle and prophet, He has apparently added "rule the world" to their job descriptions.

This may all sound a bit, well, far-fetched to those who haven't been watching this movement. Since the majority of the criticism directed at the NAR and Dominion theology has come from liberal commentators, most conservative Christians have tuned it out. And considering the moral decline of our nation, it's understandable that many Christians would find the political activism of the new apostles appealing. Witnessing to unbelievers is *hard*. It's uncomfortable. It is far more appealing—and easier—to focus on political causes and candidates that "advance the kingdom."

Given the patriotic tendencies of conservative American Christians, it is no surprise that militaristic language has found its way into descriptions of the coming kingdom of God. We fight a "culture war" to reclaim the seven mountains of civilization. But the most extreme elements of the Kingdom Now movement take the military analogy more literally. They believe that God is raising up, alongside latter-day apostles and prophets, a new generation of super-human believers who will establish God's kingdom on earth.

This "new breed," a rebranding of the many-membered Man-Child of the Latter Rain movement, is an elite group referred to as "overcomers," "forerunners," the Elijah Generation, the Joshua Generation, or Joel's Army. The latter title is based on a poor understanding (or deliberate misrepresentation) of the supernatural army described in chapter 2 of the book of Joel. These super-soldiers, it is taught, will embody the incarnate Christ, becoming the many-membered Man-Child mentioned earlier, and overwhelm all who stand in the way of establishing God's kingdom on earth[161]—beginning with troublesome Christians who won't get with the program.[162]

The problem with this exegesis—besides the heretical belief that these overcomers literally become God—is that the army described by the prophet Joel is clearly demonic, sent to punish the kingdom of Judah for its rebellion against God. Reading the entire second chapter of Joel makes it difficult to see any blessing for God's people from the destruction caused by this military force—which, incidentally, God destroys after it serves its purpose (see Joel 2:20).

The language of Joel 2 is prophetic. But rather than serving as Latter-Rain crusaders who establish the kingdom of God, Joel's Army actually bears a striking resemblance to the demonic horde released from the bottomless pit with their king Abaddon/Apollyon.

Compare this description of Joel's Army…

The appearance of them is like the appearance of horses;
and like horsemen, so shall they run.
Like the noise of chariots,
on the tops of mountains shall they leap,
like the noice of a flame of fire
that devoureth the stubble,
like a strong people set in battle array. (Joel 2:4–5)

…with this description of the horde that swarms from the Abyss during the Great Tribulation:

And the shapes of the locusts were like horses prepared unto battle; and on their heads were, as it were, crowns like gold, and their faces were like the faces of men.

And they had hair like the hair of women, and their teeth were like the teeth of lions.

And they had breastplates, as it were breastplates of iron; and the sound of their wings was like the sound of chariots of many horses running to battle. (Rev. 9:7–9)

This is the military force the apostolic-prophetic movement wants to create. It is possible that the New Apostolic Reformation and the Joel's Army movement, with the emphasis on signs and wonders and a belief that a generation is coming very soon that will literally become the incarnate Christ, were what Jesus had in mind when He warned of "false Christs and false prophets" in the last days (Matt. 24:23–24).

In 2006, the documentary film *Jesus Camp* created a stir when it revealed that children as young as six at a charismatic summer camp were being taught how to develop prophetic gifts and to "take back America for Christ."[163] While the filmmakers almost certainly had an agenda (which liberal pundits eagerly ran with), there is no getting around scenes of children in military-style camouflage clothing waving mock swords and enthusiastically shouting their desire to become soldiers for God.[164]

Bible-believing Christians can sympathize with the motives of the organizers of the "Kids on Fire" camp. It's impossible to look at the world around us without concluding that something is very wrong. In the trailer for *Jesus Camp*, it is explained that such a youth outreach is needed because "our enemies"—referring to radical Muslims—indoctrinate their children to hate us.

This identification of Islam as the enemy of Christendom, and especially American Christendom, is significant for a couple reasons. First, even though Jesus told us to love our enemies, it is easy to rationalize that command away when the media consistently subjects us to the venomous ranting of Islamic terror leaders who vow to bring death to America (and Israel).

Second, strong identification with Israel by a large segment of American Christianity may play an important role in the coming great deception. Statistics support the claim that Israel has no better friend in the world than American Christians. A recent study by the Pew Research

Center found that white evangelical Protestants are more than twice as likely as American Jews to say that God gave Israel to the Jews.[165] The survey also found that white evangelical Protestants are also more likely than American Jews to support stronger US support for Israel.

This may explain the political shift by leaders of the neoconservative movement in the United States during the 1970s and '80s. Broadly speaking, influential liberal Democrats, supporters of John F. Kennedy and Lyndon B. Johnson, many of whom were Jewish, became disenchanted with the emerging New Left during the Johnson administration. They were alarmed by the New Left's bitter opposition to President Johnson, to capitalism, and to Israel during the 1967 war.

By the time of Ronald Reagan's presidency, many leading neocons, some of whom had been socialists in their youth, found they had more in common with the Republican Party (and the growing number of politically active evangelicals) than with the new leadership of the Democratic Party.

In particular, these two groups, formerly opposed on most social and religious issues, found common ground over the matter of the Holy Land. Many influential neocons were Jewish; American evangelicals tend to see the restoration of Israel as the fulfillment of prophecy.

This support for Israel by American evangelicals, which grew in the wake of the 1967 war, was actively encouraged by Israel itself. In the 1980s, the Israeli Ministry of Tourism organized free trips to the Holy Land for hundreds of evangelical pastors. The most powerful Jewish lobbying group, the American Israel Public Affairs Committee (AIPAC), realigned itself with the American political right wing[166] just as evangelicals began flexing their political muscle.

The clout wielded by this coalition has been considerable. Retired General Wesley Clark has said in multiple interviews that neocons, after the terror attacks of September 11, 2001, unveiled a plan "to attack and remove governments in seven countries over five years: Iraq, Syria, Lebanon, Libya, Somalia, Sudan and Iran."

This was not a new idea. Clark said he had a conversation ten years earlier with prominent neocon Paul Wolfowitz, then the number-three man at the Pentagon, in which Wolfowitz said the lesson of the 1991 Gulf War was that the US could use its military to effect regime change in the Middle East without interference from Russia—and that there was a five-year window to take out the governments of Iraq, Iran, and Syria before another superpower could step up and challenge America's right to do so.[167]

The common thread that links the seven nations apparently targeted for regime change by influential people within the American government for the last quarter century is that all are predominantly Muslim, and all are reportedly hostile to American and Israeli interests.

Given the legacy of violence and bloodshed blamed on those nations or groups operating within them, such as the Marine barracks bombing in Beirut, Pan Am Flight 103, Mogadishu (*Black Hawk Down*), the Iran Hostage Crisis, support for Hezbollah, and more, it is not difficult to stir up American support for military payback.

Add to this volatile cocktail a dash of prophetic significance—for example, a threat to Israel—and patriotic American evangelicals are ready for war.[168]

It appears that certain elements within the apostolic-prophetic movement have an even stronger motive than mainstream evangelicals for adopting a protective stance toward Israel. An emerging doctrine called "One New Man" seems to be gaining traction that provides theological cover for unquestioning support of the nation-state of Israel.

The One New Man doctrine teaches that Christians and Jews will someday come together in Israel as a new body of believers—neither Jew nor Gentile, but "One New Man." This is based on chapter 2 of Paul's letter to the church at Ephesus:

Wherefore, remember that ye, being in time past Gentiles in the flesh, who are called Uncircumcision by that which is called the Circumcision in the flash made by hands—

That at that time ye were without Christ, being aliens from the commonwealth of Israel, and strangers from the covenants of promise, having no hope, and without God in the world.

But now in Christ Jesus ye who once were far off are made near by the blood of Christ.

For he is our peace, who hath made both one, and hath broken down the middle wall of partition between us,

Having abolished in his flesh the enmity, even the law of commandments contained in ordinances, to make in himself of two one new man, so making peace;

And that he might reconcile both unto God in one body by the cross, having slain the enmity thereby,

And came and preached peace to you who were afar off, and to them that were near.

For through him we both have access by one Spirit unto the Father.

Now, therefore, ye are no more strangers and sojourners, but fellow citizens with the saints, and of the household of God;

And are built upon the foundation of the apostles and prophets, Jesus Christ himself being the chief corner stone,

In whom all the building fitly framed together growth unto an holy temple in the Lord;

In whom ye also are built together for an habitation of God through the Spirit. (Eph. 2:11–22)

These passages are interpreted by One New Man teachers as prophetic, referring to God's end game rather than to events of the first century. Paul wrote his letter to Ephesus while imprisoned in Rome, awaiting trial on a false charge of escorting a Gentile past the barrier intended to keep *goyim* (non-Jewish nations) out of the Temple. Jesus destroyed that "dividing wall of hostility" on the cross, allowing Gentiles direct access to Yahweh.

Significantly, at least some teachers of the One New Man doctrine are convinced that this new body of believers will receive the land God promised to the descendants of Abraham. This includes all or parts (depending on interpretation) of the Palestinian territories, Egypt, Lebanon, Syria, Jordan, Kuwait, Saudi Arabia, Iraq, and Turkey.

Needless to say, such a radical redrawing of the map of the Middle East would be controversial, to say the least.

One New Man has become, for some in the apostolic-prophetic movement, a substitute term for Joel's Army, which was saddled with negative connotations after liberal commentators began talking about the movement during the 2012 presidential campaign. Though they do not use the term outright, the authors of the influential book *Victorious Eschatology: A Partial Preterist View*[169] cite the same passages in Ephesians 2 referenced above to describe Christ's literal incarnation inside the faithful remnant—Joel's Army/One New Man—who become "a dwelling place for God" before they go forth to destroy His enemies.

While again recognizing that this must sound bizarre to most American Christians, the influence wielded by Dominionists in American politics is actually on the rise. In recent years, prominent members of the New Apostolic Reformation have developed relationships with leading Republicans such as Newt Gingrich, Mike Huckabee, Sam Brownback, and Rick Perry. Vice presidential candidate Sarah Palin was criticized for being a member of a church with Dominionist leanings in her hometown of Wasilla, Alaska.

Demonstrating an ability to cross political boundaries, a prominent Assemblies of God pastor and member of the International Coalition of Apostles, a key group within the NAR, was invited to the White House by President Barack Obama to discuss immigration reform.

The new apostles and prophets have been mainstreaming their image in Christian circles as well, by associating with mainstream evangelicals at a variety of public events, conferences, and speaking engagements in recent years. Respected leaders such as Dr. James Dobson, Billy Graham, Ravi Zacharias, Chuck Swindoll, Max Lucado, Chuck Colson, Rick Warren, David Barton (WallBuilders), Charles Stanley, Francis Chan, and Joni Eareckson Tada, among others, have been linked to people in the apostolic-prophetic movement.

That is not to say that these respected teachers endorse Dominion theology. However, by associating with those who do, they lend their credibility to the new apostles. Unwary Christians may assume that because recognized evangelical leaders endorse a particular event, *all* of those endorsing that event are similarly sound in doctrine.

And the New Apostolic Reformation has definitely influenced mainstream evangelical Christianity in America. In May of 2010, I wrote a piece for my blog about the National Day of Prayer, noting that the mission statement of the National Day of Prayer Task Force (since removed from the group's website) was to mobilize prayer for America and its leaders "in the seven centers of power."

The seven centers of power just happen to track very closely with the 7 Mountains of Culture, or 7-M Mandate, that's promoted by the new generation of self-appointed apostles on a mission from God to rule the Earth. The only difference appears to be that "Military" has replaced "Arts & Entertainment" with the Task Force.[170]

While references to the "seven centers of power" are no longer featured on the website of the National Day of Prayer Task Force, an offshoot organization called Pray for America promotes "7x7," a campaign to encourage American Christians to "pray for our seven centers of power, seven days a week."[171]

Now, the call to pray for government leaders is biblical, so this campaign is, on its face, scripturally sound. However, the clear evidence that the Seven Mountains Mandate of Kingdom Now theology is influencing events promoted by prominent evangelical Christians is eye-opening. And the substitution of a military "center" for the arts and entertainment "mountain," given the Dominionist belief that Joel's Army is about to go forth and destroy the enemies of God, is more than a little disturbing.

It is the view of this author that the threat posed by Dominion theology is not that a charismatic Christian will win the presidency and turn the United States into a theocracy.[172] Frankly, in spite of dire warnings by progressive commentators against the likes of Sarah Palin,[173] Governor Rick Perry, and Michelle Bachmann, it seems highly unlikely that an openly Christian leader could win enough electoral votes to gain the White House.

The real danger is that well-intentioned American Christians, generally ignorant of prophecy[174] and motivated more by patriotic sentiment than by the Great Commission, will actually welcome the Antichrist with open arms—assuming, of course, that the Rapture follows the Beast's rise to power.

Consider that the enemy is exceedingly subtle.[175] Contrary to Hollywood portrayals, the Son of Perdition will not announce himself as such. It is far more probable that the Antichrist will be perceived as a charming, personable, and effective leader, open-minded and tolerant, who does wonders for the security and political fortunes of Israel.

When the Antichrist establishes a strong "covenant with many" (Dan. 9:27), it may be welcomed by those who believe that Israel, which most prophecy scholars assume will be a party to the covenant, will finally have the peace and security that has eluded the tiny nation since its restoration in 1948. It is safe to assume that many American Christians, and nearly all believers in the Joel's Army/One New Man doctrine, will see this as a good thing.

This is especially true if, as some prophecy scholars believe, the Antichrist presents himself as a Jew. While this concept runs counter to recent popular theories that the Antichrist will be a Muslim (and the prevailing view of past generations that he will be Roman and/or the Pope), it is not a new idea. Early church fathers such as Hippolytus and Irenaeus believed "[t]he Antichrist will be a Jew, and will achieve his stated objectives by being accepted as the Christ, the messianic king of the Jews, taking his seat in the rebuilt temple in Jerusalem, pretending to be God Himself, and thereby becoming the 'abomination of desolation' spoken of by the prophet Daniel and mentioned also by Jesus."[176]

This is significant. Hippolytus of Rome (170–235) was a disciple of Irenaeus (c. 130–c. 202), a disciple of Polycarp (69–155), who, Irenaeus wrote, was a disciple of John the apostle. So the notion of a Jewish Antichrist was taught by prominent Christians in the second century, and they may have received that doctrine from one of the twelve apostles, the author of the book of Revelation.

But why, you may ask, would Christians and Jews willingly support the political career of the Beast? As noted above, it is highly unlikely that the Man of Sin will identify himself as the Antichrist. Appearing rather as an angel of light, the Antichrist will draw into his orbit those who believe that his motives are good and pure, especially when viewed through a Zionist lens.

His appeal to Dominionists, and many mainstream American Christians, will be confirmed if, as prophecy student Chris White suggests, the Antichrist wages a successful war against Israel's Muslim neighbors. Assuming that the Antichrist rises to power in Jerusalem, then Daniel 11:40–45 reads like a summary of another 1967 war—a sudden attack on Israel from the south and north, with the end result a smashing Israeli victory, especially against Egypt.

As this dovetails with both the Dominionists' desire to rid the world of the enemies of God, which by definition includes Muslims, and the understandable desire for self-preservation of most Israelis, it is logical to conclude that playing the role of a strong, capable Israeli leader who finally sweeps aside the Islamic threat in the Middle East will provide a much easier path to power than the part of an outsider who somehow manages sets up his political power base in Jerusalem.

One can see the appeal to Jews and Christians alike of an Israeli leader who apparently secures his nation against the threat of hostile neighbors, especially if the victory results in expanding Israel's borders to something like the territory promised by God to Abraham. Imagine the popularity of, say, Benjamin Netanyahu or Ariel Sharon with superpowers and you begin to grasp the appeal of a Jewish Antichrist.

It is beyond the scope of this paper to detail the scriptural support for the concept of a Jewish Antichrist. I present it here because it is a plausible theory (and one held by some in the early church), and because it presents, in the current theopolitical climate of the United States, a clear and present danger to ungrounded believers.

It bears repeating: The threat is not that American Christians will seize power and establish a theocracy. Nor does Dominion theology necessarily pose a threat to the souls of those who believe it. It is possible for one to accept Jesus Christ as Lord and Savior while simultaneously misunderstanding the nature, timing, and purpose of Christ's return.

And it must be stressed that this is absolutely *not* a call for Christians to avoid the political process. The world would be a far better place if more true Christians served in government, or at least took an active role in civic affairs. It is impossible to be salt and light to a fallen world from behind the walls of a compound. Withdrawing from the world is one sure path to condemning it to tyranny.

The other path, sadly, is being traveled by a growing coalition of undiscerning charismatics, legalistic Reconstructionists, and biblically ignorant evangelicals. That road inevitably leads to forcing Judeo-Christian morality onto an unwilling world. Changing behavior without a corresponding change of heart does not please God. If it did, Jesus would have praised the scribes and Pharisees instead of condemning them.

Nowhere in Scripture did Jesus command His disciples to reclaim dominion over the earth to prepare for His return. The Great Commission was not an order to bring nations into the fold en masse. Conversion is an individual process, not something that can be conferred on entire cities, states, or nations through unbiblical practices like "spiritual mapping," "identificational repentance" for "corporate sin," or "reconciliation walks."

We serve a God whose standard of righteousness is impossible to meet. Jesus told His disciples that just hating another person is murder. He did not say it is *like* committing murder; He said it *is* murder. Given that, how can anyone believe that God is pleased by forcing unbelievers to adopt a veneer of biblical morality? It was precisely because they valued style (public displays of "holiness") over substance (contrite, repentant, loving hearts) that Jesus called the Pharisees whitewashed tombs.[177]

By focusing on political solutions to spiritual problems, Dominion theology poses several dangers to the modern church. First, it diverts time, talent, and resources away from the true calling Jesus gave us, which is to preach the gospel to all nations—not the gospel of the kingdom, but the gospel of salvation. The wages of sin have been paid for believers at the cross. Death holds no power over us, and it will ultimately be defeated for all time when Christ returns and throws it, and hell, into the lake of fire.[178]

Second, it destroys our witness, rendering our preaching ineffective. Unbelievers see the naked political ambition of Dominionists and assume that all Christians are motivated by a desire to impose biblical morality, by force if necessary, on those who do not accept the authority of the Bible.

Finally, the belief that God is calling Christians to reclaim the planet in His name, born from a misguided patriotism, a willingness to believe popular preaching rather than study Bible prophecy, and an unquestioning support for the nation of Israel, may very well deceive many professing Christians into unwittingly laying the foundation for the rise of the Antichrist.

Jesus told us, "My kingdom is not of this world." Christians focused on Kingdom Now may in fact be working for the one Jesus called the god of this world.

9

A DIVIDED HOUSE

Mainline Liberal vs. Evangelical Conservative

By Cris D. Putnam, MTS

It is widely conceded that Western culture has entered a post-Christian era. As a result, the Christian church is deeply polarized. Although some mainline churches include evangelicals and charismatics, the mainline Protestant churches are a group of churches that contrast in belief, history, and practice with evangelical, fundamentalist, and charismatic Protestant denominations. The dividing line is the authority of Scripture. On the right, one finds conservatives who uphold the doctrine of biblical inerrancy and embrace God's moral truths as timeless. On the left, one encounters folks who believe the Scriptures are an imperfect human work bound to anachronistic culture and that one must revise one's interpretation in light of today's sensibilities.

The Association of Religion Data Archives (ARDA) counts 26,344,933 members of mainline churches versus 39,930,869 members of evangelical Protestant churches in the United States.[179] Instead of being Christ's missionaries to the lost world, mainline liberals are now ostensibly the world's missionaries to the church. They devote their energy to social issues like trying to legitimize same-sex marriage; lesbian, gay, bisexual, and transgender (LGBT) equality; feminism; and being inclusive of non-Christian religions. Mainline churches include the Episcopal Church, the Evangelical Lutheran Church in America (ELCA), the Presbyterian Church USA (PCUSA), the United Methodist Church (UMC), the American Baptist Churches, the United Church of Christ (Congregationalist), the Disciples of Christ, and the Reformed Church in America, amongst others. Many of the above reject core doctrines of classical Christianity like substitutionary atonement, leading H. Richard Niebuhr to famously surmise their creed: "A God without wrath brought men without sin into a kingdom without judgment through the ministrations of a Christ without a cross."[180] Evangelicals stand in sharp relief.

Evangelicalism is defined as "the movement in modern Christianity, transcending denominational and confessional boundaries, that emphasizes conformity to the basic tenets of the faith and a missionary outreach of compassion and urgency."[181] The name derives from the Greek word for "gospel," *euangelion*, and verb *euangelizomai*, "to proclaim the good news." Examples of evangelical denominations are: Assemblies of God, Southern Baptists, Independent Baptists, Bible Church, Black Protestants, African Methodist Episcopal, African Methodist Episcopal Zion; Church of Christ, Churches of God in Christ, Lutheran Church—Missouri Synod, National Baptist Church, National Progressive Baptist Church, nondenominational, Pentecostal denominations, and the Presbyterian Church in America. Some of these are called fundamentalists.

Often maligned, the term "fundamentalist" started out simple enough. In 1846, the Evangelical Alliance was formed to unite all believers who saw nineteenth-century rise of "social gospel," theological liberalism as a denial of the faith. At a meeting in Niagara Falls, New York, the alliance listed the five "fundamentals" that could not be denied without falling into the error of liberalism. Those five were: (1) inerrancy of Scripture, (2) the divinity of Jesus, (3) the virgin birth, (4) Jesus' death on the cross as a substitute for our sins, and (5) His physical resurrection and impending return. In light of recent attacks, I propose to add (6) the doctrine of the Trinity,[182] and (7) the existence of Satan, angels, and spirits[183] to the list for a total of seven. Most evangelicals affirm all seven, even if they do not identify as fundamentalist.

While evangelicalism may sometimes be perceived as the middle ground between the theological liberalism of the mainline denominations and the cultural separatism of fundamentalism, those fundamental doctrines are what separates the sheep from the goats. While it is argued here that they are *all essentials*, numbers 2, 4, 5, and 6 cannot be denied by anyone who can in any meaningful way remain a Christian. After all, we worship a triune God with Christ at the center of Christianity; the gospel is His atoning death and resurrection; and the great hope for the believer is His promise to return and eternal life (Heb. 9:28; Titus 2:13; and Matt. 25:46). Anyone who believes anything short of that ceases to be truly Christian.

Even the outspoken antitheist Christopher Hitchens had a better understanding of Christianity than what most liberal mainline Christians express. For example, this excerpt from an interview of Hitchens by a Unitarian minister Marilyn Sewell concerning his book *God Is Not Great* reveals the bankruptcy of demythologized nominal Christianity:

> **Sewell:** The religion you cite in your book is generally the funda-
> mentalist faith of various kinds. I'm a liberal Christian, and I don't

take the stories from the scripture literally. I don't believe in the doctrine of atonement (that Jesus died for our sins, for example). Do you make and distinction between fundamentalist faith and liberal religion?

Hitchens: I would say that if you don't believe that Jesus of Nazareth was the Christ and Messiah, and that he rose again from the dead and by his sacrifice our sins are forgiven, you're really not in any meaningful sense a Christian.[184]

It is terribly unfortunate that an ardent antitheist like Hitchens understands Christianity better than a so-called minister. However, this is representative of the polarization inherent in the postmodern project.

Episcopal Bishop John Shelby Spong holds similar beliefs to the Unitarian. Notice the denial of classic Christian doctrines set out in the preface of his book, *Jesus for the Non-Religious:*

The second stream flowing through both my professional life and my writing career was the recognition that the expanding knowledge of my secular world had increasingly rendered the traditional theological formulations expressed in such core Christian doctrines as the incarnation, the atonement and even the trinity inoperative at worst, and incapable of making much sense to the ears of twenty-first-century people at best.[185]

The incarnation, atonement, and Trinity are not exactly negotiable doctrines. Under the classical definition, without them, the word "Christian" is unintelligible. As a result, they do not affirm the same values as biblical Christians. Let's examine how the liberal church challenges biblical morality and ends up having more in common with atheists like Hitchens than with those who affirm classical Christianity.

Challenges to Biblical Morality

The liberal church is challenging and rejecting God's revealed understanding of moral right and wrong as much as the secular community. Because God has revealed His moral standards in the pages of Scripture, these are necessarily challenges to biblical morality. This suggests two principle areas of attack: 1) the Bible; and 2) the existence of objective morality. The atheist denies biblical morality by definition, but these assaults come from liberal Christians as well. While they are often deployed in tandem, this chapter will examine each line of attack, the way it is used, and some of its problems. Fortunately, the denial of Gods' revealed moral standards entails suppressing the truth and inevitably leads to logical or moral inconsistency (Rom. 1:18–21). This makes our job a little easier.

The first challenge to biblical morality entails attacking the Bible. This assault assumes various forms and comes from liberal Christianity as well as from secularists. The most dangerous is the former, because it often persuades new believers and confuses less knowledgeable conservatives. Challenges from scholars like Bart Ehrman focus on the text and argue that we cannot trust it to be accurate. If we do not have God's words, we do not have His morals. Fortunately, brilliant evangelical scholars oppose the likes of Ehrman and offer a cogent defense for the reliability of the Scripture.[186] Others argue that the Bible is culturally bound and not applicable to modern culture. This spans the gap from the egalitarians who seek to usurp biblical gender roles in order to promote female clergy to radical homosexual revisionists indulging in the most incredible eisegesis to assert that the Bible is silent concerning homosexuality. As noted by Francis Schaeffer, the slippery slope argument validly applies because the former very often leads to the latter.[187]

Other nominal Christians dismiss the Bible as the deeply flawed product of an ancient patriarchal culture. Radical theologian Spong epitomizes the wholesale dismissal of biblical morality by suggesting it promotes slavery and demeans women:

> The Bible has been used for centuries by Christians as a weapon of control. To read it literally is to believe in a three-tiered universe, to condone slavery, to treat women as inferior creatures, to believe that sickness is caused by God's punishment and that mental disease and epilepsy are caused by demonic possession. When someone tells me that they believe the Bible is the "literal and inerrant word of God," I always ask, "Have you ever read it?"[188]

This exemplifies a wholesale compromise with culture. Although Spong is an Episcopal bishop, it is hard to call him a Christian in any significant way. Truthfully, he is not that far from the atheists.

Atheists deny God's morality by denying He exists. Still, they attack the Bible to support their position. Often this results in inconsistency. For instance, on one hand they will dismiss the historical narrative of the Bible as a Jewish legend, while on the other hand they will use Joshua's conquest as an example of genocide. In so doing, they claim that if He does exist, God is a moral monster. Richard Dawkins has infamously argued:

> The God of the Old Testament is arguably the most unpleasant character in all fiction: jealous and proud of it; a petty, unjust, unforgiving control-freak; a vindictive, bloodthirsty ethnic cleanser; a

misogynistic, homophobic, racist, infanticidal, genocidal, filicidal, pestilential, megalomaniacal, sadomasochistic, capriciously malevolent bully.[189]

Comparing Episcopal Bishop Spong's statement above to the one by "New Atheist" Dawkins reveals no meaningful distinction. Both men believe the Old Testament God is evil. In like fashion, Dawkins' cohort, the deceased antitheist, Christopher Hitchens, not only dismissed biblical morality, but also leveled moral judgment against it in his best seller, *God Is Not Great: How Religion Poisons Everything.* The atheist and the mainline liberal not only reject God's moral standards; they often brand them as "evil" in the process. However, conceding the existence of evil falsifies the second line of attack. If evil exists objectively, then moral relativism has a big problem.

The second major way biblical morals are rejected is by denying the existence of objective morality. A corollary of postmodernism known as "moral relativism" rules out the possibility of a transcendent moral law revealed by God. In this view, morality is culturally defined and relative to a particular group. It is often called a *cultural construct.* So, if the majority of Americans agree that same-sex marriage is morally good, then it is. God has no say, and absolutes do not apply. Thus, the majority decides what is morally virtuous and what is not. In effect, it amounts to "the mob rules." While mainline liberal denominations think this way, relativism is also associated with what has come to be known as the *emergent church.*

The emergent church is basically mainline liberalism for the twenty-something hipster. The movement is led by the likes of Brian McLaren, Gregory Boyd, and Rob Bell. McLaren is postmodern to the depths of denying the gospel in adopting a radical inclusivism—the belief that other religions lead to salvation. Boyd is an open theist—a position that God does not infallibly know the future. Bell—aptly described as classic theological liberalism in skinny jeans[190]—created a firestorm of controversy by denying the reality of hell and promoting universalism in his best seller, *Love Wins*. As a result, conservative apologists have largely concluded that these men are heretics who have abandoned the faith. For example, Peter Jones has written, "McLaren and others are taking unsuspecting evangelicals into a new flavor of the same paganism about which the apostle Paul warned us. Emergent, progressive 'Christianity' is committed to the Oneist unity of all religions."[191] McLaren does not think we should convert Buddhists to Christianity, but rather make "Buddhist followers of Jesus."[192] Buddhism is usually atheistic, so it is a relativist absurdity to make such an assertion. This led Jones to quip, "As oxymorons go, this 'oxy' is more moronic than 'military intelligence' or 'educational television.'"[193]

In keeping with the postmodern penchant for cultural relativism, McLaren argues that because evangelical systematic theology is filtered through a Western, colonialist worldview, we cannot really be sure about basic doctrines like penal substitutionary atonement. I wonder if he thinks John the Baptist was influenced by such colonialism when he exclaimed, "Behold the Lamb of God, who taketh away the sin of the world" (John 1:29)? Although it is immensely popular with emergents, secular humanists, and mainline liberals, history demonstrates that even its staunchest promoters cannot consistently live according to the tenets of relativism. There are too many obvious contradictions.

According to moral relativism, it is immoral for one group to judge another by its own standards. They deny that moral absolutes exist. This is how mainliners argue that the Bible's prohibitions of homosexuality no longer apply. They contend that one cannot use the morals of the Old and New Testaments to judge modern LGBTs. In order to discourage the practice, relativists apply discouraging labels like "homophobic." Similarly, the term "religiocentrism" denotes the conviction that one's religion is superior to others. Often these are paralleled to racism for emotional effect. They oppose biblical morality as a form of cultural imperialism by asserting that its objective moral truth claims are wrongful impositions. Although this absolute is smuggled in the back door, they ignore the inconsistency. Accordingly, they really do not live by their stated beliefs.

Relativists are only relativists when it suits them. From their stated beliefs, it follows that if the majority decides that genocide or racism benefits the group, then it should be deemed morally virtuous. Apart from an objective standard, there is no warrant to criticize atrocities like the Holocaust. Yet, the Allies appealed to an objective standard and went to war against the Nazis. Furthermore, it turns great moral reformers like Martin Luther King into immoral rabble-rousers. King also appealed to a transcendent moral standard against the prevailing tide of the culture. A consistent relativist would have to reject his claims and support the racist consensus. Most liberals idealize King, so this is a very effective defeater.

Extreme examples have a way of clarifying the issue. One might ask the relativist to name a circumstance when killing children for fun is morally virtuous. If the relativist agrees that there is not one, then he or she has conceded a moral absolute. This demonstrates that, given relativism, there are no real moral values, merely opinions, like tastes in ice cream. Given relativism, one cannot consistently say "racism is wrong" or "discriminating against homosexuals is wrong." They can only say, "I don't like it." Relativism actually destroys morals. Moral relativism is an incoherent concept that all rational people should abandon. In truth, it amounts to moral nihilism.

The culture denies biblical moral standards by attacking the Bible or the notion that moral standards are objective. They might deny God exists, that He has spoken through Scripture, or that Scripture is reliably preserved. They might also question the existence of objective morality. In so doing, they run the risk of embracing moral anarchy. These points lead to the conclusion that the apostle Paul was right in connecting the suppression of truth in unrighteousness with increasingly futile thinking and a seared conscience: "Because, when they knew God, they glorified him not as God, neither were thankful; but became vain in their imaginations, and their foolish heart was darkened" (Rom. 1:21). Since the mainline churches are performing same-sex ceremonies, in the next few years we expect discrimination lawsuits to be leveled against conservative evangelical churches refusing to perform them. In response, demonstrating that same-sex relationships are not in the same moral category as marriage could be helpful. In truth, the phrase "same-sex marriage" is a misnomer, a nonsense combining of terms like "married bachelor" or "square circle."

Homosexuality and the Dividing Line

Of all the social issues today, homosexuality seems to be the main one leveled against conservative evangelicals. The mainline churches are largely given over to it. Episcopal,[194] ELCA,[195] and PCUSA[196] not only accept homosexual unions, but put homosexual clergy in charge of their churches. At President Barack Obama's inauguration, an openly gay Episcopal bishop, Gene Robinson, expressed his horror at how specifically Christian past inaugural prayers had been, and instead prayed to the "God of our many understandings."[197] Baptist fundamentalist John MacArthur has argued this represents God's judgment on America in line with:

For this cause God gave them up unto vile affections; for even their women did exchange the natural use into that which is against nature;

And likewise also the men, leaving the natural use of the woman, burned in their lust one toward another, men with men working that which is unseemly, and receiving in themselves that recompence of their error which was fitting. (Rom. 1:26–27)[198]

Of course, liberals try to explain this away as first-century exploitation. New Testament scholar Peter Jones addressed the mainline interpretation, arguing, "Some critics say that Paul was speaking of exploitative relationships of domination and that he didn't understand homosexuality as we know it today—a loving, mature, stable commitment. But Paul argues (v. 27) that men burned with desire for each other, not that one exploited the other."[199] Another conservative evangelical pastor, John Piper, points out that these denominations are knowingly leading people to hell by approving of and modeling this behavior (1 Cor. 6:9–11).[200] It is also important to note that the 1 Corinthians passage reads "And such *were* some of you" (1 Cor. 6:11a, emphasis added), forever dispelling the notion that one cannot become a *former* homosexual. Because it is representative of the divide, this chapter will close with arguments against same-sex marriage based on a moral category distinction.

A Category Distinction

The first task is to distinguish the moral category of marriage from the moral category of same-sex relationships. This presentation will first give an overview of the biblical-theological distinctions, then it will examine the social-secular differences. Same-sex relationships are ontologically different from marriage between a husband and wife. The difference in moral category will be explored in a face-value manner. According to a standard reference, "Category differences are articulated as a way of diagnosing and avoiding various philosophical problems and confusions."[201] Western culture is deeply confused concerning the attributes of a same-sex relationship as compared to attributes of a marriage. If same-sex relationships and marriage are in different moral categories, then there can be no such thing as "same-sex marriage." It will be shown that they are not in the same moral category. For example, a same-sex relationship requires both individuals to be of the same sex, while a marriage requires gender complementarity. That alone should settle the matter, but further reasons are given. Marriage, grounded in a natural teleology and beneficial to society, is in an entirely different moral category than homosexual relationships that are inherently immoral and, from a secular perspective, pathological. Because marriage is a covenant, let's begin there.

A covenant is an oath-bound promise within which one party swears to bless or serve another party in a specified way. In the Bible, a covenant was associated with ritual sacrifice and involved splitting an animal in half and walking between the two halves, i.e., "cutting a covenant." The implication was that if one violated the covenant, the fate of the animal would be visited on the violator. Covenants are made between God and man (Gen. 9:12–15) and between humans with God as their witness (Gen. 21:22–34; 31:44–54). Marriage was established at Creation as a covenant bond between a husband, a wife, and God. David Naugle explains: "It was to be a total life union between man and woman in an exclusive and permanent covenantal relationship of faithfulness and love (Gen. 2:23–24)."[202] In modern ceremonies, the division of the groom's party on one side of the church with the bride's on the other is symbolic of the ancient practice of splitting an animal. Malachi 2:14 indicates that marriage was understood as a covenant. In marriage, one man and one woman vow to live together in a lifetime relationship (Gen. 2:24; Matt.

19:4–6) involving sacrificial love, sexual relations, and joint provision.

Therefore, marriage is a sacred institution defined by a spiritual and moral pledge rather than merely a legal contract, as held by secular society. The seventh commandment, "Thou shalt not commit adultery" (Exod. 20:14) serves to protect this sacred institution rather than mere sexual fidelity. This is illustrated by the fact that the punishment for adultery was death (Deut. 22:22), but the punishment for fornication was compulsory marriage and a fine (Deut. 22:28–29). The distinction is that the former violates a sacred covenant while the latter does not. Children are also at stake, because the bond is essential to healthy child rearing.

In the social-secular realm, the marriage relationship has a natural teleology toward procreation and child rearing. It is an uncontroversial fact of biology that only male and female couples can procreate. Data from the social sciences strongly suggests that intact marriages produce the healthiest children. Children raised in intact, married families are physically and emotionally healthier, less likely to be abused, less likely to use drugs or alcohol and to commit crimes, have a decreased risk of divorce, and are more likely to attend college.[203] In contrast, data on children reared by same-sex couples suggests they are more likely to have social and emotional problems.[204] Because married couples produce the next generation of citizens for a nation, the state has an interest in preserving and encouraging traditional marriage. This reasoning does not and cannot apply to same-sex relationships, because they do not produce children. There is no legitimate interest for the state.

In the biblical theological sphere, homosexual relationships are inherently sinful and offensive to God. The overarching category is sin or immorality, but same-sex relationships of this type are in their own specific moral category. God affirms healthy, platonic, same-sex relationships. For example, Jonathan and David cut a covenant in which Jonathan acknowledged David's right to the throne of Israel (1 Sam. 18:3; 23:18). However, contrary to liberal revisionism, this has absolutely nothing to do with the modern debate concerning homosexual couples. Same-sex relationships can be covenantal, but are not necessarily so; marriage is by definition a covenant. God's moral character does not change, and in the Torah He clearly defines homosexual acts as an abomination (Lev. 20:13). The New Testament affirms this in many passages (Rom. 1: 26–27; 1 Cor. 6:9; 1 Tim. 1:10). This scriptural categorization is clearly not arbitrary or historic-culturally bound. Even more, an argument from teleology supports the divine rationale.

Homosexuality defies God's created order. Arthur Holmes asserts, "Paul in Romans 1 speaks of some human actions as contrary to nature: he echoes the Genesis record about man and woman created in God's image, their lives and their heterosexuality protected therefore by the law of creation (Genesis 1:26–31; 2:18–25; 4:8–16; 9:1–6)."[205] It is indisputable that there is a definite biological order, indeed a necessity, when it comes to sexuality. Same-sex attraction is obviously a violation of this order and purpose. A same-sex relationship is not designed to be sexual, while a marriage relationship is designed to be sexual. A same-sex relationship cannot result in procreation, but marriage has the potential for procreation. If this is a healthy behavior as its advocates argue, then it follows that everyone should adopt healthy behaviors. The *reductio ad absurdum* is that, if universally adopted, homosexuality leads to the extinction of the human species. This strongly suggests homosexuality is a sexual attraction *disorder*. Jones wrote, "Homosexuality is a creational dysfunction and homosexual marriage an oxymoron."[206] In contrast, normal marriage generally benefits the survival of the human species. Accordingly, it follows in the social-secular sphere that same-sex relationships are in a different moral category than marriage.

Marriage can be generally classified in secular terms as a procreative contract. Marriage is supposed to be a lifelong commitment, "until death do us part." Some same-sex relationships are dissoluble, whereas marriage is defined to be indissoluble. It seems that marriage is something described rather than defined. One observes the natural procreative order and describes the coupling commitment for child rearing in terms of marriage. It is not something defined to suit popular affinities, but rather a description of natural teleology. Those who wish to redefine marriage to include same-sex relationships are engaging in a futile exercise. Philosopher Frank Beckwith has quipped, "You can eat an ashtray but that doesn't make it food."[207] Semantics aside, same-sex relationships can never really be "marriage."

Marriage is within a different moral category than same-sex relationships. Marriage is in the category of a covenant bond between God, a husband, and a wife for the purpose of raising children and caring for one another. Only a male can be a husband and only a female can be a wife; this rules out "same-sex marriage" by definition. Homosexual relationships fall in the category of sin and pathology, as they violate God's law, His biological design, and they do not contribute to repopulation. These ideas are supported by biblical theology demonstrating the establishment of the marriage covenant by God and His prohibitions against homosexuality. In the secular sphere, traditional marriage is good for society, because it produces the next generation, and children are better off with heterosexual parents. Same-sex relationships do not produce new citizens, and even same-sex adoptions are less than ideal. Hence, there is no good reason for the state to endorse or promote them. These facts lead to the conclusion that the idea of "same-sex marriage" is an immoral absurdity that has been deceptively hoisted on a naively liberal culture. Mainline churches that perform these ceremonies are willfully opposing the God they claim to worship.

The Solution

It is extremely unfortunate that what is called the Christian church is so divided. Even so, this chapter has shown that not all that is labeled "Christian" actually is consistent with classical Christianity. Liberals suffer from unbelief. The only solution is the gospel. That's right, I said it: They need the gospel. How can I say that? The gospel entails sincerely believing that Christ died for my sins (1 Cor. 15:3) and that Christ resurrected from the dead on the third day (1 Cor. 15:4). We have seen many examples of emergent (McLaren) and mainline (Spong) pastors and leaders who explicitly deny those very truths. Some do so by folly and ignorance and others by malintent: "And no marvel; for Satan himself is transformed into an angel of light. Therefore, it is no great thing if his ministers also be transformed as the ministers of righteousness, whose end shall be according to their works" (2 Cor. 11:14–15). Thus, we should approach liberal Christians as nonbelievers, keeping in mind that "the natural man receiveth not the things of the Spirit of God; for they are foolishness unto him: neither can he know them, because they are spiritually discerned" (1 Cor. 2:14). Unfortunately, they have chosen the wide gate Jesus warned of (Matt. 7:13).

I am not saying there are no saved people in liberal, mainline, or emergent churches, but that the theology expressed by their leaders does not lead to it. This should not be terribly surprising, as Jesus' brother Jude warned back in the first century:

> Beloved, when I gave all diligence to write unto you of the common salvation, it was needful for me to write unto you, and exhort you that ye should earnestly contend for the faith which was once delivered unto the saints.

For there are certain men crept in unawares, who were before of old ordained to this condemnation, ungodly men, turning the grace of our God into lasciviousness, and denying the only Lord God, and our Lord Jesus Christ. (Jude 3–4)

Although it is more blatant, there is nothing new here. It seems this chapter's title was somewhat misleading; the church is not a "divided house," but rather, many who claim to be under its roof, in truth, are married to the world (Rev. 3:17). These "in name only" Christians will most likely lead the persecution of the believing church, already labeled as bigoted and homophobic.

The Great Harlot and the Return to Pagan Rome

It is not that homosexuality is a special sin more deserving of revulsion than other transgressions, but I have yet to witness an "adultery pride" parade. Homosexuals flaunt and expect everyone else to celebrate "gay pride." Because its defenders refuse to admit it is a sin, homosexuality is the primary social issue used to marginalize folks who take the Bible seriously. Already, the celebration of same-sex unions is being pressed, indeed forced, upon those who believe it to be immoral.

The year 2013 marked a dramatic shift in American jurisprudence, one with foreboding implications. In 2006, Elane Huguenin of Elane Photography declined Vanessa Willock's request to photograph and help celebrate a same-sex marriage ceremony between Willock and her partner. Huguenin declined the request because her and her husband's Christian beliefs would not allow them to participate in good conscience.

Even though Willock easily found another photographer for her ceremony, she nevertheless filed a complaint with the Human Rights Commission against Elane Photography. The case eventually rose to the New Mexico Supreme Court. On August 22, 2013, the high court ruled against Elane Photography and concluded that the Huguenins "now are compelled by law to compromise the very religious beliefs that inspire their lives," adding "it is the price of citizenship."[208] This was despite the fact that same-sex marriage was not even legal in New Mexico at the time.

It is important to recognize that a wedding photographer is not merely an impartial observer, but rather a cocelebrant in a wedding ceremony. Can the state really force people to celebrate something they believe is wrong? Senior Defense Counsel Jordan Lorence lamented, "The idea that free people can be 'compelled by law to compromise the very religious beliefs that inspire their lives' as the 'price of citizenship' is a chilling and unprecedented attack on freedom," and "Americans are now on notice that the price of doing business is their freedom."[209]

The judge's decision basically boils down to saying, "You are free to believe whatever you like in your private life, as long as it doesn't affect how you live in the real world." The government is quite literally forcing Christian business owners to either celebrate a sin that the Bible teaches leads to hell (1 Cor. 6:9) or go out of business. The legal precedent set by this case lays the legal groundwork for further persecution. Like with the first-century Christians who were commanded to bow down to the Roman Caesar as god or be crucified, homosexuality is the foil to legally marginalize true, Bible-believing Christians. These developments should not surprise students of biblical prophecy.

Jesus prophesied that just prior to His return, "Shall many be offended, and shall betray one another, and shall hate one another" (Matt. 24:10). The KJV translators rendered the Greek word *skandalizō* as "offended," whereas the English Standard Version translates it as "fall away." Both are correct as far as they go, but the complete meaning likely incorporates both: "to cause to stumble, to give offense."[210] In the American church, the issue of homosexuality, more than any other, is the stumbling block that offends and leads to hatred of those who remain faithful to the Word of God. One should expect to see many more cases like the Huguenins and increasingly punitive verdicts. The liberal church is leading the charge.

The so-called Christianity of the emergents and theological liberals is one and the same as pantheistic monism of Eastern religions known as *oneism*. The defining issue is the creature/creator distinction from exegesis of: "Who exchanged the truth of God for a lie, and worshipped and served the creature more than the Creator, who is blessed forever. Amen" (Rom. 1:25). Notice that the text juxtaposes "the lie" with "the Creator."[211] The lie is oneism that "all is one." Androgyny and homosexuality flow naturally from this spiritual system, as explained in Romans chapter 1.

Biblical scholar Peter Jones explains, "The open practice and approval of homosexuality is precisely what Paul affirmed two thousand years ago—that homosexuality flows directly from the One-ist worship of creation."[212] The following bullet points are quoted directly from Dr. Jones' seminal work *One or Two: Seeing a World of Difference* (essential reading for a twenty-first century believer):

- In ancient Canaanite religions, effeminate priests served the goddesses Anat, Cybele and Rhea;
- In the Roman Empire, androgynous priests castrated themselves publicly as an act of devotion to the Great Mother;
- In Hinduism, anyone who unifies the sexes in sexual practice has reached the highest self-identity;
- In the Medieval West, Alchemists who transformed heterosexual energy into androgyny produced spiritual "gold" ("a

tremendously deepened sense of the oneness of all....beyond gender differences");

- The pagan spiritualist Jacob Böhme (1575–1624) believed the ideal human state was androgyny;
- In ancient Aztec and Inca religions, homosexual and bisexual priests were common; in American Indian religious practice, homosexual transvestite males are its shamans;
- In Latin America and the Caribbean Islands, homosexuals were magicians with supernatural powers; frequenting gay temple prostitutes was a means of sanctification;
- Jewish Kabbalah celebrates the ideal of the first cosmic androgyne, and in its modern form, is committed to "global, spiritual oneness."[213]

Thus, one should not find it so surprising that the nominal church has embraced homosexual behavior. They are primed for absorption into the great harlot one-world religion, "with whom the kings of the earth have committed fornication, and the inhabitants of the earth have been made drunk with the wine of her fornication" (Rev. 17:2). Those who dissent are already called "bigots" and "enemies of progress." Even so, all true followers of Jesus, while loving their neighbors, must stand on truth no matter the consequences. The context of pagan Rome in the book of Romans has come full circle, and the end-time believer will eventually find himself or herself in the same predicament: martyrdom or compromise.

10

WHEN ANTICHRIST REVEALS HIMSELF IN AMERICA, WILL WE RECOGNIZE HIM?[214]

By Douglas W. Krieger and S. Douglas Woodward

To the surprise and the dismay of most Christians, it is probable that no repellent political figure in modern times ever professed faith in Christianity more than Adolf Hitler. No public official ever championed the separation of church and state more fervently than the Führer. And it is unlikely that any religious leader promoted putting faith into action with more exuberance than the leader of the National Socialist Party. Consider a small sample of Hitler's words:

This "Winter Help Work" [a social "outreach" program] is also in the deepest sense a Christian work. When I see, as I so often do, poorly clad girls collecting with such infinite patience in order to care for those who are suffering from the cold while they themselves are shivering with cold, then I have the feeling that they are all apostles of a Christianity—and in truth of a Christianity which can say with greater right than any other: this is the Christianity of an honest confession, for behind it stand not words but deeds.[215]

Luther's cover to the 1543 edition,
The Jews and Their Lies

For these substantive reasons and many more (not always so warmly swaddled in biblical ideals), the German Catholic as well as the "evangelical" church *failed to discern a glaring and provocative manifestation of Antichrist in their midst*. The best and the brightest, the priests and the theologians, all were caught up in the rush to support the cause of National Socialism. German leaders, both spiritual and political, stood side by side to bring the Fatherland back from the brink. And Adolf Hitler inspired them to come together for the common cause.

Certainly, more than "mass psychology" was influencing 1930s Germany.[216] Christian intellectuals, from the middle ranks to the upper echelons, professed faith in the Führer. In hindsight, we could be justifiably aghast about how the experts wholly missed the most obvious incarnation of the Antichrist since brutal, first-century Roman emperors fed thousands of Christians to the lions.[217] How, pray tell, could this happen?

Indeed, this particular "mystery of iniquity" (2 Thess. 2:7) astonishes us because Hitler not only convinced the hungry and unemployed masses, he gained the favor of the theologically sophisticated. Despite his outspoken rancor and the suspected occultism amongst him and his accomplices, opposition from the church never materialized in any meaningful way until almost the war's end. Hitler promoted what Germans wanted to hear—*that God was on their side.* He provoked patriotism by calls to revere the old ways. He assured the nation that the disgrace of losing "the Great War" (World War I) had nothing to do with the Kaiser's blatant imperialism. And despite outrageous anti-Semitism, Adolf Hitler was hailed as "God's man of the hour." The servants of God were simply clueless in detecting the malevolent motivating force behind Adolf Hitler. *Discernment disappeared from the church.*

Behold the uniqueness of Adolf Hitler! With contagious conviction, he voiced what the German soul could be in its manifold creative genius! His carefully orchestrated words disclosed complete commitment and utter brilliance as a leader of the people. With rapturous expressions, he invigorated a dejected Germany. He guided the rediscovery of its powerful but pagan roots, illuminating who they were and what they could become, with Almighty God guiding their steps (he saw no conflict between Odin— the Scandinavian king of gods—and Jehovah!) Hitler injected into nearly every German heart a divine imprimatur, which justified an inferno of destruction and death unmatched in human history. Its pristine message created a new Reich of *das volk,* a people destined by the triumph of their collective will to become the consummation and commencement of the kingdom of God—*das thousande jahre Reich* (the millennial reign, a one-thousand-year kingdom initiated in the German spirit of Charlemagne, the emperor of the First Reich, the Holy Roman Empire inaugurated at Christmas, AD 800).[218]

This infamous would-be Kaiser/Caesar/Antichrist arose in Germany over a ten-year time frame, from the end of 1924 until he became chancellor in March 1933, and soon thereafter, becoming the supreme leader—having combined the offices of president and chancellor into "führer and reichskanzler" upon the death of President Paul von Hindenburg.

There were those, however, who possessed the ability to discern the real meaning of National Socialism. They possessed the necessary time and skill to analyze the political, social, and spiritual events leading up to the Nazi takeover. But they steadfastly refused to respond to their better judgment. No doubt their failure in part stemmed from a latent (and all-too-often blatant) anti-Semitism widespread amongst the German population, arguably stimulated by Martin Luther's strong anti-Semitic perspectives.[219] Nevertheless, even the dramatic incidents of hate expressed toward Jews (one thinks of *Kristallnacht, Crystal Night* or *the Night of the Broken Glass,* November 9–10, 1938) failed to supply the spiritually astute with insight into what was going to happen. The appeal of Hitler satisfied a number of concerns related to national pride, providing simple answers to very complex questions, promising economic rebirth to a nation dead in its fiscal tracks, and the rehashing of the nation's favorite Teutonic folk myths stirring the soul of its people.

Gott Mit Uns: "God with Us"

We don't have space to concern ourselves with *all* the causes for the *apokalypsis* of Antichrist in Germany.[220] Instead, we will focus on the spiritually based sentiments Hitler explicitly expressed, promising that his ideology and his government supported the Christian faith—that there was no conflict between National Socialism and Christianity. It was this relationship—an overtly rank expression of "religio-political apostasy"— that so disturbs us. From his countless statements made directly to Christian audiences, we will learn why Adolf Hitler was so extremely dangerous. Surprisingly (we think you will agree ours is not the standard interpretation), it was not because he could scheme so treacherously. To the contrary, the key to Hitler's sleight-of-hand was due to his own self-delusion: He possessed unwavering faith that his was a righteous calling from God above—wrought by "providence."

Our point in this piece: Beware! Similar circumstances are present in our land today. Americans must be on guard—especially at this most portentous time—with depressed economic conditions, a high unemployment rate, and smooth-talking politicians long on promises and short on accomplishments. Our vigilance cannot be dulled even by the most sincere-sounding statements of faith and vision from prominent public figures. Our observations must be focused not on just what is said, but on what is being done. A superficial assessment will not suffice. We must consider all the evidence carefully and draw conclusions in pious contemplation. The church (both liberal and conservative) is poised to fail miserably in recognizing who the real enemy is.

Our concern boils down to this poignant question: *If Antichrist were to be revealed in America, would the faithful recognize him?* Would Americans committed to spiritual values miss the same clues disclosing Antichrist's true nature as did the Germans with Hitler?

Reichskirche Flag

There is little doubt that if a figure paraded himself in front of the American people resembling an easily stereotyped leader of the Third Reich—with a mousy moustache, an armband with a hypnotic logo, and wearing a brown shirt—his character and agenda would be obvious to almost everyone. Mounting the podium with an emotional appeal to our national loyalty, the adamant display of venom and vitriol against the enemies of the state, the promise of the restoration of our American "empire" through a continuing buildup of military might, the stark name-calling identifying an appropriate scapegoat to fault for our problems—all of these factors would, at best, betray a would-be Antichrist figure as a false messiah—or at worst, spotlight an artless actor who undoubtedly took us for fools.

We can be certain the *apocalypse* of (that is, the *revealing* of) Antichrist in America, an event we believe will transpire in the years just ahead, will be a one-of-a-kind challenge requiring spiritual discernment worthy of only the most circumspect and attuned "code breakers" whose specialty is exposing wolves in sheep's clothing. We call the church to take up this mission. We believe the church of Jesus Christ, the true church that understands the authentic meaning of Jesus' message, the coming of the kingdom of God, stands as the last line of defense.

Orchestrating the Madding Crowd

Remember, Hitler achieved a meteoric rise to prominence and power because he understood the soul of his people. He could relate. He knew what made them tick. He realized how to couch his message in the context of the political situation and how to engage those who would be but mere spectators by relating to their financial pain and anxiety over the future. Hitler understood crowd psychology and how to manipulate it. To mesmerize his audience, he utilized the power of emphatic facial expressions and energetic hand gestures. He compelled unquestioning allegiance by conveying solutions plainly and confidently no matter how oversimplified or extreme his answers might be. In fact, the more oversimplified and uncompromising his solutions were, the better to persuade the people of their usefulness. His greatest weapon was that "wretched Treaty of Versailles" and its national humiliation—its guilt-ridden condemnation upon the German people, coupled with horrific war reparations heaped upon the German people (which capitalists in America were only too happy to finance).

What is the lesson for us? If the Antichrist were to arise in America at this moment, we would be foolish to expect him to be anything but a consummate American. He would look like us. He would talk like us. He would think—for the most part—like us. And with a straight face he might even assert a profession of Christian faith, and why he believes the teaching of Jesus Christ is so well suited for society. Following Adolf Hitler's lead, he would appeal to the most devout class of Christian, the evangelical. He would offer opportunities to bring biblically based believers "out front"—to escape the shadows of social disdain and distance themselves from the hackneyed portrait showcased by the media and affirmed by the intelligentsia, supposing that those who call themselves evangelical are intellectually bankrupt. He would convince Bible-believing conservatives that they should no longer see themselves as simple *plebeians* (common folk). Their self-image should be elevated so they regard their value no less in status than the progressive patricians of sophisticated national institutions.[221] Not that he would identify himself with the elite or propose that the common man should be ashamed of his laborer status. Rather, he would argue that he remains a man "of the people," yet holds himself sufficiently apart to sanctify his status as our formidable if not *fearless* leader.

This positioning reflects the example of Herr Hitler in many respects. Likewise, the tone and substance coming from the mouth of the Führer, although etched in the *zeitgeist* of that age, begs for comparison to what we hear today from select political leaders promoting the American version of the New World Order,[222] especially those who were, are, or would be our president. Consider for a moment: Might it not be a factor in the false Christ's persuasiveness—the fact that he could deceive, if possible, even the elect? (Matt. 24:24).

The sham to fool evangelicals will make use of more than patronizing remarks. It will turn the words of our most popular preachers against us. The ideology that should prohibit the arising of Antichrist—the Christian religion and its worldview—will be a powerful tool co-opted to capture the "believing" masses and to encourage through a moral veneer and political resolution an agenda resonating within the heart of the "folks" in these United States. Indeed, the future philosophy of Antichrist will convince us that we should resolve to be nothing less than what *our most prominent spiritual leaders teach us to be—successful, healthy, and committed to classic American ideals* (although our most noble notions of individual liberty, *a la* Henry David Thoreau and Thomas Jefferson, have long since quietly departed for destinations unknown).

In like manner, Antichrist would deftly implore citizens to follow his lead. He would criticize Christians for their failure to follow the most "positive" aspects of our faith. Indeed, it would be similar to Hitler's "positive Christianity"—a Christianity that is proactive, expressed in "unselfish service" to others, characteristic of true Americans.

He would call us to be the best Americans we can be—a worthy aspiration for the greater good of all Americans. The health of our nation, he would argue, depends upon living productive lives that contribute to economic prosperity for all. Morality, like ethics, should be shaped to improve our communities in light of standards established by the majority. Religion, true religion, will instill these values. It will not conflict with political objectives because *positive* faith goes hand in hand with constructive political ideology. The manifesto of "the public good" will brand any substantial opposition worthy of elimination. True believers will be activists—but for causes that conform to the will of the many—all the better to reflect his "image," with "great signs and wonders" to deceive (Matt. 24:24).

The Cross and the Swastika

On the surface, the nature of these ideals will seem consistent with the Bible. After all, who would argue that the spiritually inclined should be unproductive, immoral, unethical, a burden on the public's well being, and incapable of contributing to the community's economic health? And yet, upon a more cautious objective inspection, there will emerge a thin but distinctive line between a laudable social compact (built upon beneficial principles for both the individual and the nation) and an overreaching "state" that demands unquestioned obedience (aka *cooperation*)—commanding allegiance above all other causes no matter how worthy. One thinks of the pro-life stance denying women the right to choose. American society has chosen pro-abortion. There are more than fifty million dead Americans who never made it outside the womb to gain some semblance of civil rights. Those who point out this sorry fact are liable to be labeled "social dissidents."

Moreover, the challenge to discern the agenda of the Antichrist will be difficult for many reasons, not just intellectual. Social pressure to conform will be "maxed out." The path to achieve clarity will be a lonely one, for our peers will be only too ready to encourage complicity. Any complaint and disparagement will be interpreted as unpatriotic, a threat to social order, and harmful not only to our own health, but to those we love and care about. An "untoward behavior" will be viewed as "self-alienation," first frowned upon and then doggedly condemned, since it fails to benefit "the many." One's consciousness-raising must be done in stealth so as not to draw attention to an expressed awareness that the enemy of Christ speaks profanely in our presence. It would not be easy to resist even if we were to come to the realization that we have been asked to serve Antichrist. *Our peers will plead with us not to rock the boat, not to question falling in line, not to label the state as anything but what is best for one and all.* To be "the best Christian one can be" will appear synonymous with being the perfect US citizen. Fear will lead families to betray one another: Brother will betray brother, and children will betray their parents—all in the name of doing what is "for the common good of all." The words of Jesus from the Gospel of Matthew must be seen for what they really are: a sign of His soon coming.

And the brother shall deliver up the brother to death, and the father the child; and the children shall rise up against their parents, and cause them to be put to death.

And ye shall be hated of all men for my name's sake, but he that endureth to the end shall be saved. (Matt. 10:21–22)

Needing to recognize political and religious rhetoric as a potential harbinger of the evil one to come, study the words of Hitler below. He seems most open-minded. Consider just how difficult it will be to discern the voice of Antichrist when it reverberates in America:

We demand liberty for all religious denominations in the State, so far as they are not a danger to it and do not militate against the morality and moral sense of the German race. The Party, as such, stands for positive Christianity, but does not bind itself in the matter of creed to any particular confession.[223]

The National Government regards the two Christian Confessions as the weightiest factors for the maintenance of our nationality. They will respect the agreements concluded between them and the federal States. Their rights are not to be infringed… It will be the Government's care to maintain honest co-operation between Church and State; the struggle against materialistic views and for a real national community is just as much in the interest of the German nation as in that of the welfare of our Christian faith. The Government of the Reich, who regard Christianity as the unshakable foundation of the morals and moral code of the nation, attach the greatest value to friendly relations with the Holy See and are endeavoring to develop them.[224]

The partnership of church and state constructed by Hitler was remarkable in many ways, for he appealed to Christians' proclivity to self-righteous aspiration, beguiling them through awarding accreditation as possessors of the very "moral soul" of the nation. To enhance his appeal, *he vowed that without a Christian moral foundation, there would be no German morality.* In light of this, the reader of the Gospels can stop wondering why Jesus (in Matt. 24) was so repetitious regarding "deception and being deceived," "false prophets and false messiahs," and the like in reference to the "state of society" at the end of the age.

At the time, Hitler's audience was Catholic, but his announcement of the Concordat with Rome (the papal agreement, July 5, 1933) had meaning to Protestants as well. The message was obvious and clear: Friendly relations—relations that are inclusive of the church—must be the norm in a resurgent Germany. "The fact that the Vatican is concluding a treaty with the new Germany means the acknowledgement of the National Socialist state by the Catholic Church. This treaty shows the whole world clearly and unequivocally that the assertion that National Socialism [Nazism] is hostile to religion is a lie."[225]

Hitler was even more effusive about the value of Nazism to benefit the church:

While we destroyed the Center Party [a Catholic political party[226]], we have not only brought thousands of priests back into the Church, but to millions of respectable people we have restored their faith in their religion and in their priests. The union of the Evangelical Church in a single Church for the whole Reich, the Concordat with the Catholic Church, these are but milestones on the road, which leads to the establishment of a useful relation and a useful co-operation between the Reich and the two Confessions.[227]

The Division of Labor in the Third Reich

Furthermore, it was essential *to separate the realms of personal faith from political action.* Hitler's "spheres of function" were altogether essential insofar as the church's dominion was concerned, for without the spiritual health of Germany, there would be no political health. But he also took a hard line to distinguish their responsibilities: The church was to look after the spiritual and moral health of the flock—the state would tend to its material need:

> The German Church and the People are practically the same body. Therefore there could be no issue between Church and State. The Church, as such, has nothing to do with political affairs. On the other hand, the State has nothing to do with the faith or inner organization of the Church.[228]

> The National Socialist State professes its allegiance to positive Christianity. It will be its honest endeavor to protect both the great Christian Confessions in their rights, to secure them from interference with their doctrines (Lehren), and in their duties to constitute a harmony with the views and the exigencies of the State of today.[229]

> So long as they concern themselves with their religious problems the State does not concern itself with them. But so soon as they attempt by any means whatsoever—by letters, Encyclical, or otherwise—to arrogate to themselves rights which belong to the State alone we shall force them back into their proper spiritual, pastoral activity.[230]

In other words, both church and state must reassure its denizens the institution exists to provide for their well-being. But it is, from Hitler's perspective, necessary that they split duties. Keep the church's message personal and positive while the state should keep on its message of economic welfare for all. And of course, the supremacy of the state must be upheld. It was never to be questioned. The state dictated the role of the church. Furthermore, it mandated that any criticism of the state would not be tolerated.

Moreover, upon close inspection, Hitler would "gerrymander" the territory of the state whenever it suited him. Some theological modifications would be necessary. In a Germany liberated from the "old-fashioned" faith, the church should dismiss any talk of humankind's sinful inclinations and its need for repentance. *Evil must be mitigated—more specifically, downgraded—and reduced in substance to "mistakes" and not the more menacing notion of sin.* Defects in human behavior amount to little more than "poor choices." Thus, with sin redefined and evil eliminated as a "metaphysical reality,"[231] the gospel was compromised and the church complicit. It could then pray reverently with the Führer:

> We want honestly to earn the resurrection of our people through our industry, our perseverance, and our will. We ask not of the Almighty, "Lord, make us free!"—we want to be active, to work, to agree together as brothers, to strive in rivalry with one another to bring about the hour when we can come before Him and when we may ask of Him: "Lord, Thou seest that we have transformed ourselves, the German people is no longer the people of dishonor, of shame, of war within itself, of faintheartedness and little faith: no, Lord, the German people has become strong again in spirit, strong in will, strong in endurance, strong to bear all sacrifices."

"Lord, we will not let Thee go: bless now our fight for our free-dom; the fight we wage for our German people and Fatherland."[232]

Furthermore, while the Führer did not directly confront Christian sensibilities, his prayer led one to conjecture as to what "positive Christianity" involved, and exactly what its opposite—"negative Christianity"—would entail. No doubt his listeners let the matter drop without questioning the meaning behind his exhortation for accentuating a "positive Christianity." In contradistinction, like observing a lit firecracker failing to pop, we should be very alarmed when such a loaded phrase lies dormant for too long. Observers must be asleep if they have no apprehension about when the firecracker *will* detonate.

To the wary spectator, Hitler's statement anticipated a pause "for the other shoe to drop." And yet, assuming nothing but good intent from the Führer, the audience did not worry one iota that another shoe would hit the floor (or worse, that the fecal matter would collide with the oscillating rotor!). Instead, they were enraptured by Hitler's acclamation:

MY LORD AND SAVIOR...IN THE BOUNDLESS LOVE AS A CHRISTIAN...HE HAD TO SHED HIS BLOOD UPON THE CROSS. My feelings as a Christian point me to my Lord and Savior as a fighter. It points me to the man who once in loneliness, surrounded only by a few followers, recognized these Jews for what they were and summoned men to fight against them [Peter should take up his sword, rather than put it away]. This is God's truth! He was greatest not as a sufferer but as a fighter. In boundless love as a Christian and as a man I read through the passage which tells us how the Lord at last rose in His might and seized the scourge to drive out of the Temple the brood of vipers and adders. How terrific was His fight for the world against the Jewish poison. Today, after two thousand years, with deepest emotion I recognize more profoundly than ever before in the fact that it was for this that He had to shed His blood upon the Cross. As a Christian I have no duty to allow myself to be cheated, but I have the duty to be a fighter for truth and justice.[233] (emphasis added)

The notion that the Messiah was himself NOT Jewish was a view propounded by Richard Wagner, the famous German composer whose operas were expressions of the nineteenth-century German *zeitgeist* (the "spirit of the age"). Unquestionably, Hitler's favorite composer, Wagner, stirred Hitler's soul to envision a revived, irrepressible, and vengeful Germany. During World War II, Wagner's legacy lived on as his music filled the putrefied air of Holocaust death camps. As a result, survivors would forever associate Wagner with Auschwitz. This was no disservice to Wagner—for he believed that Christ was Aryan, not Jewish. And like Friedrich Nietzsche, the "Philosopher Emeritus" of the German people (a good friend of Wagner until their falling out), he believed the German soul must not be dragged down by the "slave mentality" of the Jew. Consequently, it logically followed that Jesus could never be considered a Jew. To the aspiring German mindset, the Jews were a millstone about their necks. The Hebrew religion bestowed nothing but restrictive laws and depressive guilt. It was time for Germany to cast aside the Jewish mentality and its stifling effect upon the soul of humankind, but especially their Aryan race!

As to Nietzsche, he famously asserted a philosophy known as *the will to power.* To the extent Jesus allowed Himself to be crucified, *to that same extent Jesus was Himself the anti-Christ.* For Nietzsche, Jesus' commitment to die for the sin of the world was nothing but a *death wish* to be condemned and repudiated. For him, Jesus' willingness to lay down His life remains the source of so much nonsense contaminating the true purpose for religion. Instead, a "true confession" encourages struggle! *(Mein Kampf,* of course, means "My Struggle.") For Nietzsche, suffering saves no one. Moreover, this must be the stalwart creed of all true believers. The gospel of Wagner, Nietzsche, and especially Adolf Hitler held in common a disdain for the Jew.

The duty to be a fighter for truth, justice, (and the German way) comprises, of course, the motto of Superman, the quintessential American superhero. Indeed, less feted translators often seek to convey the meaning of Nietzsche's *Übermensch* with the expression "superman." However oversimplified this one-word translation (especially vulgar to the sophisticated), nonetheless, it likewise urges those loyal to Old Glory— the red, white, and blue—to stand and be counted! America boasts the greatest military ever assembled. Any concept of redemptive suffering preached from the Bible by ignoble vicars of Christ surely misses the mark. Turning the other cheek (Matt. 5:39) cannot be what Christ actually meant. "Fight back! Don't get mad—get even!" Of course, the German people in the 1920s and 1930s were a frustrated, defeated people, wearing anger on their sleeves right below their swastikas.

Americans do not feel compelled to take such overt military action. Discretion is the better part of valor. We much prefer to keep our battles on the "down low," equipping our intelligence services to act covertly (witness the 2013 conflict regarding the National Security Agency's mining of private phone and Internet data, spying on multiple foreign [friendly] governments, accessing and cataloguing private data of one hundred million Americans, as well as the intrusive behavior of the Treasury Department's Internal Revenue Service), requiring our special forces to operate in darkness, and necessitating US sorties of the aeronautical kind be carried out in stealth mode. As the military is wont to say, "We own the night." Unlike the saints to whom Paul addressed his letters, one could argue (and Woodward has in his books, *Power Quest—Books One and Two*), that in the last one hundred years, the US government has seldom sought to be mistaken for *children of the day*.

Hating in the Name of Christ and Country

The unity of the church was important to Hitler. He could not consummate his grand plan without the support of the church. He required his backside be covered. Consequently, it was crucial that disputes in the church be silenced, if for no other reason than to keep quarrels from bubbling over into matters of state and distracting the populace from the bellicose but sacred duty before them.

> It will at any rate be my supreme task to see to it that in the newly awakened NSDAP [Nazi Party], the adherents of both Confessions can live peacefully together side by side in order that they may take their stand in the common fight against the power, which is the mortal foe of any true Christianity [as Hitler would define it].[234]

> This is for us a ground for satisfaction, since we desire that the fight in the religious camps should come to an end…all political action in the parties will be forbidden to priests for all time, happy

because we know what is wanted by millions who long *to see in the priest only the comforter of their souls and not the representative of their political convictions.*[235] (emphasis added)

Furthermore, Hitler required that the church's energy contribute to the Fatherland's *fighting spirit*. Christ must not be seen as the Prince of Peace. Religious fires must burn brightly on his (Hitler's) behalf.

So far as the Evangelical Confessions are concerned, we are determined to put an end to existing divisions, which are concerned only with the forms of organization, and to create a single Evangelical Church for the whole Reich… And we know that were the great German reformer [Martin Luther] with us today he would rejoice to be freed from the necessity of his own time and, like Ulrich von Hutten [1488–1523, an outspoken German scholar, poet, and reformer], his last prayer would be not for the Churches of the separate States: *it would be of Germany* that he would think…and of the Evangelical Church of Germany [Hitler loved putting words in the mouth of Martin Luther].[236]

After all, to Hitler, the real enemy was the "international Jew." Christianity must unite, Catholics and Protestants, laity and priesthood—"against the power"—i.e., the international Jewish conspiracy that, he argued, warred against the church of Jesus Christ and the German people. Not that this tactic was especially risky. His approach was tried and true: Unite around a well-defined, mutual foe. Foment hatred against the scapegoat. Exaggerate images to make plain their villainous ways. Build the faithful into the "hammer of God"—make it an instrument of *righteous indignation!*

Impulse for a New Christian Ecumenism?

In comparison, today's political leadership in America and Europe has it somewhat easy; *it does not need to manufacture a fanatical enemy.* RADICAL Islam has served itself up as the despicable lunatic fringe fighting against Christendom and the state. The political leadership message must be made plain to the public: The radical Muslims are not at war not with the actions of the American government; they hate us because of our "way of life." Their enmity is personally directed at Americans. It could not be due to protectionism of American corporations supervised by the political system and safeguarded by the military. It could not be because we have military bases in their land. Nor could it be because we have helped ourselves to their petroleum. The words of our politicians insist that it is our sacred values of freedom and faith in the Bible of both Old and New Testaments. From the speeches of our governing leaders, their disdain for *Americana*[237] is the primary reason Islam hates Americans. Islam views the church's toleration of secular society as an abhorrent mixture of the *sacred and profane*—not so much an expression of political unity, but a compromised expression of religious weakness.

Subsequently, the more Islam frightens the free world, the more its enemies (secular and religious) understandably and justifiably unite. Other than twisting its ulterior motive (making it about the differences in religion as the root cause for animosity),[238] why do we need to create falsehoods about the opposition when of its own accord it provokes with carefully crafted words of hate, carries out cowardly acts of terror, and callously celebrates death when it completes its missions of murder? Radical Islam deserves disdain. Their terrorist acts are deplorable. Still, there are some legitimate reasons why they hate the United States.

Notwithstanding the subtleties in analyzing the causes for Islamic hatred of the USA, the pathway to co-opt the church in America today first requires the encouragement of unity within the varied hallowed institutions, then secondly, aligning them according to the preferred political agenda. The broad strategy for managing religious institutions has not changed all that much over the past eighty years—although selected tactics do differ.

So what is the method to achieve an ecumenical union? It involves reconstructing the Christian message. Building unity in the contemporary church comprises a modern-day equivalent to building the tower of Babel. *The most relevant message, what will really bring us together as one, requires the church to substitute the content of the gospel with a message of confusion, which is what "Babel" means.* How can this be accomplished? By creating confusion over *the nature of good and evil.* We could say that reaching new heights in cooperation with other beliefs and faiths is not based upon clear communication and seeing things eye to eye. *It is about not seeing things at all.* "Coming together" necessitates closing one's eyes to *see no evil, hear no evil,* and *speak no evil.* The less said the better. We must dispense with controversial matters, uniting against intolerance, epitomized in militant Islam. We can do no less. Indeed, regarding traditional Judeo-Christian values, the nature of sin, and the reality of evil in particular, stand out like sore thumbs. Therefore, church leadership in its aspiration seeks to be mainstream. Americans must paper over the notion of sin and evil with platitudes of self-improvement, overcoming self-doubt, as well as proclaiming health and wealth to magically make their congregations (and especially them) wealthy. In today's evangelical church, it is most certainly about expressing a positive Christianity! Hitler would feel especially vindicated if he attended the typical mega church and listened to the sermons there.[239] Christianity has been effectively shorn of biblical discernment and blinded to the reality of evil as it presents itself in our world today.

Diminishing doctrine as an essential element in "confessional Christianity" is hardly new. Liberal Christian churches dispensed with meaningful theological content decades ago. They embraced a social gospel, replete with platitudes of pluralism, while promoting the practice of social good works, unwittingly leading to greater government intervention and involvement in the church. When American theologians sentenced God to death in the 1960s, they simultaneously (albeit unwittingly) assigned their own ecclesiastical institutions to death row. Fifty years ago, they reduced the gospel to what was left over after so-called science ravaged the Bible. Theology became nothing more than existential philosophy. The meaning of being a Christian amounted to repeating holy words in ritual ceremonies. It did not matter how far out (i.e., how "supernatural") the notions of the original creeds or "Psalters" were. *Theology became applied psychology.* It was reconstructed to be a frame of mind or, better yet, a mental state. Once the creeds had been ransacked of all calls to spiritual transformation and relieved of all genuine miracles recorded in the Bible, what remained was Friedrich Schleiermacher's "feeling of absolute dependence," Paul Tillich's ruminations about God as the "ground of being," or Karl Jaspers' yearning for an "ultimate experience." Consequently, today's mainstream churches are now so emaciated it is a wonder they have not already given up the ghost.

In contrast, today's evangelical churches (that proclaim that oh-so-positive message) swarm with "believers." But the question is, "What do they believe in?" To be sure, there are many assemblies of faithful, believing Christians who keep science in its place and rightly esteem spiritual reality; who regard the Bible as God's Word; and rely upon the Spirit of Christ to be an ever-present reality in their daily lives not so much as an emotional impulse stimulating a mystical faith, but as an enabling power to conquer the challenging circumstances of everyday life. On the other hand, as we contend, the most well-known churches appear guilty of depriving their congregations of meaningful content—biblically based content. It is almost as if the gospel so successfully preached there today is derived from aphorisms in *Poor Richard's Almanac:* "Early to bed and early to rise makes a man healthy, wealthy, and wise." Or to misquote a famous mega-church preacher: "It IS about you!" Or worse yet, the evangelical message transforms spirituality into a transaction: You do "x" and God does "y." "Give and it shall be given to you"—*not out of need but out of greed.* God *guarantees* our destiny to be healthy, wealthy, and wise (although the last item in this threesome is not always requested). At issue is only whether you count yourself entitled to merchandise from the heavenly commissary, stocked wall to wall to assure your material needs are met in full.

Betraying the Meaning of the Kingdom of God

After the death of Pope Pius XI in 1939, the electoral procedure to seat another pope began. The election favored Eugenio Pacelli (1876–1958), and four days later, Pacelli made it clear that he would handle all German affairs personally. He proposed the following to Hitler:

> To the Illustrious Herr Adolf Hitler, Führer and Chancellor of the German Reich! Here at the beginning of our Pontificate, we wish to assure you that we remain devoted to the spiritual welfare of the German people entrusted to your leadership.… During the many years we spent in Germany, we did all in our power to establish harmonious relations between Church and State. Now that the responsibilities of our pastoral function have increased our oppor-

tunities, how much more ardently do we pray to reach that goal. May the prosperity of the German people and their progress in every domain come, with God's elp, to fruition![240]

The Pope's Nuncio, Archbishop Orsenigo

Pacelli was crowned pope on March 12, 1939 (becoming Pius XII). The following month, on April 20, 1939, at Pius XII's expressed wish, Archbishop Orsenigo, the nuncio (ambassador) in Berlin, opened a gala reception for Hitler's fiftieth birthday. The birthday greetings thus initiated by Pacelli immediately became a tradition: Each April 20 during the few years left to Hitler and his Reich, Cardinal Bertram of Berlin would send "warmest congratulations to the Führer in the name of the bishops and the dioceses in Germany," to which he added "fervent prayers which the Catholics in Germany are sending to heaven on their altars."[241] *The walls of the kingdom of God were thoroughly breached. The homogenization of church and state was complete.*

In the context of today's mega church, we must ask, "What does the kingdom of God mean?" It is a most unwelcomed question, since many of our ministers and theologians in America do not proclaim a "coming kingdom"—such a prophetic assertion implies a negative message. If the kingdom exists at all, many churches preach it is up to us to "take dominion" and bring it about ourselves. Like Hitler, we "struggle" (the meaning behind *Mein Kampf*) to make it real. How odd, then, that we who foresee the kingdom to be before us (in the future) to proclaim America could truly be that "City on a Hill" beckoning the "huddled masses" (yearning to be free) to come be a part of our melting pot.

This phrase, "the kingdom of God," was the theme of Jesus' ministry. It was His "call to action"—His byword, His catchphrase. Despite that being so, given what appears to be the *modus operandi* of mega churches, we question whether the coming of the kingdom of God resides at the center of today's preaching. No, the preaching of our most celebrated churches resounds with a different message.

We believe its common creed is rather crass. It is at least as materialistic as it is spiritual. It is about getting the most out of life—or better yet, making the most (money) you can! In fact, one's financial independence indicates your spiritual status. The manner of making your life count is measured in denominations of $20s, $50s, and $100s. Jesus' blunt injunction about deciding between two masters, God and mammon (material prosperity), seems intentionally withdrawn. *God wants you to have all the mammon you can muster!* If the apostles showed up in a mega church today, chances are they would wonder what the message being proclaimed has to do with the faith for which they died. Jesus told His audience (much to their astonishment) that it is virtually impossible for the rich to enter into the kingdom of God. It is easier for a camel to pass through the eye of a needle (Matt. 19:24). The real truth could not have been more out of step with their colloquial tradition. In their day, it was just common sense:

Prosperity meant God's affirmation—if you were rich, you were "in like Flynn." You were as valuable in the kingdom of God as your net worth—and not a penny less. That is why Jesus' message crashed His disciples' worldview like a brick landing on a paper airplane—or, better yet, like a margin call on an over-leveraged portfolio.

Is it any wonder that the topic of prophecy is so taboo in most mega churches today? The true biblical apocalyptic message of Jesus Christ guarantees that private property means next to nothing—the world is passing away! Riches are of no value. Wealth will be consumed in the fire of the last days! "I am come to send fire on the earth; and what will I, if it be already kindled?" (Luke 12:49).

To be sure, Jesus taught many parables based on the priority of keeping one's eyes peeled—the parables of readiness (Matt. 24:32–51 and Matt. 25) resoundingly affirm such a prescient posture: the "wise and foolish virgins," the "sheep and the goats," and the traveling "master of the vineyard" (to name but a few). Nevertheless, His point was consistent (paraphrasing, but only slightly): "Watch! For you know not when the Son of Man cometh" (Matt. 25:13). All too often, those weary of prophetic teaching cite those they deem obsessed with its message for failure to remember what Jesus said: "For you do not know the day or hour of my return…wherein the son of man cometh," as if His words were a concession to the impossibility of living life in light of His charge or as if His intent was granting license to ignore the *temporal* implication in the apocalyptic message, since we cannot tell when it will happen. But that is most assuredly the opposite of what Jesus taught. His words could not have been more plain—or provocative. "The world is ending! Be ready. Do not focus on wealth. Do not sequester treasure for yourself! Do not build bigger barns! Live one day at a time."

Indeed, the strategic plan for kingdom members amounts to

remembering that "you can't take it with you"—so better to share the wealth with your brothers and sisters (not waste it on your every whim!). To quote our Lord in His own words:

> Lay not up for yourselves treasures upon earth, where moth and rust doth corrupt, and where thieves break through and steal:
>
> But lay up for yourselves treasures in heaven, where neither moth nor rust doth corrupt, and where thieves do not break through nor steal:
>
> For where your treasure is, there will your heart be also. (Matt. 6:19–21)

A main point of prophecy and why it is indispensable to the gospel: to keep life and material things in proper perspective.

Justification by the Providence of God

In 1939, Adolf Hitler summarized why he was so confident that the Third Reich was imminent: "The National Socialist Movement has wrought this miracle. If Almighty God granted success to this work, then the Party was His instrument."[242] In retrospect, the reader would be hard pressed to find a historical leader who levered faith, however skewed, more effectively as a power tool for REALPOLITIK. Hitler was almost unparalleled in the annals of leadership as a champion for the relevance of spiritual belief. He saw man created by God, rewarded for his reliance upon God, and sustained when cooperating with Him on a grand scale. In Hitler, we confront a leader who abandoned all self-consciousness—he was so tightly coupled with his constituency that they became of one mind. Yes, he learned the craft of public speaking like few others—maybe better than anyone. But we are dangerously mistaken if we regard his fervor *as only an act*. NO, he believed in what he was doing. He lost himself in his cause.

He was not tepid in faith, darting hither and thither, equivocating whenever the opportunity afforded itself. To the contrary, the leader of the Third Reich was a champion of conviction that was so "in your face" it was contagious. If faith wavered, Hitler reinstated it, bolstering public confidence in his program for a new Germany. His power hinged on claiming that a brilliant destiny lay at Germany's feet. God's providence guaranteed success. In every darkened pathway, he claimed God would enlighten the path and keep National Socialism on track because it fulfilled the Almighty's plan. Hitler pleaded it, believed in it, and "owned" what he stridently confessed. All doubt concerning Germany's mission fled from his presence, because, as far as he was concerned, God mandated that the German people be ultimately victorious. History would demonstrate divine preference. God would honor Hitler's unfeigned devotion to his people. Listen to his confident faith:

In this hour I would ask of the Lord God only this: that, as in the past, so in the years to come He would give His blessing to our work and our action, to our judgment and our resolution, that He will safeguard us from all false pride and from all cowardly servility, that He may grant us to find the straight path which His Providence has ordained for the German people, and that He may ever give us the courage to do the right, never to falter, never to yield before any violence, before any danger…. I am convinced that men who are created by God should live in accordance with the will of the Almighty…. If Providence had not guided us I could often never have found these dizzy paths…. Thus it is that we National Socialists, too, have in the depths of our hearts our faith. We cannot do otherwise; no man can fashion world history or the history of peoples unless upon his purpose and his powers there rests the blessings of this Providence.[243]

In the final analysis, the Antichrist may be dangerous not because he is the best actor ever to mount the world stage or that he will hide insincere intent and cloak satanic motive. He will be exceptionally treacherous because, like Adolf Hitler, he will be utterly convinced that defeat is inconceivable. *Convinced of his invincibility and even more, his infallibility, the deception characterizing the man of lawlessness will be utterly commanding because he is himself deceived, believing that God is evil and Satan good.*

Only so you can appeal to your God and pray Him to support and bless your courage, your work, your perseverance, your strength, your resolution, and with all these your claim on life.[244]

In this world him who does not abandon himself the Almighty will not desert. Him who helps himself will the Almighty always also help; He will show him the way by which he can gain his rights, his freedom, and therefore his future.[245]

Such sentiments cannot be dismissed because they are disingenuous. It would be preposterous to suppose Adolf Hitler was consistently inauthentic. He believed in an "active cooperation" with the divine—his was a form of perseverance strengthened by a Calvinist-like conviction. Echoing the adage of the common man in America—*God helps those who help themselves!* Can we imagine a more *positive* way to express Christian faith? This maxim has almost been synonymous with home-grown American religion.

Perhaps it is to our advantage to listen to the words of Adolf Hitler and believe we must struggle and fight against our enemies. Perhaps we should put ourselves first. *Perhaps we should prioritize worldly riches and personal health, and not the kingdom of God.*

Maybe we would be wise to forget the self-effacing teaching of the Master: "He that findeth his life shall lose it; and he that loseth his life for my sake shall find it" (Matt. 10:39). If so, it would also follow that we should ignore the testimony of the aging apostle Paul, who was tormented by all manner of physical and emotional distress: "Therefore, I take pleasure in infirmities, in reproaches, in necessities, in persecutions, in distresses for Christ's sake; for when I am weak, then am I strong" (2 Cor. 12:10). Or maybe, to follow the logic of the gospel of the mega church, Paul was just depressed in his old age!

NO. If we believed what Paul believed, we would be willing to stand opposed to the state, be willing to sacrifice ourselves in the cause of the old-fashioned faith "once delivered unto the saints" (Jude 3), and find affliction, famine, peril, and suffering as ways to draw close to God and be remade anew from the inside out. Surely that is a confession differing in kind and color. Of this one thing we can rest assured: the Führer would not approve. Dietrich Bonhoeffer talked about this plainly in his call to consecration in *The Cost of Discipleship*. Communion with Christ is manifest best when we participate and share in Christ's sufferings. We draw closest to Him, and He to us, not in our morning Bible reading, not in our most emotional singing of choruses, but in suffering for the cause of Christ. Paul surely must have been thinking of this reality when he said to the church at Rome: "And if children, then heirs—heirs of God, and joint heirs with Christ—if so be that we suffer with him, that we may be also glorified together" (Rom. 8:17).

In closing, may we offer this call to discernment: Beware the false flag operation, the burning of the "Reichstag," the diminution or even elimination of the people's assembly (our Congress), and especially the coming of the imperial leader in the name of heightened security and peace, for we have surely seen this before. Consequently, we are compelled to ask, "Are we awake? Are we vigilant at this moment in time when the stakes have never been higher? Are we prepared to be REAL CHRISTIANS when it means calling our government to question? Do we realize that most 'Christians' will soon be at war against us when we challenge the actions of the state? Are we willing to follow the example of Dietrich Bonhoeffer and stand opposed to the Antichrist, even when he appears as the savior of the state and our way of life?"

"Those who cannot remember the past are condemned to repeat it."
—George Santayana

11

THE FINAL VICTORY

By Terry James

During the darkest days of World War II, it looked for Great Britain as if the forces of Adolf Hitler's evil regime would soon enslave the English people and all of Europe. The war was, in reality—as are all wars—satanic in origin. Lucifer the fallen one stalked about then as he does now, like a roaring lion, seeking whom he may devour (2 Pet. 5:8).

The devourer hasn't changed his desires, tactics, or methodologies. Neither have the fallen minds of humankind swerved from deliberately moving away from God's governance. War still rages, pushing all of this rebellious earth toward Armageddon.

James, Christ's disciple and half brother, put it this way:

From whence come wars and fightings among you? Come they not hence, even of your lusts that war in your members?

Ye lust, and have not; ye kill, and desire to have, and cannot obtain; ye fight and war, yet ye have not, because ye ask not.

Ye ask, and receive not, because ye ask amiss, that ye may consume it upon your lusts.

Ye adulterers and adulteresses, know ye not that the friendship of the world is enmity with God? Whosoever, therefore, will be a friend of the world is the enemy of God. (James 4:1–4)

So, at the very outset, in this examination through this chapter, we identify the root cause of the battle we see going on as given in our book's title: *Blood on the Altar: The Coming War between Christian vs. Christian.*

People within Christianity in these late days of the age have made friendship with the world. There is really no other way to put it. The Laodicean church is alive and well, and growing. And, that is perhaps somewhat of a misstatement, because such "Christianity" isn't alive at all, but spiritually dead and a nauseating spectacle to the God of heaven.

Such deadness isn't static, however. The zombies (in God's holy view) of this dead Christianity, by joining with the Christ-hating world through its acquiescence, are used as soldiers against the cross of Jesus Christ as surely as are the declared agnostics, atheists, and all false religionists.

Just like Great Britain in that darkest hour, when the Nazi Luftwaffe was firebombing to pieces the city of London, and there beat within the hearts of true British patriots the determination to defeat the evil they faced daily and nightly, there must be similar resolve within the true church. British heroes believed Winston Churchill's words that they would one day look back and say this was "England's finest hour." My coauthors have superbly explored and explained the many aspects of what this generation faces in the battle of *Christian vs. Christian.* Particularly, we are concerned with what those who are the genuine Christians of this generation face in this battle to the finish.

Like Churchill intoned about the British patriots caught up in World War II, this time of growing apostasy can be the *true* church's finest hour.

What, then, is a "true" Christian? To be a "true" Christian, one must be a "true" believer in Jesus Christ. One must be *born again:* "Jesus answered and said unto him, Verily, verily, I say unto thee, Except a man be born again, he cannot see the kingdom of God" (John 3:3). The Lord explained to Nicodemus—and to the rest of humanity down through the ages—the meaning of His words.

Jesus said that man is born of water, but he must also be born again of the spirit to ever be able to see or understand God's kingdom. Mankind, all human beings, must be born again into God's kingdom or into His eternal family to ever make it to that eternal state in the presence of God.

All human beings are born lost in sin, and must be redeemed by the shed blood of Jesus Christ. The command in order to be redeemed, thus become part of God's eternal family, is: "Believe": "That if thou shalt confess with thy mouth the Lord Jesus, and shalt believe in thine heart that God hath raised him from the dead, thou shalt be saved. For with the heart man believeth unto righteousness; and with the mouth confession is made unto salvation" (Rom. 10:9–10).

All who are redeemed constitute the church of Jesus Christ, and this is the church we are concerned about in particular. It is this body of true believers that collectively and individually is under assault by the forces of the world, the flesh, and the devil.

The spiritual bombardment by Satan and his minions, both supernatural and human, explodes around us daily. This earth and this nation are battlefields of humankind's longest-running war. The primary general waging that campaign against Christ has been battling far longer, apparently. Lucifer lost the first major battle, and was, along with one-third of God's created angelic hosts, cast out of heaven. His sin rebellion infected all the human race in the Garden of Eden, and the effort to thwart the purposes and plan of God has continued to intensify. It will culminate at Armageddon.

Today's assault on America's traditional culture is the most obvious sign of the bombardment. The authors of the chapters in this book have each addressed in a thoroughly excellent way many of the areas in which Christians confront anti-God attacks. We will examine here a number of collateral developments regarding the luciferian war being waged on Christianity in exploring the struggle during these last days.

Next for America: Corrective Measures or Accumulating Pleasures?

The latter part of the twentieth century brought profound changes to this once more morally anchored nation. Regardless of some of the less savory facts that have been brought out in recent times concerning America's founding, this nation has truly been an experiment in principle based upon biblical precepts.

The year 1963, with Supreme Court decisions determined to try to remove God from public schools, proved to be a pivotal point in the slide toward oblivion that is even now picking up speed. Let's have a brief review of the early part of that stunning century.

My research in writing the book *The American Apocalypse: Is the United States in Bible Prophecy?* (Harvest House, 2009) took me back to

God's harsh dealing with America in the 1930s. The things Americans suffered were considered by preachers and politicians alike to be God's wrath and judgment.

One well-known writer, John Steinbeck, even gave his famous novel on that depressed time in America the title *The Grapes of Wrath*. America had gone through a tremendous time of growth and relative prosperity during the "Gay Nineties." (For the younger readers, it had nothing to do with the Clinton years, nor with homosexuality. It was the 1890s, and the term "gay" still enjoyed its proper definition.)

Despite the early 1900s bringing about World War I, the nation leaped forward, and soon the "Roaring Twenties" brought forth the flappers and boisterous, even debauched, "good times." Reformers tried to squash the hedonism, and with the passage of the 18th Amendment instituted prohibition against alcohol manufacture, sale, and transportation. The action only increased rebellion against morality. American gangsters took over, and illegal booze, gambling, and every other type of nefarious activity permeated culture and society.

Then in 1929 came the stock market crash in the United States, and worldwide depression quickly followed. The wrath of God had fallen!

Or had it?

No, it had not. Neither had His judgment against America's sin fallen upon the nation, thus affecting the world—not in the sense of God's great judgment that came upon the antediluvians, the wicked, violent, even genetically corrupted earth dwellers of Noah's day. But God's mighty hand of correction through the Great Depression and the horrendous "Dust Bowl" era came down hard on the backside of this nation He so manifestly chose to accomplish great things for His great purposes. Those things would include, in particular:

1) **Developing the technologies that would spread the gospel** around the entire world

2) **Acting as midwife for the birth of modern Israel** on May 14, 1948, and becoming the Jewish peoples' closest ally—an ally that just happened to soon become the most materially blessed, most powerful, and most influential nation the world has ever known

America, despite the Great Depression and war that took thousands of young American lives, came to know a standard of living and pleasures—both unsullied and debauched—like no generation of any people in history. The thing to keep in mind is that during all of that degeneration of America and the corrective measures the Lord was employing, Christianity stood firm. The church—the "born again"—faced up to those efforts to totally debauch this United States of America. The Billy Sundays—the great evangelists—were anchors in the pews of the nation, as were a vast number of genuine Christians in the pews across the land. Even a casual perusal of the national landscape of morality today evokes the question: Is there such resistance to evil in these troubling days?

Today, other profoundly disturbing questions to ponder are: Will God choose to again correct this special nation called America? Or, will He take His hand off to an extent, allowing the US to find its own way, which is what the majority of the electorate seems to want?

I get email daily from people who fear this nation will now feel the Lord's hand of wrath. The die is cast, as one of Shakespeare's characters said. I don't necessarily subscribe to that "judgment-and-wrath-are-about-to-fall" opinion, at least not in the immediate near term the way many who send the fear-filled emails believe.

Nonetheless, God's wrath is building. It will be unleashed when the "prince that shall come" confirms the covenant with Israel and Israel's antagonists (Dan. 9:26–27).

That pouring out of God's anger won't happen until the church is removed. However, there is almost certainly a heavenly decision that has already been made, and is even now in the process of implementation. It is likely the decision to either take corrective measures as in God's past dealings with America in order to get this nation back on the moral course to complete its work in His grand prophetic design, or to give rebellious masses what they more and more demonstrate they demand. They demand freedom to choose what is right in their own eyes.

God's decision to take His hand off to some extent would be far more fearful than His again taking corrective action like world economic depression. To let the rebels do what is right in their own eyes, thus casting God away from any semblance of divine guidance, means America's work is done. That is indeed a frightening thing to contemplate.

Much of what happens next is dependent upon the true Christian church—born-again believers. How we choose to confront evil might well determine our nation's—even the world's—immediate fate.

I must say that I, with reverential consideration, don't expect immediate meltdown and correction from Almighty God. I believe with all that is within me that He has been demonstrating corrective movements over the past years and months—movements that have gone unheeded by even the majority of His people. These have chosen to bury their heads in the sands of watered-down messages that have practically no relevance to God's message of doctrinal truth. Rather than revival, there have been false, emotional outbursts that have done disservice to the Lord who purchased each and every one who has been born again. It seems to me that the church's work, like that of America, has almost run its course.

Dave Hunt once wrote a book called *Peace, Prosperity, and the Coming Holocaust.* His basic premise was that this fallen world system, and particularly the United States and even the church, would be drawn ever deeper into believing in humanistic salvation by seeming peace and prosperity. He demonstrated, then, through historical precedent and Bible prophecy both past and yet to come, that the world of fallen man will at a future time of unprecedented evil activity on earth endure a holocaust far worse than that perpetrated by Adolf Hitler. The end will bring, he concluded, God's wrath and judgment on an incorrigibly wicked world.

I believe America and the world can yet have another burst of so-called peace and prosperity—although I see it as highly unlikely. The "change" the country and the world are clamoring for through trust in human governmental entities rather than God's moral governance will certainly, if not rejected, as my friend Dave Hunt wrote, swiftly bring the holocaust of the Tribulation.

Let us, the church of the Lord Jesus Christ, pray for the president—even when it seems to do no good—and for all governmental leaders, so that we might lead peaceful lives. This is commanded of us by the Lord. But, let us work to complete whatever He puts in front of us to do for the kingdom. Let us, as Oswald Chambers entitled his book of devotions, do "our utmost for His highest" while our fleeting time remains upon this fallen sphere.

Worldview Is All-Important

The way Christians—the born again, who are in God's holy will—carry on with life's duties is all important in the battle we do against the powers and principalities in high places as outlined in Ephesians 6:12. The Christian worldview is so dramatically different from all others that it literally is the difference between daylight and darkness. It is guided by the only compass that can navigate through the deadly shoals of this earthly, tumultuous sea.

Looking at the world around us from so many different viewpoints separates and divides the human community, engendering hatreds, wars, and death. Jesus, speaking while on the Mount of Olives one day, prophesied the degree to which the differences would explode in the time just before His return: "For nation shall rise against nation, and kingdom against kingdom: and there shall be famines, and pestilences, and earthquakes, in various places" (Matt. 24:7).

It has been pointed out often that the word "nation" here is from the Greek word *ethnos,* translated "ethnic" in English. Jesus was forewarning that the Tribulation era will produce great hatreds that will center on racial and cultural differences of worldview. These unprecedented uprisings of this sort will, Jesus foretold, eventuate in famines and pestilence—the inevitable result of all-out war.

Although we of this generation are not in the Tribulation era about which Jesus here prophesied, we have diametrically differing worldviews on the national and international scenes that certainly must be setting the stage for the times Jesus foresaw. The US is mired in many ethnic problems and cultural differences within the various races themselves. Insistence on embracing multiculturalism by the politically correct, "PC" crowd, motivated to their hyper level of championing the melting-pot worldview by mainstream media, throws fuel on the fires of racial divides. The multicultural Nazis want Americans to stay separate, because most of these PC types are socialist-leaning globalists who want us to be citizens of the world rather than citizens of a sovereign nation. Hyphenating, or mixing, ethnic with national identities into unique nomenclature seems designed to make America eventually forfeit its national autonomy.

Worldview is being shaped in this nation to reflect the one-world builders' blueprint for the global village, as one well-known, probable second-time presidential candidate put it. The worldview in question has never gone away. It is the perennial worldview that has been with mankind since Nimrod attempted to build the tower to heaven not long after the Flood of Noah's day (read Gen. 11). We see that blueprint manifested in the incessant attempts to bring everyone together in the Middle East *peace process*—at Israel's expense, of course.

Jesus also prophesied that man would get himself deeper and deeper into trouble, so far as the nation-state is concerned, the closer the Second Advent comes: "And there shall be signs in the sun, and in the moon, and in the stars; and upon the earth distress of nations, with perplexity; the sea and the waves roaring" (Luke 21:25).

There can be little argument against the obvious. Nations are indeed in great distress today—with much perplexity. We don't have to look at the many nations of earth to prove this fact. Our own nation is divided right down the middle on most all issues of politics and morality. People are so distressed—even perplexed—that many have promised to leave the country if they didn't get their way in presidential election results. Others have written fictional books, venting their anger in wishful accounts of the assassination of a president they hate.

The problems involved all boil down to one issue: worldview.

Any view of life on this planet other than God's view—the Christian worldview—is, to put it bluntly, but truthfully, wrong, and is destined to produce disaster. This is true no matter the area of life involved. Worldview is all important in avoidance of trouble and in achievement of success. There isn't space here to go into the many areas in life today to which this truth applies. So, let's briefly look at one key issue in considering worldview that gets to the crux of the most important prophetic indicator of this late hour. The issue is modern Israel.

The geopoliticians are in perplexity about Israel and its hate-filled enemies. The diplomats have no idea where the anger truly comes from; therefore, they cannot begin to understand how to solve the violence and hatreds. The world's diplomats have a worldview or combination of worldviews that completely leaves the God of heaven out of the equation for peace-making. The result has been more than five thousand years of war throughout recorded history. God says, "Be governed by my rules, because I created all that is, and know what is best." The earthly rulers say, "We can handle it. If there is a God, that God is existential at best. We don't need or want Him to rule over us." This doesn't apply, of course, to Islamic fanatics who slavishly accept the bloody demands of their god to make war.

God says that everything is His, including the land of the Middle East He chose to give to the Jews—Israel. The geopoliticians say they will decide who owns the land and who doesn't. The result: a world that is quickly moving toward all-out war—Armageddon.

The same error in worldview is within the church today. The worldview of most mainline denominations today say God is through with Israel. The church—that worldview proposes—is now inheritor of all promises that the Lord covenanted with Abraham, Isaac, and Jacob. God is through with Israel and all about Israel that is in the Bible must be spiritualized, allegorized, or treated as history already accomplished.

Really?

They proclaim—through their satanically inspired worldview—that the church is going to make the world better and better until they have made it good enough through the political and diplomatic process, in conjunction with religious, do-good projects, for Jesus to come back and take over.

Really?

They aren't reading the same headlines I am. If the Lord has given up on Israel, then there sure is some coincidence going on. We are expected to believe that Israel just "happens" to be on the front-page headlines every day, in the center of a desperate cry for peace, just like God's prophetic Word forecast. Worldview—the *Christian worldview*—is all-important in God's economy. God's worldview is, as legendary football coach Vince Lombardi once put it in talking about winning, not everything. It is the only thing!

Apostates Warring with the Church

The church that will be on the scene while the end-times battle for the spiritual hearts and minds of mankind unfolds is warned by God's prophetic Word: "Let no man deceive you by any means; for that day shall not come, except there come a falling away first, and that man of sin be revealed, the son of perdition" (2 Thess. 2:3).

The "falling away" is translated from the Greek word *apostasia,* which means a "departure" from the truth of God's Word, as well as a literal "departure" from the scene. In this forewarning sense, we will look at it as it means the falling away from the biblical truth that Jesus Christ is the one and only way to God the Heavenly Father through God's redemptive process described above in this chapter.

Paul the apostle was saying that the Day of the Lord—the Tribulation, or Daniel's seventieth week (see Dan. 9:26–27)—won't happen until there is first a departure from the faith that Jesus Christ is the only way, truth, and life. In that regard, we see a profound battle shaping to deter the spiritual hearts and minds of men, women, and children from learning the truth that Christ alone died in order that they can be redeemed from sin.

Let's examine carefully some possible developments coming into view with regard to the apostasy of which Paul forewarned.

Jorge Mario Bergoglio—Pope Francis, 266th pontiff of the Catholic Church—seems to be taking the world by storm, as they say. He is, of course, the 112th pope since twelfth-century Irish Bishop St. Malachy "prophesied" that the last pope would be number 112 from the time he made the "prophecies," as we've all learned about by now.

Obviously, he hasn't overtly taken the official name "Petrus Romanus," or "Peter the Roman," as Malachy predicted would be the moniker of the final pope who would preside over the Catholic Church during an era of the greatest time of trouble in its history. Let's think again briefly upon what Malachy said he foresaw. Malachy's biographer, St. Bernard of Clairvaux, reported in *Life of Saint Malachy* that St. Malachy wrote briefly, in Latin, on each succeeding pope of the future, and then gave the document to Pope Innocent II, who had it placed in Vatican archives, where it remained for several centuries. It was rediscovered in 1590 and published.

Some scholars who have studied these predictions carefully claim that Malachy was remarkably accurate about succeeding popes right up through Pope Benedict XVI, who abdicated his papal throne in 2013. Others who have looked into these things have found that in most cases regarding the Malachy prophecies, the bishop's predictions were too oblique, too veiled, or couched in esoteric description to be validated as having been fulfilled to any great extent. Our bottom-line conclusion must be that, while most of Malachy's prophecies about the popes are questionable as to absolute proof that the bishop was accurate in every case, there is little doubt that the 112th pope from the time he wrote the predictions is a strange pope to be sure.

The world at large literally loves the guy. His popularity really jumped on a global scale—and especially in the view of national and international mainstream media, when he implied that there might be many ways to God and heaven and declared that Christians must be more tolerant of things we don't embrace or understand. At least, that was the gist of his statements.

The pope made it clear in a number of statements in various speaking forums that the Catholic Church and all of Christendom must cease condemning and excluding from God's kingdom homosexuals and those who hold other religious views than those that are Jesus Christ-centered.

That sentiment, even among a growing number within so-called Christian churches, is a visceral part of all of humanism's elite and their mouthpieces. The Christian Bible and its harsh, restrictive "one way to God" is intolerant, bigoted, homophobic, and bordering on fundamentalist insanity that desires to bring the world to Armageddon. (The pope didn't say that; I did, based upon the pontiff's stance of recent days that has won him great accolades.)

America's current president is perhaps the most recent of the global leaders to express this pope's elevated standing in his opposition to biblical restrictions. Barack Obama said recently: "I have been hugely impressed with the pope's pronouncements." He described Pope Francis as "somebody who lives out the teachings of Christ [who, by the way, claimed He is the only way to God, the Heavenly Father]. Incredible humility—incredible sense of empathy to the least of these, to the poor."

In his interview with the CNBC business news channel, Obama was asked about Francis' recent comment that the Catholic Church has become too "obsessed" with issues like gay rights and abortion. Obama said:

> [Pope Francis is] somebody who is—I think first and foremost—thinking about how to embrace people as opposed to push them away; how to find what's good in them as opposed to condemn them…. And that spirit, that sense of love and unity, seems to manifest itself in not just what he says, but also what he does. And, you know, for any religious leader, that's something—that's a quality I admire.[246]

Sure sounds good, doesn't it? Unity—that's the ticket for the coming Antichrist system. Unity means to embrace all belief systems as acceptable to God's prescription for living on planet earth, according to the globalists elite. This is the route to "peace."

We are to embrace those religionists who behead women for having been raped. We are to accept as brothers those who murder anyone with whom they don't agree.

Pope Francis met with Palestinian president Mahmoud Abbas. He wasn't prepared to give the Israeli prime minister an audience, however. Yet, he is pushing the peace process so Palestine can have its statehood on Israel's tiny land mass. The pope gave the Palestinian leader a special pen. He said when handing it to him, "Surely, you have a lot of things you have to sign." Abbas responded, "I hope to sign a peace treaty with Israel with this pen."[247]

My thought was, upon reading about the pope's generosity, that the Beast of Revelation chapter 13 will have a sidekick who will—like Mr. Big himself (Antichrist)—push the peace that will be the covenant made with death and hell (Isa. 28:15, 18).

Anti-Biblical Prophetic Trend

Troubling matters have leaped to the surface of evangelical Christianity in recent days. Movement away from some of the basic tenets of prophetic truth is being expressed by teachers many of us thought were immune to such corruption.

At the outset, I'll say that I don't intend to mention names, because I don't wish to have what I will write here seen as being personal attacks on individuals. That is not my purpose. My purpose is, rather, to point to egregious error so that readers will be aware of the false premises being foisted in these waning days of this Church Age.

The ones who are bringing the error to the surface of discourse are not neophytes to Bible prophecy. They are among the most respected and noteworthy of such teachers. Therefore, it is doubly necessary that you be aware of what is being proposed by them.

Before getting to the alarming claims by these prophecy teachers, we will look at trends that have perhaps prepared the way for false teaching along this line to emerge. Seeds have long been planted that make fertile the ground for the growth of such serious error.

First, we look at the so-called unity movement, which is more an unspoken way of doing business in the modern evangelical church than a specific, official movement. It is nonetheless a concerted, lockstep march in the same direction—a march toward the heresy of inclusiveness. Jesus Christ, as the way, the truth, and the life, and as the only way to God the Father, you see, is too harsh, too…well…exclusive. Did not Jesus Himself welcome all sinners? Did He not go into the homes of sinners—and even meet one on one with prostitutes and demon-possessed persons?

To shut out the world as we live in it—in which we must operate every day—is to keep people from coming to Christ. Those outside the fold have to be welcomed into the confines of our organized church activities. To make them comfortable, our services must be tailored to reflect that to which they are accustomed—to some extent, at least. Our music, in particular, must be instrumentally orchestrated and beat-oriented to provide the rhythmic pulsations that make all—especially the youth—feel right at home.

"Old fogey!" I can hear the challenges begin. Yes. I'll admit to probably being a "back number," as Dr. J. Vernon McGee would put it. But, my concern goes beyond personal musical preference for style of service in the sanctuary. It is the melding of the world in these unity-type churches that is at the heart of this critique. Such melding sets the stage for doctrinal corruption. And, such has already set in, in a major way. Jesus does indeed embrace all who come to Him—but on His terms, not ours, who are His creation. He told the rich, young ruler to go and sell all he had, and then come follow Him. This was not merely a call for the young man to give all he had to the poor, or to Jesus' church organization, but to divest himself of anything that would encumber the young man's worship of Christ, who would be his Savior.

The unity-type church today is saying, "Bring all of the world influences you love into the worship with you. There is little difference in this environment and the one you are so afraid you might lose by accepting Jesus as your Savior."

This movement away from sound Bible doctrine isn't only happening in fringe denominational or other groups within what is known by secular observers as Christendom. It is rampant now within worship bodies that were once spiritually sensitive to the apostle Paul's warning:

> I charge thee, therefore, before God, and the Lord Jesus Christ, who
> shall judge the living and the dead at his appearing and his kingdom:

Preach the word; be diligent in season, out of season; reprove, rebuke, exhort with all longsuffering and doctrine.

For the time will come when they will not endure sound doctrine but, after their own lusts, shall they heap to themselves teachers, having itching ears;

And they shall turn away their ears from the truth, and shall be turned unto fables.

But watch thou in all things, endure afflictions, do the work of an evangelist, make full proof of thy ministry. (2 Tim. 4:1–5)

I intended when beginning this writing to go into a number of other things that have been spawned by movement away from Bible truth in these closing days of the age—things like the "Jesus-only movement," the lie wrapped up in "dual covenant" inculcation, and especially the "many ways to salvation" championed by an exponentially growing number of people within evangelical Christianity and without. But, alas! Those will have to wait another time of examination.

I must get right to the matter of the false teaching that has surfaced in recent days by some Bible prophecy teachers whom I previously thought impervious to such corruption. I'm talking about the proposition— actually, the firmly held belief by these noted prophecy teachers, apparently—that following the Rapture, those who accept the mark of the Beast will still have a chance to be saved—that is, go to heaven. This is their claim, and it has raised quite a furor.

Here is what God's Word plainly says about those who will in that Tribulation time accept the mark of the Beast, which means they will agree to worship Antichrist as God: "And he causeth all, both small and great, rich and poor, free and enslaved, to receive a mark in their right hand, or in their foreheads, And that no man might buy or sell, except he that had the mark, or the name of the beast, or the number of his name" (Rev. 13:16–17).

That description of the process of taking the mark is followed by a precise overview of the unmistakable consequences that will result:

> And the third angel followed them, saying with a loud voice, If any man worship the beast and his image, and receive his mark in his forehead, or in his hand,
>
> The same shall drink of the wine of the wrath of God, which is poured out without mixture into the cup of his indignation; and he shall be tormented with fire and brimstone in the presence of the holy angels, and in the presence of the Lamb;
>
> And the smoke of their torment ascendeth up for ever and ever; and they have no rest day nor night, who worship the beast and his image, and whosoever receiveth the mark of his name. (Rev. 14:9–11)

We must hold firm to absolute truth given in God's Word, no matter whether it seems fair or whether considering any other human divergence from what is written by the holy hand of God. Here's what the Creator of all things has to say about His Word—especially His prophetic Word:

> For I testify unto every man that heareth the words of the prophecy of this book, If any man shall add unto these things, God shall add unto him the plagues that are written in this book;
>
> And if any man shall take away from the words of the book of this prophecy, God shall take away his part out from the tree of life, and out of the holy city, and from the things which are written in this book. (Rev. 22:18–19)

Key to Final Victory

The battle is more vicious than was the battle for Britain that had Winston Churchill declaring that men would look back one day and say that this was Britain's finest hour. The present battle in which the church of Jesus Christ is enjoined involves the eternal souls of men, women, and children. Never have the stakes been higher in a war of any magnitude!

There are those who believe and claim angrily that the church must go through the Tribulation—the hour of God's wrath and judgment, the last seven years of human history just before Christ's Second Advent (Rev. 19:11). Christians, they claim, must wash their robes clean so that they can stand before a holy God and reap the rewards of heavenly glory.

This declaration is ludicrous, of course, because they apparently believe believers must endure that time of horror in order to prove themselves worthy. This is the very thing Jesus Christ has done for each and every believer. He did all of the cleansing for those who believe in His once-and-for-all sacrifice on the cross at Calvary. Believers simply accept that sacrifice and are cleansed of all sin that separates them from God the Father in the eternal sense. We are cleansed of all sins, past, present, and future, through the shed blood of our Lord, who died for us and rose again on the third day.

But, the detractors say, Christians will go through that time of Tribulation. They use the following verse to prove their point. They, speaking of Antichrist, say that he will greatly abuse Christians: "And it was given unto him to make war with the saints, and to overcome them; and power was given him over all kindreds, and tongues, and nations" (Rev. 13:7).

Indeed, there will be a group of saints who will go through that terrible time, and Antichrist will put them to *physical* death because of their belief in Christ and refusal to take Antichrist's beastly mark. However, there are many sets of saints throughout God's Holy Word, the Bible. While the saints mentioned above are *Tribulation* saints who will have to suffer and die for their beliefs under Antichrist, Jesus spoke of *saints* of our own dispensation—the *Church Age* or *Age of Grace.*

The Lord spoke to His disciples who had just answered His question, "But who say ye that I am?" Peter answered, "Thou art the Christ, the Son of the Living God." Jesus told Peter that he was right and had gotten that knowledge from the Heavenly Father. The Lord then said: "And I say also unto thee, That thou art Peter, and upon this rock I will build my church, and the gates of hell shall not prevail against it" (John 16:18).

So, we see the two, distinct sets of saints: the Tribulation saints and the church believers of this present dispensation. The church will not be "overcome" by the Beast, or Antichrist. But, the saints of that other period or dispensation will be overcome—so far as physical life is concerned—by Satan's great dictator. They will, however, be forever with Christ in heaven.

To grasp this truth, we only have to understand that while many, many millions of believers throughout time have suffered horribly and died for their belief in Christ, and many are even dying for the cause of Christ right at the moment of your reading this, many millions of Christians have never had to suffer horribly and die for the cause of Christ. American Christians have for the most part lived and died in almost pampered circumstances.

Does this mean those who haven't suffered and died horribly or who haven't lived through those terrible times haven't washed their robes clean, thus aren't going to receive rewards or even life in heaven with the Father? Of course not. It's a ludicrous concept. The Lord did the cleansing; He, alone, is the benchmark for whether one goes to heaven.

So, despite all of the trials and tribulations—the degeneration and debauchery of culture and society—the attack on the church itself during these darkening days through which we are living, *the church, not the gates of hell, will prevail!* The final victory is already ours! Jesus Christ is the key to victory!

ENDNOTES

CHAPTER 1—Forgotten Aspect of Bible Prophecy: The Lucifer Effect and the Coming War between Christian vs. Christian
by Thomas Horn

1. Awr Hawkins, http://www.breitbart.com/Big-Peace/2014/01/08/ Report-Number-Of-Christians-Martyred-For-Their-Faith-Nearly-Doubled-In-2013.
2. Http://www.pewforum.org/2014/01/14/ religious-hostilities-reach-six-year-high/.
3. Http://www.nationalreview.com/article/368796/ us-and-christian-persecution-raymond-ibrahim.
4. Heather Clark, http://christiannews.net/2014/01/25/legal-group-reports-dramatic-increase-in-hostility-toward-christian-students-in-public-schools/.
5. Benjamin Fearnow, http://charlotte.cbslocal.com/2014/02/02/ nc-high-school-football-coach-ordered-to-cease-baptisms-leading-prayers/; emphasis added.

6. Http://www.americanthinker.com/2014/01/establishing_a_us_state_religion.html.

7. Deborah Wrigley, http://abclocal.go.com/ktrk/story?section=news/local&id=9377070.

8. Http://dailycaller.com/2014/01/03/house-committee-obama-administration-banned-christmas-carols-and-cards-for-veterans/.

9. Http://www.charismanews.com/opinion/clarion-call/42019-blogging-gays-urge-murder-castration-of-christians.

10. Bob Unruh, http://www.wnd.com/2014/02/violence-inspiring-hate-map-continues-to-incite-2/.

11. Gillian Flaccus, http://news.yahoo.com/atheist-mega-churches-root-across-us-world-214619648.html.

12. John Bingham, "Christians Called to 'Martyrdom' Says Welby," *The Telegraph*, January 14, 2014, http://www.telegraph.co.uk/news/religion/10572539/Christians-called-to-martyrdom-says-Welby.html.

13. Ruth Gledhill, "Church Faces Implosion and Life Underground," Virtue Online, December 10, 2004, http://www.virtueonline.org/portal/modules/news/article.php?storyid=1782#.UvFfmvldXKc.

14. A. W. Tozer, *The Dangers of a Shallow Faith: Awakening from Spiritual Lethargy* (Gospel Light Publications, 2012) Google eBook, 14–15.

15. Alastair Leithead, "Stanford Prison Experiment Continues to Shock," BBC News, August 17, 2011, http://www.bbc.co.uk/news/world-us-canada-14564182.

16. "Stanford Prison Experiment," Wikipedia, http://en.wikipedia.org/w/index.php?title=Stanford_prison_experiment&oldid=605102500 (accessed April 21, 2014).

17. Edward Marriott, "Torture as Second Nature," April 28, 2007, http://www.theguardian.com/books/2007/apr/29/politics1.

18. Philip Zombardo, "Who Was Lucifer and How Did He Become the Devil," Lucifer Effect, http://www.lucifereffect.com/lucifer.htm.

19. Ibid.

20. Harold M. Schulweis, *Conscience: The Duty to Obey and the Duty to Disobey* (Jewish Lights Publishing, 2010) Google eBook, 106 (retrieved February 6, 2014).

21. Ibid.

22. http://en.wikipedia.org/wiki/Milgram_experiment#cite_note-7.

23. Ibid.

24. Stanley Milgram, The Perils of Obedience," http://www.physics.utah.edu/~detar/phys4910/readings/ethics/PerilsofObedience.html.

25. "The Milgram Experiment," Wikipedia, http://en.wikipedia.org/wiki/Milgram_experiment#cite_ref-11.

26. Charles L. Sheridan and Richard King Jr., "Obedience to Authority with an Authentic Victim," http://www.holah.co.uk/files/sheridan_king_1972.pdf.

27. Rory Cellan-Jones, "First Human 'Infected with Computer Virus,'" BBC News, May 27, 2010, http://www.bbc.co.uk/news/10158517.

28. C. Christopher Hook, *Human Dignity in the Biotech Century* (Downers Grove, IL: InterVarsity, 2004) 92.

29. Ibid., 93.

30. Mihail Roco and William Sims Bainbridge, ed. *Converging Technologies for Improving Human Performance* (New York: Kluwer Academic, 2003) emphasis in original.

31. Rebecca Evans, "The Internet Unlocked Something Dark in Humanity," March 24, 2013, http://www.dailymail.co.uk/news/

article-2298600/The-internet-unlocked-dark-humanity-Top-author-Anthony-Horowitz-uses-speech-make-claims.html.

32. Ibid.

33. Thomas Horn, Nita Horn, *Forbidden Gates* (Crane, MO: Defender, 2010) 92.

34. David Wilkerson, "Witchcraft in the Church," Believers Web, May 2, 2003, http://www.believersweb.org/view.cfm?ID=735.

35. Research in Review, http://rinr.fsu.edu/spring96/features/evil.html.

36. Lee Rannals, "Scientists Discuss the Possibility of a Zombie Apocalypse," Red Orbit, October 31, 2013, http://www.redorbit.com/news/science/1112964783/zombie-virus-could-be-reality-exclusive-100213/.

37. Ibid.

38. Rick Weiss, "Of Mice, Men, and In-Between," MSNBC, November 20, 2004, http://www.msnbc.msn.com/id/6534243/.

39. Http://news.yahoo.com/s/cq/20090315/pl_cq_politics/politics3075228.

40. *American Journal of Law and Medicine*, vol. 28, nos. 2 and 3 (2002), 162.

41. Chuck Missler, *Prophecy 20/20: Profiling the Future through the Lens of Scripture* (Nashville: Thomas Nelson, 2006) 225–226.

42. Ibid.

43. "Judge Orders Colorado Cake Maker to Serve Gay Couples," CBS Denver, December 6, 2013, http://denver.cbslocal.com/2013/12/06/judge-orders-colorado-cake-maker-to-serve-gay-couples/.

CHAPTER 2—The Good and Bad of What's Coming
by Chuck Missler

44. Cf. WND "Whistleblower" articles, etc.

45. Q.V. J. Vernon McGee, *Thru the Bible,* 2 Tim. 3:12.

46. This incredible history has been detailed in *The Pilgrim Church—Tracing the Pathway of the Forgotten Saints from Pentecost to the Twentieth Century, 1931,* by E. H. Broadbent, a classic covering episodes from Acts chapter 2 through the beginning of the 1930s. It was out of print for many years, and we are indebted to the efforts of Dave Hunt to have it in print again. (Some of these remarks were taken from Dave's foreword to the recent edition.)

47. Broadbent deals with more than seventy; they are summarized on p. 422.

48. From Dave Hunt's foreword to Broadbent's book (emphasis added).

49. Edmund Hamer Broadbent, *The Pilgrim Church—Tracing the Pathway of the Forgotten Saints from Pentecost to the Twentieth Century, 1931* (Port Colborne, ON: Gospel Folio Press) ISBN 9781882701537, www.gospelfolio.com. A must-read book for every serious Christian.

50. Rev. 2 and 3.

51. Translated from the German from an inscription on a cathedral door in Lubeck, Germany, by Dr. William Welty, director, ISV Foundation.

52. Acts 2:2.

53. Acts 2:46, 5:42, 8:3, 9:11, 12:12, 16:40, 18:7, 20:20, 21:8; Rom. 16:5; 1 Cor. 16:19; Col. 4:15; 1 Tim. 5:13–14; and Philem. 1:2.

54. 1 Tim. 2:5.

55. Rev. 2:6, 15.

56. Probably only a minority of Christians really know what that term means: "Good News" is just a comfortable evasion. Note Paul's specifics in 1 Cor. 15:1–4.

57. These specifications embroider the entire Old Testament. Can you

find the occasions alluding to the "third day" specification? There are ostensibly six more supplementing the allusion to Jonah's "whale of a tale" in Matt. 12:40.

58. Eph. 4:12.

59. Rev. 2:6, 15.

60. Acts 18:2–3, 20:34–35; 1 Cor. 4:11–13; et al.

61. ("The thing speaks for itself") as an attorney might cite.

CHAPTER 3—By the Typing of Our Thumbs, Something Wicked This Way Comes
by Sharon Gilbert

62. Conversation between Commander John Adams and scientist Morbius in final scene of *Forbidden Planet*, a 1956 science fiction film from MGM. For more on this film, see Wikipedia entry: http://en.wikipedia.org/wiki/Forbidden_Planet (accessed December 25, 2013).

63. William Shakespeare's *MacBeth*, Act IV, Scene I, Lines 44–45. "By the pricking of my thumbs, Something wicked this way comes."

64. Linda S. Gottfredson, *Mainstream Science on Intelligence: An Editorial with 52 Signatories, History, and Bibliography* (first published *Wall Street Journal*, December 13, 1994, but accessed online on January 6, 2014, at http://www.udel.edu/educ/gottfredson/reprints/1997mainstream.pdf).

65. *Cogito ergo sum*, Rene Descartes. Descartes was a seventeenth-century philosopher who strove to sum up mankind's self-awareness in *Principles of Philosophy* (1644).

66. Steven A. Benner, "Defining Life," *Astrobiology*, December 2010, pp. 1021–1030. Archived at http://www.ncbi.nlm.nih.gov/pmc/articles/PMC3005285/ - (accessed January 6, 2014).

67. Synthia, also known as Mycoplasma laboratorium, derived from Mycoplasma genitalium. See more at http://en.wikipedia.org/wiki/Mycoplasma_laboratorium (accessed January 6, 2014).

68. The numerical value of a letter is obtained by equating a sequence of letters in any language (in this case, English) to the numbers 1 through 9.

69. "Intergalactic Computer Network," Wikipedia, http://en.wikipedia.org/w/index.php?title=Intergalactic_Computer_Network&oldid=602778300 (accessed April 25, 2014).

70. Stephen Levy, "Zuckerberg Explains Internet.org, Facebook's Plan to Get the World Online," Wired, August 17, 2013, http://www.wired.co.uk/news/archive/2013-08/27/mark-zuckerberg-internet-org (accessed January 6, 2014).

71. For more on Tasha Lem, see: http://tardis.wikia.com/wiki/Tasha_Lem (accessed February 5, 2014).

72. Paraphrase of conversation between Kirk and Spock in *The Wrath of Khan,* Paramount Pictures, 1982. Spock has just saved the entire ship by sacrificing his own life. This is a theme that runs through the entire film: that the body requires sacrifice. This is an eerie counterpoint to a Star Trek original series episode in which a computer named "Landru" forces individuals to sacrifice their freedoms to join the BODY (Episode 21, "The Return of the Archons," original airdate February 9, 1967).

73. The Turing Test was described by Alan Turing as a means to "test" the intelligence of machines by having humans try to tell the difference between a computer and a human through text questions and answers. Today's computers can speak in nearly all languages, fluently and naturally. For more on the Turing Test, see: http://en.wikipedia.org/wiki/Turing_test (accessed February 5, 2014).

74. Reuters and AP sources, "Watch Out for That Truck! Cars to 'Talk' to Each Other by 2017 Under U.S. Plan to Significantly Reduce Accidents on the Road," http://www.dailymail.co.uk/news/article-2551217/Government-wants-manufacturers-install-transmitters-vehicles-2017-cars-talk-other.html (accessed February 5, 2014).

75. Http://www.globalresearch.ca/artificial-intelligence-and-death-by-drones-the-future-of-warfare-will-be-decided-by-drones-not-humans/5353699 (accessed January 7, 2014).

76. *Unmanned Systems Integrated Roadmap* is a DoD document released to the public in December 2013. To read the entire report, go to http://www.defense.gov/pubs/DOD-USRM-2013.pdf (accessed on January 7, 2014).

77. Http://www.rt.com/usa/drones-own-decisions-soon-156/ (accessed January 7, 2014).

78. "The Game," the 106th episode of *Star Trek, The Next Generation*. Originally aired October 28, 1991. For more, see: http://en.memory-alpha.org/wiki/The_Game_(episode) (accessed January 7, 2014).

79. Ian Johnston, "EU Funding 'Orwellian' Artificial Intelligence Plan to Monitor Public for 'Abnormal Behaviour,'" The Daily Telegraph Online, September 19, 2009, http://www.telegraph.co.uk/news/uknews/6210255/EU-funding-Orwellian-artificial-intelligence-plan-to-monitor-public-for-abnormal-behaviour.html (accessed January 7, 2014).

80. Http://en.wikipedia.org/wiki/List_of_artificial_intelligence_projects (accessed January 7, 2014).

81. Http://en.wikipedia.org/wiki/BRAIN_Initiative (accessed January 7, 2014).

82. There are many variations of the story of the golem found in the Babylonia Talmud, the *Standard Jewish Encyclopedia*, the *Encyclopedia Judaica*, and the *New Jewish Encyclopedia*.

83. Susan Young, "Entire Book Written in DNA," *Technology Review*, http://www.technologyreview.com/view/428922/ an-entire-book-written-in-dna/.

84. Http://www.telegraph.co.uk/health/dietandfitness/10161854/ Exercise-can-alter-your-DNA-study-claims.html.

85. *Strong's Enhanced Lexicon; BibleWorks for Windows 9.0* (Norfolk, VA: BibleWorks, 2013) #H02403.

86. Ibid., "#H05771.

87. Brian Greene, "A Theory of Everything?" http://www.pbs.org/wgbh/ nova/elegant/everything.html.

88. Nick Begich, *Weapons of the New World Order*, video (Topeka, KS: The Prophecy Club, 2000).

89. British Geological Survey, "Reversals: Magnetic Flip," http://www. geomag.bgs.ac.uk/education/reversals.html.

90. Leonard Horowitz, *The Controlled America Lecture* (Sandpoint, ID: Tetrahedron, LLC, 2002).

91. R. T. Kendall, *Understanding Theology*, Vol. 1 (Ross-shire, Great Britain: Christian Focus, 1996) 15, emphasis added.

92. *Strong's*, # G4352.

93. Carl E. Olsen, "Pope Francis Just Concluded Vatican III and Declares 'All Religions Are Right,'" *The Catholic World Report*, January 5, 2014, http://www.catholicworldreport.com/Blog/2826/ pope_francis_just_concluded_vatican_iii_and_declared_all_ religions_are_true.aspx#.Uy8XlvldV8E.

Chapter 6—War of the Apostates
by Larry Spargimino

94. "Famous Christian Charity Hiring Married 'Gays,'" WND, March 25, 2014, www.wnd.com/2014/03/famous-christian-charity-hiring-married-gays.

95. Napp Nazworth, "Those Who Promote Global Warming Skepticism Should Be Imprisoned, Professor Argues," *Christian Post,* March 18, 2014, www.christianpost.com/news/those-who-promote-global-warming-skepticism-should-be-imprisoned-professor-argues-116331/.

96. Ibid.

97. Mark Hitchcock, *The End: A Complete Overview of Bible Prophecy and the End of Days* (Carol Stream, IL: Tyndale House, 2012) 361–362.

98. Mal Couch, Gen. Ed., *Dictionary of Premillennial Theology,* "Babylon" (Grand Rapids: Kregel, 1996) 61.

99. Walid Shoebat, *God's War on Terror. Islam, Prophecy and the Bible* (US: Top Executive Media, 2010) 292.

100. Mal Couch, Gen. Ed., *A Bible Handbook to Revelation* (Grand Rapids, MI: Kregel, 2001) 279.

101. Shoebat, 409.

102. Www.lighthousetrailsresearch.com/blog/?tag=let-us-reason-ministries.

103. January 23, 2006, www.christianitytoday.com/parse/2006/january/brian-mclaren-on-homosexual-question-finding-pastoral.html.

104. John MacArthur, as interviewed by Phil Johnson, "What's So Dangerous about the Emerging Church?" Grace to You, 2006, www.gty.org/resources/sermons/GTY107.

105. Brian McLaren, *A Generous Orthodoxy* (Grand Rapids, MI: Zondervan, 2004) 74.

106. MacArthur.

107. Ibid.

108. "Q & R: Second Coming from Sweden," brian d. mclaren, Brianmclaren.net/archives/blog/hello-brian-i-hope-youre.html.

109. Ibid.

110. Mark Biltz, *Blood Moons: Decoding the Imminent Heavenly Signs* (Washington, DC: WND Books, 2014).

111. Andy Crouch, "The Emergent Mystique," November 1, 2004, www.christianitytoday.com/ct/2004/november/12.36.html?start=2.

112. "Global Warming Petition Project, www.petitionproject.org.

113. D. James Kennedy and E. Calvin Beisner, *Overheated: A Reasoned Look at the Global Warming Debate* (Ft. Lauderdale, FL: Coral Ridge Ministries, 2007) 23.

114. "Pope Calls on Leaders to Protect People, Environment," Voice of America, www.voanews.com/content/new-pope-installed-with-formal-mass.

115. Reuters, "Pope Urges All Religions to Unite for Peace, Justice," March 20, 2013, www.voanews.com/content/pope-justice/1625457.html.

116. John W. O'Malley, "Opening the Church to the World," *New York Times*, October 10, 2012. Accessed: www.nytimes.com/2012/10/11/opinion/vatican-ii-opened-the-church; see archived article here: http://www.nytimes.com/2012/10/11/opinion/vatican-ii-opened-the-church-to-the-world.html?_r=0.

117. E. Calvin Beisner, "The Competing World Views of Environmentalism and Christianity," Cornwall

Alliance, www.cornwallalliance.org/articles/read/
the-competing-world-views-of-environmentalism-and-christianity/.

118. Ibid.

119. Paul H. Rubin, "Environmentalism as Religion," April 22, 2010,
www.wsj.com.

120. Beisner, "Competing World Views."

121. Michael Crichton, "Environmentalism as Religion,"
September 15, 2003, www.michaelcrichton.net/
speech-environmntalism-as-religion.

122. Hollie McKay, FoxNews.com, February 21, 2014.

123. Scott Lively, *Redeeming the Rainbow: A Christian Response to the
"Gay" Agenda* (Springfield, MA: Veritas Aeterna, 2009) 19.

124. Ibid., 20–21.

125. Ibid., 23.

126. Jared Keever, "Case against Anti-Gay Minister Scott
Liverly Still Being Pursued," Opposing Views, March
4, 2014, www.opposingviews.com/i/society/gay-issues/
case-against-anti-gay-minister-scott-lively-still-being-pursued.

127. Zack Ford and Annie Rose Strasser, "Rick Warren: I Regret
Coming Out in Support of California's Anti-Gay Marriage
Proposition," Think Progress, November 28, 2012, http://
thinkprogress.org/lgbt/2012/11/28/1250921/rick-warren-i-
regret-coming-out-in-support-of-californias-anti-gay-marriage-
proposition/.

128. Ibid.

129. Ibid.

130. Ibid.

131. "Joel Osteen Finally Comes Out on 'Gay' Issue," WND,

October 3, 2013, http://www.wnd.com/2013/10/
joel-osteen-god-approves-of-homosexuals.

132. Ibid.

133. Lively, 153.

134. Albert Mohler, "Can Evangelical Chaplains Serve God
and Country?—The Crisis Arrives, AlbertMohler.com,
September 17, 2013, www.albertmohler.com/2013/09/17/
can-evangelical-chaplains-serve-god-and-country-the-crisis-arrives.

135. Ibid.

136. Major Brian L. Struckert, School of Advanced Military Studies,
Fort Leavenworth, KS, "Strategic Implications of American
Millennialism," www.dtic.mil/cgi-bin/GetTRDoc?Ad=ADA48551
1&location=u2&doc=getTRDoc.pdf, 51.

137. Paul Wilkinson, *The Church at Christ's Checkpoint* (Cheshire, UK:
Hazel Grove Full Gospel Church, 2012) 1.

138. Ibid, 2.

139. Ibid., 5.

140. Ibid., 7.

141. Ibid., 10.

142. Www.algemeiner.com/2014/04/04/former-israeli-ambassador-pins-
dead-peace-process-on-American-thinking.

143. Brian McLaren, "June 2011 Archives," brian d. mclaren,
brianmclaren.net/archives/2011/06.

144. Joshua Massey, "The Use of the Word 'Allah,'" People of the
Book," www.thepeopleofthebook.org/Massey-Allah.html.

145. Http://archive.constantcontact.com/fs/177/1102797716062/111.

146. Www.christianitytoday.com/ct/2013/january-february/
my-train-wreck-conversion.

Chapter 7—The Evangelical Church, Apostasy, Change Agents, and the Destiny of America in the Last Days
by Paul McGuire

147. Francis Schaeffer, *The Great Evangelical Disaster* (Wheaton, IL: Crossway, 1984) 37.

148. "Our theological bedrock is what has been known as Dominion Theology. This means that our divine mandate is to do whatever is necessary, by the power of the Holy Spirit, to retake the dominion of God's creation which Adam forfeited to Satan in the Garden of Eden. It is nothing less than seeing God's kingdom coming and His will being done here on earth as it is in heaven." (Dr. C. Peter Wagner, letter to his Global Harvest Ministries, May 31, 2007.)

149. "Manifest Sons of God," Reachout Trust, http://reachouttrust.org/doctrine/manifest-sons-of-god/ (retrieved January 26, 2014).

150. See Gal. 1:6–9; 2 Peter 3:15–16; Rev. 22:18–19. Also, see 1 Cor. 15:8–9, where Paul implies that he was the last of the apostles since he was the last to whom Jesus Christ appeared. Other New Testament apostles, such as Barnabas and Silas, may have been among the five hundred believers to whom Jesus appeared in Galilee after the resurrection.

151. Http://www.7culturalmountains.org/ (retrieved on January 4, 2014).

152. Ibid.

153. A fundamental misinterpretation of Matt. 25:31–46. For example, see Rick Joyner (January 26, 2014), "Sheep and Goat Nations: Be a Part of What God is Building," http://www.elijahlist.com/words/display_word.html?ID=13050 (retrieved January 26, 2014).

154. Deut. 18:22.

155. "Word of the Lord for 2007—Released through the Apostolic Council of Prophetic Elders," http://www.elijahlist.com/words/display_word/4655 (retrieved January 4, 2014).

156. For example, http://goo.gl/846aFy.

157. Kenneth L. Gentry, "Summary of Postmillennial Features," August 14, 2012, Postmillennialism, http://postmillennialism.com/2012/08/postmillennialism-features/ (retrieved January 4, 2014).

158. Kenneth L. Gentry, "The Man of Lawlessness," Covenant Media Foundation, http://www.cmfnow.com/articles/pt550.htm (retrieved January 4, 2014).

159. Dr. Greg Bahnsen, "What Is 'Theonomy'?," Covenant Media Foundation, http://www.cmfnow.com/articles/pe180.htm (retrieved January 5, 2014).

160. In this, Christian Reconstructionists differ from the Hebrew Roots Movement, which emphasizes observing the Mosaic Law, especially the festivals, but stops short of advocating the death penalty for transgressions such as idolatry, blasphemy, witchcraft, and homosexuality.

161. John Crowder, *Miracle Workers, Reformers, and the New Mystics* (Shippensburg, PA: Destiny Image, 2006) 256–57.

162. See, for example, Rick Joyner, "Civil War in the Church," http://www.morningstarministries.org/resources/prophetic-bulletins/1996/civil-war-church#.Usy9y_RDuSo (retrieved January 7, 2014).

163. Tom Watts, "Ewing Believes in Jesus Camp," *Real Detroit Weekly*, October 4, 2006. Archived from the original: http://web.archive.org/web/20080416225825/http://www.realdetroitweekly.com/article_1885.shtml (retrieved January 7, 2014).

164. See the trailer for *Jesus Camp*: http://youtu.be/sC_yzUWIfzs (retrieved January 7, 2014).

165. Michael Lipka, "More White Evangelicals than American Jews Say God Gave Israel to the Jewish People," Pew Research Center, October 3, 2013, http://www.pewresearch.org/fact-tank/2013/10/03/more-white-evangelicals-than-american-jews-say-god-gave-israel-to-the-jewish-people/ (retrieved January 8, 2014). Pew reports that 82 percent of white evangelical Protestants agreed with the statement, compared to 40 percent of American Jews.

166. Timothy P. Weber, "On the Road to Armageddon: How Evangelicals Became Israel's Best Friend," http://www.beliefnet.com/Faiths/Christianity/End-Times/On-The-Road-To-Armageddon.aspx (retrieved January 8, 2014).

167. James Huang "Classic Why: Real Reason for Syria War Plans from Gen. Wesley Clark," WhoWhatWhy, August 31, 2013, http://whowhatwhy.com/2013/08/31/classic-why-real-reason-for-syria-war-plans-from-gen-wesley-clark/ (retrieved January 8, 2014).

168. Five years after invading Iraq on the basis of flimsy evidence, a majority of evangelical leaders still supported the war. Ethan Cole, "Most Evangelical Leaders Still Support Iraq War," Christian Post, February 12, 2008, http://www.christianpost.com/news/most-evangelical-leaders-still-support-iraq-war-31154/ (retrieved January 8, 2014).

169. *Victorious Eschatology* by Harold R. Eberle and Martin Trench has been endorsed by C. Peter Wagner, who named the New Apostolic Reformation and actively promotes the Seven Mountains Mandate.

170. Derek Gilbert, "National Day of Dominion," May 6, 2010, http://derekpgilbert.com/?p=3687 (retrieved January 18, 2014).

171. Http://commit2pray.com/7x7/ (retrieved January 18, 2014).

172. As if such a thing was even possible.

173. Who, based on the evidence, probably buys into at least some aspects of Dominion theology.

174. If William Koenig is correct, approximately a hundred million Americans, based on the official positions of the twenty-five largest Christian denominations in the USA, who belong to churches that teach replacement theology (or supersessionism, the belief that Christians have replaced Israel regarding the plan, purpose, and promises of God)—if they teach on prophecy at all. See http://watch.org/showart.php3?idx=64261& (retrieved January 18, 2014).

175. See Gen. 3:1 and Ezek. 28:11.

176. David Dollins, "The Early Church Fathers Belief about the Antichrist," Christian Post, July 29, 2011, http://blogs.christianpost.com/bibleprophecy/the-early-church-fathers-belief-about-the-antichrist-6524/ (retrieved January 21, 2014).

177. See Matt. 23.

178. Rev. 20:14.

Chapter 9—A Divided House: Mainline Liberal vs. Evangelical Conservative

by Cris Putnam

179. Association of Religion Data Archives, http://www.thearda.com/mapsReports/reports/mainline.asp (accessed February 6, 2014).

180. H. Richard Niebur, *The Kingdom of God in America* (New York: Harper and Row, 1959) 193.

181. Walter A. Elwell, *Evangelical Dictionary of Theology: Second Edition* (Grand Rapids, MI: Baker Academic, 2001) 405.

182. See "Reply to Rob Skiba on the Denial of the Personhood of the

Holy Spirit," http://www.logosapologia.org/?p=5144 (accessed February 6, 2014).

183. "Most American Christians Do Not Believe that Satan or the Holy Spirit Exist," Barna Group, https://www.barna.org/barna-update/faith-spirituality/260-most-american-christians-do-not-believe-that-satan-or-the-holy-spirit-exis#.UvPwX7SNJc8 (accessed February 6, 2014).

184. "The Hitchens Transcript," Portland Monthly, http://www.portlandmonthlymag.com/arts-and-entertainment/category/books-and-talks/articles/christopher-hitchens/ (accessed September 29, 2011).

185. John Shelby Spong, *Jesus For the Non Religious* (New York: Harper Collins, 2007), ix.

186. Daniel Wallace, "The Reliability of The New Testament," YouTube, http://www.youtube.com/watch?v=JRYxgPvYHFU (accessed February 6, 2014). Also see debate here: http://www.youtube.com/watch?v=kg-dJA3SnTA.

187. Francis A. Schaeffer, *The Great Evangelical Disaster* (Westchester, Ill.: Crossway, 1984) 136.

188. John Shelby Spong, "Q & A on the Bible as a Weapon of Control," cited at http://www.religioustolerance.org/imm_bibl.htm (accessed October 23, 2013).

189. Richard Dawkins, *The God Delusion* (Great Britain: Bantam Press, 2006) 31.

190. James White, "Rob Bell's Love Wins Chapter 4 Examined," YouTube http://www.youtube.com/watch?v=29J4JGJz6Dg (accessed October 30, 2013).

191. Peter Jones, *One or Two: Seeing a World of Difference* (Escondido, CA: Main Entry Editions, 2010) Kindle edition, 537–539.

192. Brian D. McLaren, *A Generous Orthodoxy: Why I Am a Missional, Evangelical, Post/protestant, Liberal/conservative, Mystical/poetic, Biblical, Charismatic/contemplative, Fundamentalist/calvinist, Anabaptist/anglican, Methodist, Catholic, Green, Incarnational, Depressed-yet-hopeful, Emergent, Unfinished Christian* (El Cajon, CA: Zondervan/Youth Specialties, 2006) 264.

193. Jones, *One or Two*, 2116.

194. "LGBT in the Church," *The Episcopal Church,* http://www.episcopalchurch.org/page/lgbt-church (accessed February 6, 2014).

195. "ELCA Assembly Opens Ministry to Partnered Gay and Lesbian Lutherans," *ELCA News Service,* http://www.elca.org/Who-We-Are/Our-Three-Expressions/Churchwide-Organization/Communication-Services/News/Releases.aspx?a=4253 (accessed December 08, 2011).

196. Eric Marrapodi, "First Openly Gay Pastor Ordained in the PCUSA Speaks," *CNN News,* October 10, 2011, http://religion.blogs.cnn.com/2011/10/10/first-openly-gay-pastor-ordained-in-the-pcusa-speaks/.

197. Laurie Goodstein, "Gay Bishop Is Asked to Say Prayer at Inaugural Event," *New York Times*, January 12, 2009, http://www.nytimes.com/2009/01/13/us/13prayer.html?partner=rss&emc=rss&pagewanted=all&_r=0 (accessed February 6, 2014).

198. John MacArthur, "When God Abandons a Nation," *Grace to You*, August 20, 2006, http://www.gty.org/resources/sermons/80-314.

199. Jones, *One or Two*, 2578–2580.

200. John Piper, "The Tornado, the Lutherans, and Homosexuality," *Desiring God*, August 19, 2009, http://www.desiringgod.org/blog/posts/the-tornado-the-lutherans-and-homosexuality.

201. Amie Thomasson, "Categories," *The Stanford Encyclopedia of*

Philosophy, Edward N. Zalta, ed. (Fall 2013) http://plato.stanford.edu/cgi-bin/encyclopedia/archinfo.cgi?entry=categories (accessed September 20, 2013).

202. David K. Naugle, *Reordered Love, Reordered Lives: Learning the Deep Meaning of Happiness* (Grand Rapids, MI: William B. Eerdmans, 2008) Kindle edition, 281–282.

203. Bradford Wilcox, "Why Marriage Matters: 26 Conclusions from the Social Sciences," Institute for American Values, www.familyscholars.org/assets/Why-Marriage-Matters-summary.pdf (accessed September 16, 2013).

204. Mark Regnerus, "How Different Are the Adult Children of Parents Who Have Same-Sex Relationships? Findings from the New Family Structures Study," *Social Science Research,* 41:4 (July 2012) 752–770; available here: http://dx.doi.org/10.1016/j.ssresearch.2012.03.009.

205. Arthur F. Holmes, *Ethics Approaching Moral Decisions,* 2nd ed. (Downers Grove, IL: IVP Academic, 2007) 65–66.

206. Jones, *One or Two,* 2963–2964.

207. Tim Barnett, "Is Same-Sex Marriage Really About Equality?" Clear Thinking Christianity, http://www.clearthinkingchristianity.com/blog/same-sex-marriage-really-about-equality (accessed September 16, 2013).

208. Todd Starnes, "NM Court Says Christian Photographers Must Compromise Beliefs," *Fox News,* August 22, 2013, http://radio.foxnews.com/toddstarnes/top-stories/nm-court-says-christian-photographers-must-compromise-beliefs.html (accessed February 25, 2014).

209. "NM Supreme Court: Price of Citizenship Is Compromising Your Beliefs," Alliance Defending Freedom, August 22, 2013, http://

www.adfmedia.org/News/PRDetail/8469 (accessed February 25, 2014).

210. Robert L. Thomas, *New American Standard Hebrew-Aramaic and Greek Dictionaries: Updated Edition* (Anaheim: Foundation Publications, 1998).

211. Jones, *One or Two*, 1307–1308.

212. Ibid., 2702–2703.

213. Ibid., 2656–2665.

CHAPTER 10—When Antichrist Reveals Himself in America, Will We Recognize Him?
by Douglas W. Krieger and S. Douglas Woodward

214. This chapter was adapted from *The Final Babylon: America and the Coming of Antichrist*, by Douglas W. Krieger, Dene McGriff, and S. Douglas Woodward (Seattle, WA, Charleston, SC: Create Space Independent Publishing Platform, 2013).

215. Adolf Hitler, speaking of the Winter Help Campaign on October 5, 1937.

216. "The main idea of Sigmund Freud's crowd behavior theory is that people who are in a crowd act differently towards people from those who are thinking individually. The minds of the group would merge to form a way of thinking. Each member's enthusiasm would be increased as a result, and one becomes less aware of the true nature of one's action." See http://en.wikipedia.org / wiki/ Crowd_psychology.

217. The study of who understood Hitler and fled and who did not is an intriguing study in itself. Walter Stein, student of Rudolph Steiner, whom Trevor Ravenscroft credits with the story behind *The Spear of Destiny*, fled to England. Paul Tillich, who later became a

major voice in American theological liberalism, supposedly looked into the eyes of Hitler, saw the demonic, and left for Switzerland. Dietrich Bonhoeffer is the most noteworthy theologian who saw Hitler for what he was—a mass murderer. Eventually he lost his life for participating in an assassination attempt on Hitler. He is the most famous Christian martyr of the twentieth century, although only one of millions as we have learned that the martyr death toll in the last twenty years may now exceed the total number of martyrs since the first century.

218. Recall his true name was German, Karl the Great, in the line of Pepin, representing the dynasty of the Carolingians.

219. Luther's *The Jews and Their Lies* (1543, Von den Jüden und iren Lügen) stands as the seminal statement on anti-Semitism. According to friend and scholar Gary Stearman, Luther makes his hatred for the Jews crudely plain.

220. The Greek word, *apokalypsis*, means "the revealing," particularly the revealing of deep secrets, from whence the word "apocalypse" derives.

221. We might even have one of our most noteworthy evangelical leaders be asked to give the prayer at a presidential inauguration!

222. Hitler spoke of bringing about the new order as did Franklin D. Roosevelt.

223. Item #24 of the German Worker's Party "Program" circa 1920s.

224. Adolf Hitler, in his speech to the Reichstag on March 23, 1933.

225. Adolf Hitler, July 22, 1933, writing to the Nazi Party (quoted from John Cornwell's *Hitler's Pope*.)

226. "The **German Centre Party** (German: *Deutsche Zentrumspartei* or just *Zentrum*) was a Catholic political party in Germany during the *Kaiserreich* and the Weimar Republic. In English it is often

called the Catholic Centre Party. Formed in 1870, it battled the *Kulturkampf* which the Prussian government launched to reduce the power of the Catholic Church. It soon won a quarter of the seats in the Reichstag (Imperial Parliament), and its middle position on most issues allowed it to play a decisive role in the formation of majorities. "When the Nazis came to power the party dissolved itself on 5 July 1933 as a condition of the conclusion of a Concordat between the Holy See and Germany." See en.wikipedia.org/ wiki/Centre_ Party_ (Germany).

227. Adolf Hitler, in his New Year message on January 1, 1934.

228. Adolf Hitler, answering C. F. Macfarland about church and state (in his book, *The New Church and the New Germany*).

229. Adolf Hitler, on June 26, 1934, to Catholic bishops to assure them that he would take action against the new pagan propaganda.

230. Adolf Hitler, in a speech delivered in Berlin on the May Day festival, 1937.

231. By this we mean a reality in its own right, although C. S. Lewis was likely onto something by describing *evil* not as essential to reality as "good" is, but akin more to "spoiled goodness"—lest we inadvertently fall into the conundrum of a Zoroastrian dualism in which good and evil are on equal footing.

232. Adolf Hitler, giving prayer in a speech on May Day, 1933.

233. Adolf Hitler from his speech of April 12, 1922.

234. Adolf Hitler, in an article titled "A New Beginning," February 26, 1925.

235. Adolf Hitler, in a speech to the men of the SA at Dortmund, July 9, 1933, on the day after the signing of the Concordat (agreement with the Roman Catholic Church, the Papacy).

236. Adolf Hitler, in his Proclamation at the *Parteitag* at Nuremberg on September 5, 1934.

237. The Microsoft dictionary supplies this definition: "All things peculiar to the United States' culture and people; anything that is a symbol of American life."

238. Not that we believe Islam is "the religion of peace," as many of its followers maintain. Allah appears merciful only to his devout followers. Those who reject Islam deserve to lose their heads, at least according to the interpretation of the Koran from a large segment of the Muslim faithful. Tolerance is not a strong suit of Mohammed's teaching. If you doubt it, just express the fact that Islam is intolerant and see how much intolerance it summons from Islamic followers.

239. Indeed, evangelical spiritual sentiment may be content to connect with nothing more than the name "Jesus." Without specific assertions, we possess nothing distinct or definite. Thus, the name of Jesus may stand for nothing. It is the ultimate use of the Lord's name in vain. There are those in leadership within the church who would prefer to pray only to Jesus and talk about nothing but Jesus to avoid any sectarian debate. After all: *dogma divides; love abides.* Of course, that adage presumes *intuition* replaces *reason* as the sole religious faculty or means to discover reality. As Francis Schaeffer once conveyed, Evangelicals have their own form of religious mysticism that is just as elusive and ineffable as Buddist *koans*. In the final analysis, only *true truth* prevails (an awkward Schaefferian tautology meant to convey truth that is objective and universal— i.e., the opposite of relative "truth" or truth that is "caught" not "taught"). "Doctrineless sound bites" bite us all in the end.

240. BBC News, "Pope Defends WWII Pontiff's Role," September 20, 2008, Red Ice Creations, http://www.redicecreations.com/article. php?id=4837.

241. John Cornwell, *Hitler's Pope: The Secret History of Pius XII* (New York: Viking, 1999) 209.

242. Adolf Hitler, in his proclamation to the German people on January 1, 1939.

243. Adolf Hitler, in a speech at Wurzburg on June 27, 1937.

244. Adolf Hitler, in a speech at Frankfurt on March 16, 1936.

245. Adolf Hitler, in a speech at Hamburg on March 20, 1936.

CHAPTER 11—The Final Victory

by Terry James

246. David Jackson, "Obama 'Hugely Impressed' With Pope Francis," *USA Today,* October 2, 2013, http:// www.usatoday.com/story/theoval/2013/10/02/ obama-pope-francis-cnbc-abortion-gay-rights/2911067/.

247. "Abbas Meets Pope, Invites Him to Visity Holy Land," video transcript, Reuters.com, October 17, 2013, http://in.reuters.com/video/2013/10/17/ abbas-meets-pope-invites-him-to-visit-ho?videoId=274194592.